ISLAMIC SURVEYS

General Editor
C. HILLENBRAND

D1343724

Islamic Science and Engineering

Donald R. Hill

EDINBURGH UNIVERSITY PRESS

© Donald R. Hill, 1993
Edinburgh University Press Ltd
22 George Square, Edinburgh
Reprinted 2001, 2003 (twice)
Typeset in Linotron Trump Mediaeval
by Koinonia Ltd, Bury, and
printed in Great Britain by
Antony Rowe Ltd, Eastbourne

A CIP record for this book is available
from the British Library

ISBN 0 7486 0455 3 (paper)
ISBN 0 7486 0457 x (cased)

Contents

CONTENTS

List of Illustrations

Note on the Transliteration
of Arabic Words

The transliteration system of the *Encyclopaedia of Islam* has been followed with three exceptions: 'j' not 'dj' is used for *jim*; 'q' not 'k' is used for *qaf*; and consonants which are single in Arabic and double in Roman – e.g. 'kh' and 'sh' – are not underlined.

Preface and Acknowledgements

This book does not demand extensive technical knowledge; when necessary, technicalities are explained. Similarly, sufficient historical information is provided to enable readers to visualise the social and cultural environment in which Islamic scientists and engineers worked. Knowledge of Arabic is unnecessary, but for those wishing to undertake further research, most of the works listed in the Bibliography cite numerous Arabic sources.

Four exact sciences are dealt with, that is to say, sciences which are now almost wholly quantified but which in medieval times incorporated both quantified and qualitative elements. The engineering chapters are concerned with the various types of construction that were built or manufactured in the medieval Islamic world.

It will help to explain the methodology I used in preparing this book if I describe briefly how I came to an interest in Islamic technology. Being a working engineer, but also holding a PhD in Arabic studies, in 1970 I attended a conference at the School of Oriental and African Studies, University of London, which was also attended by the late, great historian of technology, Lynn White Jr. Having learned of my somewhat unusual qualifications, Lynn persuaded me, gently but firmly, that my first duty was to prepare an annotated translation of al-Jazarī's machine book. This I did, following it up with a similar work on the Banū Mūsà and with other books and articles. In the engineering chapters of the present book I have therefore been able to draw directly and extensively on the Arabic sources.

The same cannot be said of the sciences. Although in the passage of over two decades I have read a good deal of material on these, I have not had the time to read more than a handful of primary sources. There are, however, a number of eminent historians of science who, building on established traditions, have made profound studies of the Arabic sources and have published their results, sometimes based upon previously untapped manuscript sources. It is upon the works of these scholars that I have largely relied in preparing Chapters 2–5, my main guides being Professors Ted Kennedy, David King, Roshdi Rashed, A. I. Sabra, A. S. Saidan, George Saliba, Julio Samsó and Juan Vernet. I also record my appreciation of Professor Ahmad Y. Al-Hassan, not only for his collaboration with me in the past, but because his work on industrial chemistry was invaluable to me in preparing Chapter 5.

The illustrations are an important and integral part of this work and I am very grateful to Mr C. Wakefield, Senior Assistant Librarian, Bodleian Library, for allowing me to reproduce illustrations from the MS Greaves 27 of al-Jazarī's book, without the payment of a fee. Similar generous facilities were afforded to me by Dr Norman Smith of Imperial College, Professor Thorkild Schiøler of Copenhagen, and Mr Francis Maddison, Curator of the Museum for the History of Science, Oxford. All these scholars not only made their own illustrations available to me, but also gave me valuable advice on their technical and historical relevance. The British Library kindly allowed me to use the three illustrations to Chapter 5 without payment of a reproduction fee. I am also grateful to Colonel Gerald Napier and his staff of the Royal Engineers Museum, Chatham, for advice on quantity surveying and for bringing some valuable books to my attention that would otherwise have escaped my notice.

I thank the Editors of the *Encyclopaedia of Islam* for allowing me to use parts of the article 'Ma'din' in Volume V.

I acknowledge with gratitude the generosity of the Royal Society in furnishing me with financial assistance over a number of years to help me in my researches into the history of Islamic technology.

As always, I express my deepest gratitude to my dearly loved wife Pat for her unfailing encouragement and support.

CREDITS FOR ILLUSTRATIONS

Biblioteca Laurenzia, Florence, 7.11; Bodleian Library, Oxford, 6.5, 6.6, 6.7, 6.11, 7.1, 7.3, 7.6, 7.12, 7.14; British Library, 5.1, 5.2, 5.3; Michael Harverson, 6.15; Museum of the History of Science, Oxford, 3.9, 3.11; Thorkild Schiøler, 6.1, 6.3, 6.9, 6.10, 6.14(a); Norman Smith, 8.4, 8.5, 8.6, 8.7, 8.8, 9.4.

PHOTOGRAPHS AND DRAWINGS FROM PUBLICATIONS

Farmer (see bibliography), 7.13; A. Y. Al-Hassan, *Arabic Mechanical Engineering*, Aleppo 1976, 11.2; Al-Karajī, *Search for Hidden Waters*, Hyderabad, Deccan 1945, 10.4, 10.5, 10.6, 10.7, 10.8 (drawings adapted, Arabic captions changed to English); Al-Khazini-N.-Khanikoff (see bibliography), 4.1, 4.2, 4.3; David A. King, *Islamic Mathematical Astronomy* (see bibliography), 3.3; Kussmaul and Fischer (see bibliography), 8.2 (redrawn, German captions translated into English); H. N. Saunders, *The Astrolabe*, Bude, 1971, 3.12; Sir Aurel Stein (see bibliography), 8.3; R. R. Wright (see bibliography), 10.10.

Other drawings by the author.

1

Introduction

The roots of every new civilisation must be nourished by the achievements of its precursors. In the case of Islam these precursors were to be found in the Hellenistic, Roman and Byzantine civilisations, with lesser, but still significant, influences from India and China.

When Alexander the Great died in 323 BC his conquests stretched from Greece, Asia Minor, Syria and Egypt through Persia and Afghanistan and as far as the River Indus. Although his empire did not survive his death as an entity, he had managed to impose a single political unit on a larger part of the western world than anyone before him. After he died the major part of the empire was divided among his generals: Antigonus ruled Asia Minor, Syria and Palestine; Seleucus ruled Mesopotamia, Persia and the eastern parts to the borders of India; and Ptolemy ruled Egypt and Libya. The division lasted to the battle of Ipsus in 301 BC, when Seleucus added Asia Minor and Syria to his possessions. The Seleucids only managed to hold such a vast expanse of territory for some fifty years, before the Parthians took control of eastern Mesopotamia and eventually – around the end of the third century BC – most of the eastern parts of the Seleucid kingdom.

The Greek kingdom of Bactria, however, arose in 254 BC – hence almost at the same time as Parthia. It was founded by a Greek governor, Diodatus, who made himself independent of the Seleucids. Little is known about this kingdom, which was centred on the Rivers Oxus and Sughd (on which are the cities of Bukhārā and Samarqand) and at one time extended to the north Indian plain. Eventually, after endemic warfare with the Seleucids and Parthians, the Bactrian Kingdom was incorporated into the Parthian domains about 140 BC. To us the importance of Bactria lies in its position as a commercial nexus between East Asia and India on the one hand, and the Middle East and Mediterranean on the other. Although we know little of its history, it is highly probable that it was an important channel for the diffusion of ideas between East and West. Other Greek cities are known to have survived inside the Parthian dominions long after the extinction of Greek rule over the region as a whole. Prominent among these were Susa, in what is now the Iranian province of Khuzistan, and Seleucia on the west bank of the Tigris some forty-five miles north of ancient Babylon. Seleucia remained a Greek colony until it was wantonly destroyed by the Romans in AD 165, on one of their periodic incursions into Parthia.

Another Greek dynasty was that of the Attalids, who ruled much of Asia Minor from the city of Pergamum in the second century BC. They were nominally independent, but in later years Pergamum came increasingly under the domination of Rome, until in 133 BC the Attalid dynasty was extinguished and Pergamum was brought under direct Roman rule. Although little is known of the cultural life of Pergamum in the days of its independence, it seems likely that intellectual life flourished: there is known to have been a library of 200,000 volumes in the capital.

The rise of Rome was a fairly gradual process, beginning with the reduction of the Greek cities of southern Italy to the status of client states by about 275 BC. A long series of wars with Carthage lasted from 246–146 BC and ended with the destruction of Carthage and the assumption by Rome of complete control over the central and western Mediterranean: Spain was in Roman hands by 205 BC; Greece and Macedonia by 147 BC. Rome gained a foothold in Asia Minor in 133 BC with the cession of Pergamum. Jerusalem was captured in 63 BC , and Egypt became a Roman province in 30 BC. Rome became an Empire in 27 BC when Octavian took the imperial throne under the title of Augustus.

At its greatest extent in the first century AD the empire included most of western Europe as far as the Rhine and Danube, the Balkans, Asia Minor, Egypt and the North African coastal regions, and Syria. Internal and external wars were a feature of life in both republic and imperial times, but in the heyday of the empire Roman power usually ensured that commercial, social and cultural communications were uninterrupted.

In AD 330 the emperor Constantine removed his capital to Byzantium on the Bosphorus, which henceforward bore the name of Constantinople. In the fourth and fifth centuries the western part of the empire was subject to invasions by Germanic peoples; during the fifth century Britain, Gaul, Spain and north Africa slipped from the empire's weakening grasp. The last sole ruler of the Roman Empire was Theodosius the Great (379–95). The eastern half of the Empire, known to history as the Byzantine Empire maintained its hold on the Balkans, Asia Minor, Syria and Egypt. Under Theodosius it became the Orthodox Christian State, its language being Greek apart from some legal documents and military expressions. Despite the temporary recovery under Justinian (527–65) of Italy, North Africa and parts of Spain, the extent of the Byzantine Empire on the advent of Islam was much as it had been in the fifth century.

In Persia the Parthians were overthrown in AD 226 by Ardashīr, founder of the Sasānid dynasty, which remained in power until it was extinguished by the Arab armies in the seventh century. For much of the period from the death of Alexander until the Arab conquests there were hostilities between Persia and the West – Seleucids, then Rome, then Byzantium. The Euphrates was the normal frontier, though it was breached from time to time in both directions. More important were the cultural interpenetrations that took place between the two sides.

The conquests of Alexander and the division of his empire among his successors caused radical changes in the cultural pattern of the Eastern Mediterranean and the Middle East. It was a world in which Hellenism was to be the most important factor in the administrative, commercial and cultural life of the region, not only in the Hellenistic period but throughout the region until the Arab conquests of the seventh and eighth centuries. A new form of Greek, the *koine*, became the common possession of civilised men. Greek might take a man from Marseilles to India, from the Cataracts to the Caspian. In the cities schools, libraries, theatres, Greek temples and gymnasia were established. It is neither possible nor necessary to discuss the ethnic origins of the scholars and scientists of this Hellenised world. Many were, of course, pure Greek, speaking the language as a mother tongue; others were indigenous peoples of Asia with Aramaic, for example, as their mother tongue but with Greek as the vehicle to be used in commercial and cultural dealings.

The science of the Hellenistic period is differentiated in a number of ways from its classical predecessor, the most obvious being that we are no longer dealing with purely Greek science. To take but one example, Seleucus, the only astronomer we hear of who followed Aristarchus of Samos in adopting the heliocentric theory, was a Chaldean or Babylonian, a native of Seleucia on the Tigris. From the third century BC onwards the cross-fertilisation between Babylonian and Greek astronomy is increasingly important; in the second century Hipparchus, for example, evidently had access to Babylonian eclipse records and used them extensively.

A more important distinguishing feature of the social background to Hellenistic science is the increase in kingly patronage, however inconsistent and capricious the granting of such patronage could be. The motives behind such patronage are not always easy to discern. Some of them were doubtless purely practical: kings needed scientists and engineers as physicians, astrologers, architects and designers of engines of war. At the same time, there does seem to have been real prestige in having eminent scientists attached to one's court, even if much of their work was purely speculative and theoretical. At all events, certain scientists at certain times and in certain places

3

received substantial support, both in terms of money and in other ways from some of the rulers. Prominent in this respect were the Ptolemies of Egypt and the Attalid kings of Pergamum. It was largely due to the Ptolemies that Alexandria, which had been founded in 331 BC, rapidly became the chief centre of scientific research in the third century BC.

Two institutions, both established under royal patronage early in the third century, were instrumental in gaining for Alexandria its pre-eminence as a centre of intellectual activity. These were the Library and Museum. Both institutions, and the complex of buildings associated with them in the royal quarter of Alexandria, were built by the Ptolemies, who also paid regular stipends to the Librarian and other scholars. The Museum was not primarily a teaching establishment, but one devoted to research, in which the community worked and, to some extent, lived together. Although similar institutions were founded in other cities of the Hellenistic world, it was mainly the Museum and the Library that attracted such a large proportion of the scientists of the period to Alexandria. By no means all the scholars of the Hellenistic world, however, were supported by royal patronage. Many of them earned their living, or at least supplemented their incomes, by practising such professions as medicine or architecture.

We shall be considering the great scientists of the Hellenistic period when we examine the translation of Greek works into Arabic later in this chapter, and also in the chapters on the individual sciences. It is therefore unnecessary to enumerate them now. It is important, however, to emphasise that there was a gradual decline in the sciences through the period of the Roman Empire and into early Byzantine times. Although Greek retained its pre-eminence in the eastern empire, from the third century onwards there were few scientists of real originality. Academic effort was largely confined to editing and writing commentaries upon the works of the great Hellenistic scientists. Many Greek manuscripts were preserved in the cities of the Byzantine Empire, but perhaps the most important contribution made to the dissemination of science in the early Christian era came from members of the schismatic churches. Greek schools were established in Asia Minor soon after the Council of Nicaea in AD 325. The Nestorian church made one of these schools, that of Edessa, their scientific centre. In AD 489 this school was transferred to Nisibīn, then under Persian rule, with its secular faculties at Jundīshāpūr in Khuzistan. Here the Nestorian scholars, together with pagan philosophers banished by Justinian from Athens, carried out important research in medicine, astronomy and mathematics. To assist in instruction a number of Greek works were translated into Syriac. At about the same time the sect of the Monophysites, who like the Nestorians were subject to persecution by the Orthodox church, were working on similar lines in Syria. They too made translations of philosophical and scientific works into Syriac. A group who were to provide some of the greatest translators and scientists of Islam were the Ṣabians of Ḥarrān in Mesopotomia. (The Ṣabians were pagans, but by a convenient fiction were classified as among the 'Peoples of the Book' and hence tolerated by the Muslims, who valued their intellectual gifts.) Their liturgical language was Syriac, and a number of their intellectual elite also knew Greek and possessed a wide knowledge of Greek literature and science.

The foregoing is perhaps sufficient to explain how the treasures of Greek science were available as a legacy to the Muslims. So far we have said little about the science of other nations, such as the Persians and the Indians, apart from a reference to Babylonian influence on Greek astronomy and to the importance of Jundīshāpūr as a meeting point of cultures. In subsequent chapters we shall have occasion to mention the passage of Persian and Indian ideas into Islam. As will become clear in those instances, however, our knowledge of Pahlevi and Sanskrit material from the centuries before the advent of Islam is very scanty, and the questions of diffusions from those cultures will often be conjectural.

In technical, as opposed to scientific, matters our knowledge of achievement in the ancient world comes mainly from non-literary sources. There are a few very valuable treatises on machines, or rather on ingenious devices such as trick vessels, automata and self-trimming lamps. As we shall see, the most important of these treatises became known to the Muslims, and provided the inspiration for a few books on fine technology that exhibit some notable improvements on the works of their Greek predecessors.

In the case of astronomical instruments, the origin of the astrolabe can be dated to the early years of the sixth century AD in Alexandria, at which time we have the first complete and accurate description of the instrument. This knowledge was transmitted to the Arabs in a Syriac treatise, also written in Alexandria, at about the time of the Arab conquest of Egypt. No examples of the instrument from pre-Islamic times have survived, but it is probable that some were available in the first centuries of Islam. Fragments of other types of astronomical instruments dating to Hellenistic or Byzantine times still exist today. Some of these kinds of instruments may have become known to the Muslims from surviving examples. It is also apparent, from remarks made by Muslim scientists, that Greek treatises on some instruments were translated into Arabic, but no such treatises have come down to us.

Turning to the more robust, everyday structures – mills, water-raising machines, canals and qanats, masonry structures of various kinds – we have no knowledge of any detailed written descriptions of these installations dating from pre-Islamic times. They were such common constructions that no scholars thought it worthwhile to record details of their design. Lack of written records would, however, have occasioned no difficulties in the diffusion of these technologies into the world of Islam. The utilitarian technologies were not interrupted by the advent of Islam. Their practitioners continued to follow their professions when the Muslims took over, and in due course their descendants became Muslims themselves, often with Arabic as their mother tongue. The ease with which these technologies were integrated into the Islamic world (and frequently improved with the passage of time) contrasts with the present-day attempts to understand and reconstruct pre-industrial technology. In some cases, notably water-raising machines, we can examine machines that are still in use. In other technologies, however, we must rely upon sketchy archaeological results or upon the descriptions, often brief and obscure, in the works of geographers, travellers and other writers.

THE ADVENT OF ISLAM

The spread of Islam beyond the borders of Arabia began in AD 634 with the invasion of Syria and Iraq by large raiding parties. The success of these forces against the armies of the Byzantium and Persia was facilitated by the exhaustion of the two empires after a prolonged war between themselves and – in Syria, Egypt and Iraq – by the hostility of the indigenous populations to their imperial masters. Very soon the campaigns became wars for permanent conquest, fed partly by the desire for booty and partly by genuine religious fervour. By about AD 645 Syria, Egypt, Cyrenaica, Iraq and Upper Mesopotamia had been effectively subjugated. Resistance was stiffer in the Iranian heartland and in the Berber country of north-west Africa, but the first was conquered by about AD 660 and the second by the end of the seventh century. The conquests were then extended into Spain and Central Asia, and by the middle of the eighth century the Arab empire had attained its greatest expansion, stretching from the Amu Darya river (Oxus) to the Pyrenees.

A number of Mediterranean islands were occupied by the Arabs, the most important being Cyprus and Sicily. Large-scale raids were mounted on Cyprus in the second half of the seventh century. It was never fully wrested from the Byzantine Empire, but for 250 years from the end of the seventh century it had an intermediate status between the Caliphs and the Byzantine Emperor. Sicily was finally subjugated in 847 by forces from North Africa and remained under Muslim rule until it was conquered by the Normans in 1072. The southern Italian mainland was itself subjected to large-scale raids during the ninth, tenth and eleventh centuries; indeed the towns of Bari and Taranto were occupied by the Muslims for several decades in the ninth century.

At the other end of the Islamic world, the province of Sind, on the Indian sub-continent, was captured in 712, but it was little more than a trading post, and caliphal authority was almost extinct by 871. No further major incursions occurred until the rule of Maḥmūd of Ghazna (in what is now Afghanistan). Maḥmūd, who ruled from 999 until 1027; made a number of destructive raids into northern India, but these resulted in no permanent establishment of Islam, except for the Punjab, which became the Ghaznavids frontier province. From our point of view, the fact that the great scientist al-Bīrūnī accompanied Maḥmūd on several of his expeditions is more important than the military results of these undertakings. He learned Sanskrit and several dialects and the result of the incalculable sum of knowledge that he obtained on these visits was his major work *The Description of India*, containing invaluable information on historical, geographical and scientific subjects. Muslim rule was extended gradually over northern India in succeeding centuries.

The Arab armies made contact with Chinese civilisation during their conquest of Central Asia. The subjugation of Bukhārā and Samarqand and the consolidation of Arab power beyond the Oxus was a process that lasted fifty years, from 705 until 755. The importance of the region lies mainly in its position as an entrepot centre on the 'silk road', between China on the one hand and Persia and the West on the other. China had long had commercial and diplomatic representatives in the area, and was accustomed to interfering in the political and military affairs of the local Iranian and Turkish princes when it suited her purposes. The final confrontation was at the battle of Atlak in 751, between the Chinese with their Turkish auxiliaries, and the Arabs. This battle marked the end of Chinese hegemony in Central Asia. The Arab governor, however, seems to have realised the importance of maintaining relations with the Chinese court, and after the battle of Atlak a succession of embassies from the Arabs is reported in Chinese sources.

At first the Arab conquests were directed by the Caliphs in Medina, but in AD 660 the Umayyad dynasty assumed power and made their capital in Damascus. In 750 the Umayyads were in turn overthrown by the 'Abbāsids and the centre of gravity of the empire shifted to Iraq where the second 'Abbāsid Caliph, al-Manṣūr, built the splendid new city of Baghdad as a fitting capital for his empire. The 'Abbāsids were only able to maintain the empire as a cohesive political unit for about one hundred and fifty years, after which is split up into a number of separate states, some nominally owing allegiance to the Caliphs but all virtually independent. In the second half of the ninth century the Caliphs themselves became the puppets of their Turkish military commanders and never regained temporal power. In the eleventh century Baghdad was incorporated into the empire of the Seljuk Turks and was finally destroyed by the Mongols under Hülägu in 1258.

By their conquest of Egypt and Syria the Arabs fell heirs directly to the Greek civilisation of those two countries. This heritage was eventually to bear fruit in the transmission of scientific literature and in the diffusion of traditions in the construction of machines, hydraulic works and masonry structures. In Persia also, the Arabs came into contact with some written material and, perhaps more importantly, with a long tradition of utilitarian engineering. A knowledge of Indian culture was gained not only in the scientific centre of Jundīshāpūr but also during the occupation of Sind and later much of the rest of northern India. The most fruitful source of intercultural relations with China seems to have been in Central Asia. We shall later have occasion to discuss the transmission into Islam of Chinese technologies in the fields of paper-making, siege machines and alchemy. In North Africa, Spain and Sicily the Arabs were able to inspect the results of Roman skills in civil engineering, particularly in the building of dams, bridges and aqueducts.

The legacy of scientific and technological knowledge from the conquered regions was eventually to produce remarkable results in the new society, but first a period of consolidation was necessary. In the period from the early conquests to the end of the Umayyad dynasty the Arabs were concerned with military affairs , with the pacification of the occupied lands, and with the setting up of administrative, fiscal and legal systems. The Arab conquerors formed a ruling elite, in receipt of financial and other privileges that were denied to the conquered peoples, even when these became Muslims, although in this case discrimination was contrary to the teachings of the Koran. Islam slowly became the faith of the majority and Arabic superseded the native languages everywhere, except in Spain and Iran, although even in those countries Arabic became the main vehicle for written communication and remained so for several centuries. The Arabs were never more than a small minority of the population of the empire and as they intermarried with women from the native populations the numbers of those who could claim pure Arab decent diminished, while the status of the indigenous peoples gradually improved. The Empire of the Arabs became the World of Islam. It was by no means a homogeneous world: racial and linguistic differences remained, there were sizeable minorities of Christians, Jews and other religious groups, and the Muslims themselves were split by religious schisms, the deepest and most enduring of which was that between the ortho-dox Sunni believers and the Shia, followers of 'Alī, the son-in-law of the Prophet. Nevertheless, and despite political fragmentation, Islam was a real entity, held together by the bonds of religion and language.

With the translation from Greek and other languages there was a tremendous openness in the early centuries of Islam. The cosmopoli-tan character of the movement that fostered knowledge of the sciences was very marked under the great 'Abbāsid Caliphs, who regarded the integration of the cultural achievements of the conquered peoples, many of whom were now converted to Islam, as a central mission of the dynasty. The increasingly systematic sponsorship of translation during these reigns reflects the policy of the Caliphs and their minis-ters of adopting the most useful elements of the pre-Islamic cultures as a matter of expediency or even urgency. In encouraging these activities rich men from the higher strata of society played a part.

TRANSLATION OF SCIENTIFIC WORKS INTO ARABIC

The Greeks took an encyclopaedic view of knowledge, a view from which their Muslim successors did not diverge. It must be emphasised, therefore, that in considering science and technology compart-mentally, in accordance with modern practice, we are guilty of anach-ronism. This is not to say that the Greeks and Muslims failed to appreciate the necessity for dividing science into its various branches. Indeed, the Muslims in particular were assiduous in compiling 'Classi-fications of the Sciences', the precise contents of which need not concern us here (in any case the lists vary from author to author, though the basic premises underlying them do not change radically).

The essential feature to be borne in mind about these lists, and about the attitude of the Greeks and Muslims in general, is that their use of the word 'science' – '*ilm* in Arabic – differs radically from our own, even allowing for our changing view of science when compared to the assumptions of the nineteenth century. The Muslim classifica-tions, while including subjects that we would certainly classify as sciences – astronomy and mechanics for example – also include sub-jects such as theology, philosophy, logic and metaphysics. The schol-ars themselves would have found the modern concept of specialisation alien, and seen nothing strange in combining speculative philosophy with, say, medicine or astronomy. Clearly, the pressures of patronage and economics would to a certain extent determine the scope of the scholars' activities, just as they had done for their Hellenistic predecessors, but this scope was in most cases extensive. (There were, however, some genuine specialists, whose work will be considered in the appropriate chapters.) We are considering the sciences in their modern guises, and with modern demarcations, since any other treatment would make this work impossibly unwieldy. Inevitably, therefore, we shall do injustice to the work of the translators, since we shall mention, in general, only those works that are relevant to the later chapters of this book.

When the second 'Abbāsid Caliph al-Manṣūr (reigned 754–75) supervised the setting out of the foundations of Baghdad he was attended to by two astrologers, Nawbakht and Māshā'allāh. The first was a Persian – formerly a Zoroastrian – and the second was a Jew from Balkh in Khurāsān. Nawbakht, a translator from Pahlavi, wrote works on astrology and related subjects. Māshā'allāh wrote on astral 'sympathies'. Their task was to plan the city to optimise such influences. Clearly, al-Manṣūr felt no qualms about using non-Arabs in this enterprise. Incidentally, it must not be supposed that al-Manṣūr, because he employed astrologers to assist him in determining the plan of the city, allowed himself to be unduly influenced by psuedo-sciences. During the actual construction he maintained such a close supervision over the contractors, especially in matters of cost, that he came to be known as the 'Father of the farthings'.

A non-Arab family who wielded great influence in the courts of the early 'Abbāsids were the Barmakids, among whom was Khālid b. Barmak, the vizier of al-Manṣūr. He came from a long line of Buddhist abbots of Balkh who became Zoroastrians not long before the Islamic conquest. As Muslims the Barmakids were ministers, commanders and governors, reaching the acme of their power in the reign of Hārūn al-Rashīd before their downfall in 803. The family had an extensive knowledge of Greek culture and were an important influence in the beginnings of the translation movement under the early 'Abbāsids. As the eighth century drew to a close, manuscripts were sought out, and objective standards and philological methods came to govern the translation procedures.

One of the first translators of the 'Abbāsid period was a writer of Persian origin named Ibn al-Muqaffa' (d. 756) who translated from the Pahlavi the Indian book of fables *Kalīla wa Dimna*. He is also credited with the translation of a group of works representing the ancient history, culture and civilisation of Iran. His son Muḥammad was

10

among the first translators of Greek works on logic and medicine into Arabic. Ibrāhīm al-Fazārī was an expert on astronomy and the calendar, and was the first Muslim to construct an astrolabe. He began work on the *Siddhan*ta, an astronomical treatise and tables by the Indian mathematician Brahmagupta (b. AD 598). The translation of this work was completed by his son Muḥammad.

The Caliph Hārūn al-Rashīd (786–809) enlarged translation activity and put it on a more formal basis. Large collections of Greek manuscripts were in the booty of Amorium and Ankara. Other Greek books on the physical sciences were acquired by a diplomatic request to the Byzantine emperor. The library, *Khizānat al-Ḥikma* (*The Treasury of Knowledge*), became a reference tool for astronomers and physicians and was large enough to need a librarian. Hārūn appointed to this post a translator of Persian works, al-Faḍl, son of Nawbakht who had been employed by this grandfather in the founding of Baghdad.

Hārūn's son Ma'mūn (813–33), however, went far beyond his father in providing support for the translators of scientific works, which by his time were predominantly Greek in origin. Al-Ma'mūn founded the *Bayt al-Ḥikma* (*House of Wisdom*), a far more ambitious institutional undertaking compared with the library of Hārūn. It can be described as a research institute, and it was under its aegis that most of the translations and original scientific works were undertaken.

A key role in the sponsorship of science and technology under al-Ma'mūn and his immediate successors was played by the Banū Mūsà, three brothers in order of seniority Muḥammad, Aḥmad and al-Ḥasan. Their father, Mūsà b. Shākir, had been a noted astronomer and a close companion of al-Ma'mūn when he was residing in Khurāsān before becoming caliph. On Mūsà's death the brothers became the wards of al-Ma'mūn, who sent them to the House of Wisdom to complete their education. After leaving this institution they were used by al-Ma'mūn and his successors in a variety of undertakings, including geodetic surveys. They also became contractors in public works undertakings and it was probably by this means, and in other entrepreneurial activities, that they became rich and powerful. In his later years Muḥammad became involved in palace politics, at a time when real power was passing from the caliphs to their Turkish army commanders.

It is their intellectual activities, however, that constitute their major contribution to the genesis of Arabic science. They devoted much of their wealth and energy to the quest for the works of ancient writers and sent missions to Byzantium to seek out such material and bring it back to Baghdad. Muḥammad is said to have made a journey to Byzantium in person. The renowned translator Thābit b. Qurra accompanied Muḥammad on his return to Baghdad and began his work in

Muḥammad's house. The brothers used to pay about 500 dinars a month to a group of translators who worked in the House of Wisdom. These scholars also made important original scientific contributions. The Banū Mūsà were probably the most effective independent agents in encouraging the assimilation of foreign works into Arabic, but they also did important original work themselves. As recorded in the sources, they wrote some twenty books, including treatises on mathematics, astronomy and mechanics. Of these works three are known to have survived. One, which was largely the work of Aḥmad, is a valuable treatise on machines and ingenious devices (see Chapter 7).

The Ḥarrrānian tradition, as represented by Thābit b. Qurra, was a surviving vestige of the astral religions widely popular in late antiquity. Because philosophy, including mathematics and astrology, was essential to the continuing traditions of the Ṣabians, Thābit did not work in isolation, but founded a school of mathematics and astrology, continued by his son, two grandsons and a great-grandson. Among other works, they translated Archimedes and Apollonius of Perga, who are valuable for geometry and mechanics, but also contain useful information on engineering practices. The neo-Pythagorean number theory developed by the neo-Platonist Nicomachus of Gerasa (end of the first Century AD) was well-known to Thābit, who produced an Arabic version of Nichomachus' *Introduction to Arithmetic*. After leaving the employment of the Banū Mūsà, Thābit became astrologer to the caliph al-Mu'taḍid. His translations from Greek and Syriac included improved versions of Ptolemy's *Almagest* and Euclid's *Elements*. He also commented on Aristotle's *Physics* and wrote a book on *The Nature and Influences of the Stars*, to give the conceptual backgrounds of the astrological arts.

Ḥunayn b. Isḥāq is the most significant individual translator of ninth-century Baghdad, and the most prolific. Son of a Nestorian Arab pharmacist of al-Ḥīra, in southern Iraq, Ḥunayn was bilingual in Syriac and Arabic. After an early period of study in Baghdad he may have travelled to Byzantium or Alexandria. At all events, when he reappeared in Baghdad he had mastered Greek. Preferring to work for independent patrons, such as the Banū Mūsà, he translated works on medicine, philosophy, astronomy mathematics and magic. He also supervised translations by his son Isḥāq, his nephew Ḥubaysh b. al-Ḥasan and various disciples. As none of his collaborators had Ḥunayn's mastery of Greek, he usually did a primary translation into Syriac or sometimes Arabic. Isḥāq and Ḥubaysh gave their work to Ḥunayn for checking. Ḥunayn exercised control throughout his life over his disciples, but their work should not be underestimated.

12

Hubaysh was an important medical translator, while he and others took overall responsibility for translating philosophical and mathematical materials, including nearly all of Aristotle. Hunayn compiled a list of the works of Galen that were available in his time, of which Hunayn named about 100 works that he translated personally into either Syriac or Arabic. Apart from these translations, his prodigious output included translations of Hippocrates and other medical writers. Among other works he is also known to have written are books on ophthalmology, the nature of light and alchemy.

In addition to his crucial role as translator, scientist and teacher, Hunayn made a most important contribution to the advancement of Arabic culture by his efforts, mainly successful, at creating an Arabic and Syriac technical vocabulary. Recognising the necessity for good texts, he worked with his colleagues on the collation of critical texts, taking account of variant readings, before beginning translation. He emended his translations where variants turned up later. Such methods set the standard for later translations.

After Hunayn, the translation of Greek works continued in the late ninth century and throughout the tenth. Prominent among the translators was Qusṭā b. Lūqā, a Christian from the town of Baʿlabakk in the Lebanon. In Baghdad, where he worked for some time as a doctor, scientist and translator, his reputation was as high as that of Hunayn. He died in Armenia in 912. Some of Qusṭā's translations are extant, for example those of Diaphantus, Theodosius, Autolycus, Hypsicles, Aristarchus and Hero. He also wrote a number of original works, many of them on medical subjects but also including several astronomical treatises, two commentaries on Euclid's *Elements*, a treatise on algebra, a commentary on the book of Diaphantus on algebra, and works on the steelyard, weights and measures, and on burning mirrors. The biographers are unanimous in praising his skill as a translator of Greek works into Arabic, and in the light of surviving translations their esteem seems to be fully justified.

Much of the other work done in the tenth century was concerned with philosophical and theological writings, particularly translations and commentaries on Aristotle. It should be mentioned, however, that the authors of some of the most important texts, from our point of view, are unknown. They could have appeared at any time during the translation movement and indeed we do not even know, in some cases, whether they are Greek or Arabic in origin. Such texts – for example the pseudo-Archimedes treatise on a water-clock – are considered in later chapters.

The translation movement continued until the middle of the eleventh century, both in the East and in al-Andalus, where the Umayyad

Caliph al-Ḥakam II (reigned 961–76) is said to have gathered a library of some 400,000 volumes, acquired by agents throughout the eastern lands. Although it has been suggested that translation was halted by a religious reaction, a more likely explanation is simply that the translators had completed their work. By about 1050 all the significant scientific works of the Hellenistic period were available in Arabic. As original work in Arabic led to improvements and extensions to Greek scientific systems, so did Muslim scholars tend to refer to their Arabic predecessors, whose works were a synthesis of Greek and Muslim thought, rather than directly to the Greek originals.

2

Mathematics

The Islamic heritage in mathematics incorporated a vast body of learning from earlier civilisations, but it is almost impossible to unravel the various strands that were eventually to be woven into the complex tapestry of Islamic mathematics. Only one of these strands, that provided by the Hellenistic world, can be identified with any confidence. The Hellenistic sources, which were rendered into Arabic in the ninth and tenth centuries, either directly from the Greek or through the medium of Syriac, included most of the major works of Greek mathematics. Thus we have translations of the *Elements* and *Data* of Euclid; the *Conics, The Section of a Ratio* and the *Determinate Solution* of Apollonius of Perga; the *Spherics* of Theodosius of Tripoli; the *Introduction to Arithmetic* of Nicomachus of Gerasa; and the *Spherics* of Menelaus, together with the works of Hero, Theon and other important Alexandrian mathematicians and commentators. Of particular importance for Islamic mathematics (and mechanics) is Archimedes, almost all of whose writings, such as *The Sphere and the Cylinder, The Measurement of the Circle, The Equilibrium of Planes* and *Floating Bodies* were translated into Arabic. There are also a number of works in Arabic, either by Archimedes or attributed to him, for which there is no original Greek. Some of the works were translated more than once and the more influential of them, such as the *Elements* of Euclid and the *Conics* of Apollonius, had a number of commentaries written about them over the centuries. The Greek tradition, both written and oral, embodied Babylonian practices, reflecting the highly developed mathematics and astronomy of Babylon. One of the most important mathematical legacies of Babylon to the Greeks and later to the Muslims, was the sexagesimal system.

The story of the transmission of Indian mathematics into Islam, a crucially important factor in the development of mathematics in general, is not easily disentangled from legend. According to an Arabic source, an Indian well-versed in the learning of his country, arrived at the court of the caliph al-Manṣūr in Baghdad in 773. This man, the report goes, knew the method of the *Sindhind*, concerning the movements of the stars and the mathematics needed for their analysis. He had composed an abridged version of a work pertaining to these matters. The caliph ordered that this work be translated into Arabic, a task that was undertaken by al-Fazārī (d. c.777), his son Muḥammad and by Yaʿqūb b. Ṭāriq (d. c.796). The traditional scholarly belief was that direct contact of Islam with Indian astronomy and mathematics, in particular the Hindu numerals, started at this time, but Arabic sources in general do not support this belief. The word *Sindhind* is the Arabic version of the Indian *Siddhanta*, but it is not known precisely which, if any, of the *Siddhantas* were translated into Arabic in the late eighth or early ninth centuries. It should be pointed out that Arabic works give no references whatsoever to any Sanskrit text or Hindu arithmetician, nor do they quote any Sanskrit term or statement. The currently most acceptable theory is that Hindu mathematics (as usual closely associated with astronomy) drifted gradually into the Middle East and the southern coasts of the Mediterranean from the seventh century onwards. Much of this material passed through Persian channels.

Unfortunately, we lack Pahlevi books on scientific subjects; Persian knowledge was incorporated into Arabic adaptations and translations prominent among which were some astronomical tables called *Zīj al-Shah*, turned into Arabic and used, among others, by al-Fazārī. Persian knowledge seems to have been an amalgam of Greek and Indian learning from which it is now impossible to isolate any purely Persian elements.

The Muslims therefore inherited a very rich and diverse body of knowledge from their predecessors: Babylonians, Greeks, Indians and Persians. From these varied elements they were to develop a mathematics that became a sophisticated and flexible tool in the pursuit of both theoretical and practical objectives.

ARITHMETIC

The Muslim mathematicians fell heir to three separate systems of numeration and calculation from their predecessors, and successive generations of scholars laboured hard to produce a unified system that was superior to any of the earlier ones. It cannot be said, however, that there is any arithmetical work in Arabic that finally and authoritatively describes an integrated system that was henceforward regarded as canonical by all practitioners. Rather it became the case that, while the whole corpus of arithmetical knowledge was known to the best mathematicians, they felt free to use those elements that best suited their purposes and inclinations. The point can best be appreciated by briefly examining the three different systems. It must be emphasised at this point that although we shall be using modern notation throughout this work for convenience, this is frequently anachronistic. As we shall see, Muslim scientists used notations that seem strange to our eyes, often for example numbers and algebraic quantities were expressed in words.

The sexagesimal scale is known to have been used by the Babylonians since remote times. Among them *sixty* played the role that *ten* now plays in whole numbers and decimal fractions. The traces of the system of course remain in our division of the hour into minutes and seconds and in the expression of a complete rotation as 360°, each degree being divided into minutes and seconds. The system was almost universally used by astronomers, both ancient and Muslim, and indeed one of its names in Arabic is *ṭarīq al-munajjim* (the way of the astronomers). The advantage of the system, compared with decimal notation, is that 60 has 11 factors (1, 2, 3, 4, 5, 6, 10, 12, 15, 30, 60) whereas 10 has only four (1, 2, 5, 10). The same advantage can be claimed for pre-decimal British money, which prior to the invention of cheap electronic calculators was easier to use in mental calculations than decimal money – but mental arithmetic seems to be a dying art anyway. In the sexagesimal system whole numbers were counted on the decimal scale, the numbers being assigned to the letters of the Arabic alphabet, as they had previously been assigned to the letters of the older Semitic alphabets and to the 24 Greek letters. The 28 Arabic letters were assigned to the following values, reading from right to left:

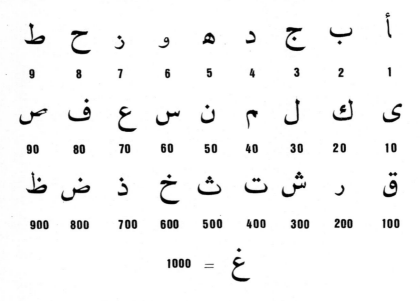

FIGURE 2.1 Arabic *abjad* letters (used as numerals).

17

The system is known as *jummal* or *abjad*, the latter 'word' derived from the first four letters. As already mentioned, astronomers almost invariably use the *abjad*/sexagesimal system; for instance astrolabes are almost always marked out with *abjad* letters. It also occurs in a number of Arabic arithmetical works and even today the system is not quite obsolete. Although it is no longer used in calculations, in some Arabic countries it is used, for example, in numbering paragraphs in official documents.

Whereas the *abjad* letters were used for integers, fractions were transferred on to the scale of 60. For instance, a Muslim reckoner would traditionally express $\frac{23}{25}$ as 55½ parts of 60. The next step would be to split 55½ into parts whose ratio to 60 is of the form $\frac{1}{n}$. Thus the result would be 30+ 20 + 4 + 1 ⅕.

Only a broad outline of the second system – finger-reckoning – can be given; the system is not described in detail in any Arabic book on arithmetic. In Arabic texts it is called *ḥisāb al-yadd* (hand arithmetic) to distinguish it from *'ilm al-ḥisāb* (the science of arithmetic) which was used to denote Indian arithmetic. One of the characteristics of the system was that it had no numerical notation – numbers were written in words. Calculations were done mentally, taking into account the rules $10^m \times 10^n = 10^{m+n}$, $10^m \div 10^n = 10^{m-n}$, and $\sqrt{10^{2m}} = 10^m$, together with a number of short cuts in general use. In manipulation, however, there would arise intermediate results that the scribe had to remember. These he indicated by placing his fingers in certain conventional positions good enough to distinguish numbers from 1 to 9999. This placement is called *'aqd*, plural *'uqūd*. Thus the finger-reckoner understood numbers as formed of places, namely units, tens, hundreds, etc., each place having one or the other of the nine *'uqūd*: one, two, ... nine. With this understanding the word *'uqūd* came to mean what we should now call digits. But in practice *'aqd* and place were not always clearly distinguished.

Another characteristic of the system of finger-reckoning appears in the way it tackles fractions. It contained three sets of fractions. Sexagesimal fractions constitute one set, proving a Graeco-Babylonian element in the system.

Another set expresses fractions in terms of the subdivisions of the units of measurements and money. For example, where one *dirham* is 24 *qīrāṭs*, 7 *qīrāṭs*, may stand for $\frac{7}{24}$. Many of these units varied from place to place, but the authors usually defined the units they were using.

The third set of fractions may be designated as 'Arabic' for want of a better name, since the Arabic language has a single-word name for each of the nine fractions ½, ⅓, ... ⅒ and a phrase to name other fractions such as ⅗, ⅟₁₁, ⅟₁₂.

18

Operating on fractional quantities was also done mentally, bearing in mind the rules:

$$\frac{a}{b} = \frac{ac}{bc}, \quad \frac{a}{b} + \frac{c}{d} = \frac{ad + bc}{bd}, \quad \frac{a}{b} \times \frac{c}{d} = \frac{ac}{bd} \text{ and } \frac{a}{b} \div \frac{c}{d} = \frac{ad}{bd} \div \frac{bc}{bd} = \frac{ad}{bc}$$

The system of finger-reckoning gave way to Indian arithmetic. This does not mean that it was completely discarded; the good points in it – and the sexagesimal system – were retained, thus creating a new system that was richer than any of its predecessors, including the transmitted Indian system. Although it was modified and improved by Muslim scholars, however, the new system is still designated as Indian arithmetic.

It is not yet sufficiently known how the figures commonly called Arabic numerals, and attributed by Muslim writers to the Indians, reached the Islamic world. The first reference to these numerals outside India appears in a statement made in 662 by Severus Sebokht, a bishop from western Syria.

The earliest Muslim scholar to have written about Indian arithmetic was Muḥammad b. Mūsà al-Khuwārazmī (d. c.847) who was active in Baghdad in the reign of the caliph al-Ma'mūn. His work on arithmetic is lost, however, and we have instead four Latin works. These are alleged to be partial translations of al-Khuwārazmī's work, and indeed the use in three of them of Latinised versions of al-Khuwārazmī's name, Algorizmi or Alchorismi has given rise to our expression *algorithm*. From these manuscripts, which may go back to an earlier, lost Latin version of al-Khuwārazmī's *Indian Reckoning*, it seems that neither the numeral forms nor the manipulational schemes given by al-Khuwārazmī agree with what spread later in Islam under the name of Indian arithmetic.

Two sets of numerals spread in the Islamic world, one in the east and one in the west. The eastern set were the forerunners of the present-day Arabic numerals: ١, ٢, ٣, ٤, ٥, ٦, ٧, ٨, ٩ with the sign 0 for zero, although this is now generally written as a dot. The western numerals developed into those described nowadays as 'Arabic' numerals, namely, 1, 2, 3, 4, 5, 6, 7, 8, 9, 0.

The earliest text of Indian arithmetic discovered so far was written in Damascus in 952/3 by Aḥmad b. Ibrāhīm al-Uqlīdisī. The subject is dealt with in a masterly way; the author enriches the system with elements from other systems and even attempts to modify it for use with paper and ink, since it came into the Islamic world with the dust-board as its distinguishing feature. Hence as well as being called by the Muslims *al-ḥisāb al-hindī* it was also called *ḥisāb al-ghubār* (dust arithmetic). The reckoner spread dust on his board and wrote on it with a stylus or with his finger. Manipulation depended upon rubbing out digits and shifting others, since the nature of the medium made the digits too large for all of them to be retained throughout a calculation. To see the system in operation we shall take three basic types of calculation: multiplication division and the extraction of square roots.

To multiply 324 by 564, they are first arranged thus:

$$324$$
$$567$$

The 3 is multiplied successively by 5 (hundreds), 6 (tens) and 7 (units). The following pictures appear on the board, one replacing the other:

$$15\,324 \longrightarrow 168324 \longrightarrow 170124$$
$$567 \qquad\qquad 567 \qquad\qquad 567$$

Now the lower line is shifted one place to the right, for the 2 to be multiplied in succession by 5, 6 and 7:

$$170124 \longrightarrow 180124 \longrightarrow 181324 \longrightarrow 181444$$
$$567 \qquad\quad 567 \qquad\quad 567 \qquad\quad 567$$

Finally the lower line is once again shifted to the right, for the 4 to be multiplied in turn by 5, 6 and 7:

$$181444 \longrightarrow 183444 \longrightarrow 183684$$
$$567 \qquad\quad 567 \qquad\quad 567$$
$$\longrightarrow 183708$$

Division was carried out by a method very similar to the modern one, except for the necessity for sequential erasures. For example, during the division of 1169976 by 328 the following pictures appear in succession on the board:

$$3$$
$$1169976 \qquad \text{(deduct } 3 \times 328 = 984 \text{ from 1169)}$$
$$328$$

$$35$$
$$\longrightarrow 185976 \qquad \text{(deduct } 328 \times 5 = 1640 \text{ from 1859)}$$
$$328$$

$$356$$
$$\longrightarrow 21976 \qquad \text{(deduct } 328 \times 6 = 1968 \text{ from 2197)}$$
$$328$$

$$3567$$
$$\longrightarrow 2296 \qquad \text{(deduct } 328 \times 7 = 2296 \text{ from 2296)}$$
$$2296$$

The quotient is 3567, with no remainder.

For the extraction of square roots one first of all divided the number into pairs, starting from the right. One began the process with the digit or pair of digits on the left-hand side:

for example, $\sqrt{5625}$:

$7 \times 7 = 49$ (the closest square to 56)

7

$5625 \longrightarrow 725 \ (7 \times 2 = 14)$

49

7

$\longrightarrow$ 725

14

$(5 \times 14 = 70, 5 \times 5 = 25)$

75

725

$\longrightarrow$ 70

25

So the square of 5625 is 75 (the number of steps has been reduced in this example).

Perhaps the most significant fact about al-Uqlīdisī's arithmetic is that he used decimal fractions, an innovation that was until very recently attributed to al-Kāshī, about five centuries later. While al-Kāshī realised the importance of decimal fractions more fully than al-Uqlīdisī, the latter had used a decimal sign – a stroke above the numeral in the units place – which is superior to al-Kāshī's way of indicating the decimal part of the number. He did this, for example, by writing it in a different colour or in a column or columns other than that of the integral part.

The Muslim achievement in the amalgamation and unification of several concepts drawn from various civilisations can hardly be overestimated. The confident handling of the basic arithmetical operations for both whole numbers and fractions, the use and interchangeability of decimal and sexagesimal numbers, the extraction of square roots and the first tentative operations with irrational numbers are all part of a system that was refined and elaborated by successive generations of Muslim scholars. The extraction of cube roots was first described by Kushyār b. Labān, a Persian mathematician who flourished in Baghdad about the year 1000. He may also have known the binomial coefficients and the extraction of the fourth and higher roots, but it was 'Umar Khayyām (d. 1123) who systemised these problems.

A branch of arithmetic with which the Muslims were concerned was the theory of numbers, *'ilm al-'adad* in Arabic. This was a field which was closely connected to the study of magic squares and amicable numbers; these were applied to various occult sciences from alchemy to magic. Magic squares, which have talismanic values, are characterised by the fact that the sum of the numbers which they surround, whether read in columns, lines or diagonals is constant. For example:

12	17	10
11	13	15
16	9	14

FIGURE 2.2 Magic square.

Two numbers are called amicable if one of them is the sum of the divisors of the other; for example 220 and 284

$$220 = 142 + 71 + 4 + 2 + 1$$
$$284 = 110 + 55 + 44 + 22 + 20 + 11 + 10 + 5 + 4 + 2 + 1$$

But 142 etc. are the factors of 284, and 110 etc. are the factors of 220. The study of these and other numerical relationships led to the analysis of arithmetical and geometrical progressions.

ALGEBRA

The oldest Arabic work on algebra was composed by Muḥammad b . Mūsà al-Khuwārazmí. The work is entitled *Kitāb al-mukhtasar fī ḥisāb al-jabr wa'l-muqābala (The Book of summary concerning calculating by transposition and reduction)*. The last two words cannot be accurately translated, but their meaning is clear enough. They concern the auxiliary processes by which problems are reduced to six basic equations:

1. $ax^2 = bx$ 2. $ax^2 = c$ 3. $ax = c$
4. $ax^2 + bx = c$ 5. $ax^2 + c = bx$ 6. $bx + c = ax^2$

The definitions of the technical terms *jabr* and *muqābala* differ very slightly from one writer to another. In general, the first word meant the transposition of terms in order to make them all positive.

22

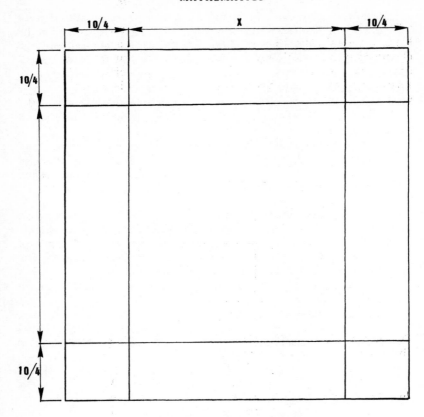

FIGURE 2.3 Completing the square.

Thus:

$$6x^2 - 36x + 60 = 2x^2 - 12$$

is transformed by *jabr* into

$$6x^2 + 60 + 12 = 2x^2 + 36x.$$

By *muqābala* is meant the reduction of similar terms. The equation

$$4x^2 + 72 = 36x$$

is simplified by dividing throughout by 4, giving

$$x^2 + 18 = 9x.$$

The differentiation between these two terms seems somewhat artificial to us, as do the terms used for different parts of an equation. As already mentioned, our system with the letters of the alphabet was not used by the Muslims. Instead, the expressions used reflect the origins of algebra in commerce and in dealing with complex questions of

23

inheritance. The word *māl*, literally 'capital', was originally used for the unknown quantity in linear equations but later came to mean the square as opposed to the root – *jidhr*. The word *shay'*, literally 'thing', was applied to the quantity sought, the unknown. In al-Khuwārazmī's algebra, developed for the six canonical equations given above, *māl* is represented by the area of a square, the *jidhr* by the area of a rectangle having the side of the square as its length and the unit as its width. Not only negative, but also irrational values were excluded from the numerical examples.

The resolution of the complete quadratic equations is given by al-Khuwārazmī in the verbal terminology described above, as rules for the extraction of roots. He then gives geometrical demonstrations and numerical proofs. For example, the equation

$$x^2 + 10x = 39$$

is found, together with many other examples from al-Khuwārazmī, in almost all the Arabic and European algebraic manuals of the Middle Ages. The geometric solution consisted of constructing a square of sides x, along each side of which one drew a rectangle of width $1\frac{0}{4}$. The corners were filled in with squares of side equal to $1\frac{0}{4}$.

The main square thus has an area of x^2, the rectangles of $2\frac{1}{2}x$ each and the small squares of $(1\frac{0}{4})^2$ each.

The total area of the large square is therefore $x^2 + 4. (1\frac{0}{4})x + 4. (1\frac{0}{4})^2$. The first two terms are $x^2 + 10x$ and we already know that this is equal to 39. Hence the area of the square is 39 + 25 = 64. Its side is therefore 8 = x + 2 $(1\frac{0}{4})$ whence x = 3. (See Figure 2.3.)

The equivalent, in modern algebraic notation, is as follows:

$$x^2 + px = q.$$

Carry out the following manipulations

$$x^2 + 4 (\tfrac{p}{4}) + 4(\tfrac{p}{4})^2 = q + 4(\tfrac{p}{4})^2$$
$$(x + 2.\tfrac{p}{4})^2 = q + 4 (\tfrac{p}{4})^2$$
$$x + 2.\tfrac{p}{4} = \sqrt{q + 4(\tfrac{p}{4})^2}$$

whence $\quad x = \sqrt{q + (\tfrac{p}{2})^2} - p/2.$

In the example given earlier, q = 39, p = 10

whence $\quad x = \sqrt{39 + 25} - 5 = 3.$

The equation is of course equal to our general solution for

$$ax^2 + bx + c = 0$$

of $\qquad x = \dfrac{-b \pm \sqrt{b^2 - 4ac}}{2a}$

but in his numerical example al-Khuwārazmī ignored the other root, i.e. –13.

The procedure has been given at some length, not because the problems were intrinsically difficult, but because modern readers will be unaccustomed to geometrical solutions of algebraic problems.

The first part of al-Khuwārazmī's treatise was translated into Latin in 1145 by Robert of Chester under the title *Liber algebrae et almucabala* hence of course the passage of the word 'algebra' into European languages.

Shortly after al-Khuwārazmī the Egyptian scholar abū Kāmil al-Shujā' (d. *c.*930) also exercised a considerable influence in the development of Western algebra, making valuable contributions to the theory, which he turned into a powerful instrument for geometrical research. He solved systems of equations involving up to five unknown quantities. He discussed problems of a higher degree, but only those which could be reduced to quadratic equations. He admitted irrational quantities as solutions.

The algebraists learned new methods from the translations of Greek mathematical works. The scholar known as Ibn al-Baghdadī, who lived in the first half of the tenth century, carefully discussed the theory of irrational quantities. The work of Apollonius on conic sections became the general instrument for the algebraists. For example, Abu Ja'far al-Khāzin (d. 961 or 971) solved the equation $x^3 + a = bx^2$ with the help of the theory of conic sections. On the other hand, the new theory provided the basis for reducing many geometrical problems to constructions by means of conic sections. Thus the eminent physicist Ibn al-Haytham (d. Egypt 1039) was able to solve a problem of the fourth degree and to deal with a special problem of the fifth degree. The general development culminated in the work of 'Umar Khayyām who discussed all cases of equations up to the third degree in a very systematic manner. He distinguished clearly between algebraic and geometrical proofs, both of which he considered necessary, although he stated that he was unable to give algebraic solutions for equations of the third degree. Negative solutions were still excluded.

GEOMETRY

'Ilm al-handasa, the science of geometry, was introduced to the Arabs, as in the case with other branches of mathematics, through the translation of Greek works, especially Euclid's *Elements*, and through the Indian *Siddhantas*. The period of translation and initiation in the ninth century was succeeded by a time of creativity (tenth to fifteenth centuries) during which the translated material was progressively annotated, discussed and corrected. Although masters such as Euclid, Apollonius and Archimedes were accorded a respect amounting almost to reverence, Arabic writers were not afraid of disputing and in some cases correcting their results. Arabic scholars also made notable contributions to theoretical geometry. The most remarkable works of theory are those of Jawharī (ninth century), of Abharī and Nayrīzī

(tenth century), of Ibn al-Haytham and 'Umar Khayyām (eleventh century) and Naṣr al-Dīn al-Ṭūsī (thirteenth century). These works were translated into Latin and Hebrew and their influence is evident in Western treatises of late medieval and Renaissance times.

More than the other branches of mathematics, however, geometry impinges on various sciences and technologies. Trigonometry (see next section), so essential for astronomy, is virtually an extension of geometry and geometrical proofs were applied to optics and algebra. Geometry was also applied to geodetic measurements and to land surveying, especially for fiscal purposes and for various transactions by landlords. It is difficult to imagine any building, civil engineering or mechanical engineering constructions that do not need the aid of geometry. In later chapters we shall have occasion to describe how constructional geometry was applied to land surveying and to hydraulic works. Indeed, so important is the geometrical element in engineering that the word *handasa*, originally denoting only geometry, in modern Arabic usually has the meaning of 'engineerng'. This is unfortunate, not only as a possible source of ambiguity, but because it reflects an attitude, common among theoretical scientists, both medieval and modern, that engineerng is 'applied science'. Certainly, it is true that engineering makes use of mathematics and science, but that does not mean that it is simply an application of those disciplines. There are many skills required to design and build engineering structures, and a number of those skills are unrelated to theoretical science.

There is one aspect of practical geometry that cannot readily be dealt with in connection with other subjects, and that is the science of measurement. The word *misāḥa* can have two meanings, the measurement of plane and solid figures, and techniques of surveying. We shall consider briefly the first of these two meanings; the second is dealt with in Chapter 10. The contents of the works on *misāḥa* as a rule comprise introductory remarks, rules for calculating areas and volumes and the most important lengths found on them, and occasionally also practical exercises. (It should be stressed, once again, that the Arabs had no language of mathematical formulae; the rules for measuring were always written out fully in words.)

A. Introductory remarks. These are as a rule:
    1. Definition of the term *misāḥa*
    2. Explanation, description and systematic classification of the geometrical figures to be discussed
    3. Definition and list of the most common units of measurement

B. Rules of calculation
    I. Plane surfaces (and the lengths occurring on them)

1. Quadrilaterals (square, rectangle, rhomboid, trapezium, trapezoid, quadrilateral with salient angle)
2. Triangles (equilateral, isosceles, scalene, right-angled, acute-angled and obtuse-angled)
3. Polygons (regular and irregular)
4. Circle, segments of circle (semicircle, segment, sector, circumference and related areas)

II. Solids (and the areas and lengths that occur on them)
1. Prism (ordinary, straight and oblique prism, square columns, rectangular columns, triangular prism)
2. Cylinder
3. Pyramids (straight and oblique, sections of pyramids)
4. Cones (straight and oblique, sections of cones)
5. Sphere and sections of sphere (hemisphere, segment, sector and zone)
6. Regular and semi-regular bodies
7. Other bodies, particularly those occurring in architecture, such as cylindrical vaults and hollow domes

C. Practical exercises

TRIGONOMETRY

Trigonometry occupied an important place in Muslim mathematics and was the branch to which the Muslims made the greatest original contributions. It also constituted an important link with astronomy through the establishment of calendars and gnomics – the theory and practice of sundials – the construction of which was widespread throughout the Islamic world.

The basis of Islamic trigonometry (and astronomy) was in three works: the Indian *Siddhanta*, the *Almagest* of Ptolemy and the *Spherics* of Menelaus. The Alexandrian astronomers had however, only introduced a single trigonometric function, that of the chord of an arc. The Indians replaced the chord by the sine, adding the cosine and the versed sine. The mathematicians of the Islamic world adopted these new trigonometric functions, studied their characteristics, and found solutions for every problem in plane and spherical triangles.

Muḥammad b. Mūsà al-Khuwārazmī wrote a work on astronomy, based upon Indian and Greek sources. This work contained the first Arabic tables of sines and tangents. It is not certain, however, that the table of tangents was by al-Khuwārazmī, since the work has survived only in a version adapted by the Spanish Muslim al-Majrītī (d. Cordoba c.1007). There is also a Latin translation of this version, made in the twelfth century by Adelard of Bath. In any case, it is certain that tangents and cotangents were known to the contemporary and colleague of al-Khuwārazmī, Ḥabash al-Ḥāsib al-Marwazī who came from the city of Marw in Khurāsān, but worked mainly in Baghdad, where he died about 870.

The tangent and the cotangent, together with the secant and the cosecant had originally been introduced as functions generated by the lines within a circle, but were used in gnomics for the ratios of right-angled triangles. In Figure 2.4 if h is considered as the height of a vertical gnomon (the stylus of a sundial), then the ratio of h to the length t of the shadow it projects depends upon the sun's altitude. The cotangent of θ = t/h, or t cotθ = h. Ḥabash al-Ḥāsib took h as unity and calculated a tale of values for the shadow t for θ = 1°, 2°, 3° ... with an accuracy down to seconds of arc. This table, expressed in cotangents, allowed the altitude of the sun to be determined by the length of the shadow.

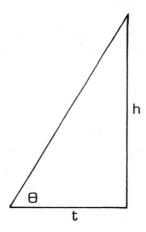

FIGURE 2.4 Shadow triangle.

The tables of cotangents and tangents compiled by Ḥabash were a considerable contribution to facilitating trigonometrical functions. Already in the works of Ḥabash, however, the use of the tangent and other trigonometrical functions was not restricted to gnomics. He also expressed the relationship of the Right Ascension α of the sun, the declination δ and the inclination ϵ of the ecliptic by the formula:

$$\sin \alpha = \tan \delta \cot \epsilon.$$

The famous astronomer al-Battānī (d. Samarra 929) listed a number of trigonometrical relationships (which were, however, already known to Ḥabash).

28

These included:

$$\tan a = \frac{\sin a}{\cos a} \qquad \sin a = \frac{1}{\cosec a}$$

$$\sec a = \sqrt{1 + \tan^2 a}$$

He also solved the formula sin x = a cos x, discovering the formula

$\sin x = \dfrac{a}{\sqrt{1 + a^2}}$ (for arcs of the first quadrant).

In the tenth century Abu'l-Wafā' (d. Baghdad 998) brought considerable progress to trigonometry. He established the relations:

$$\sin (a+ b) = \sin a \cos b + \cos a \sin b$$
$$2 \sin a = 1 - \cos 2a$$
$$\sin 2a = 2 \sin a \cos a$$

Another eminent astronomer Ibn Yūnus (d 1009) demonstrated the formula cos a cos b = ½ [cos (a + b) = cos (a – b)], permitting the passage from a sum to a product, which was to be of importance in the logarithmic system of calculation invented later.

On a clear night we have the impression that the stars are all sparkling points of light, apparently situated on the surface of a vast sphere, of which the individual observer is at the centre. Spherical Astronomy is concerned essentially with the *directions* in which the stars are viewed, and Spherical Trigonometry is the tool for solving problems of Spherical Astronomy

Any plane passing through the centre of a sphere cuts the surface in a circle which is called a *great circle*. If we are given any three points

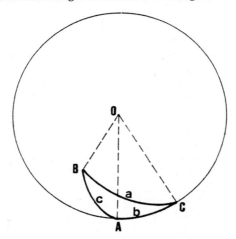

FIGURE 2.5 Spherical triangle.

on the surface of a sphere, then the sphere can be bisected so that all three points lie on the same hemisphere. If the points are joined by great circle arcs all lying on this hemisphere, the figure obtained is called a *spherical triangle*. If we consider the spherical triangle ABC (Figure 2.5), the angles $\widehat{ABC}$, $\widehat{ACB}$, and $\widehat{BAC}$ are defined as the angles between the tangents of the great circles intersecting at A, B and C. For all great circle arcs on the sphere the radius R is constant and can be considered as unity. The lengths of the sides – AB, AC and BC are therefore defined by the angles they subtend at the centre O of the sphere, namely $\widehat{AOB}$, $\widehat{AOC}$ and $\widehat{BOC}$. The sides are usually identified by lower-case letters, in this case a, b and c, in the usual trigonometrical convention. The solution of spherical triangles is by far the commonest method for obtaining astronomical and geodetic results.

In the notation given above, the fundamental formula of spherical trigonometry in use today is:
$$\cos a = \cos b \cos c + \sin b \sin c \cos A \qquad (A)$$
There are clearly two companion formulae:
$$\cos b = \cos c \cos a + \sin c \sin a \cos B$$
$$\cos c = \cos a \cos b + \sin a \sin b \cos C$$
The formula is usually known as the *cosine formula*. From (A) and its two companion formulae all the other formulae in use can be derived. The most widely used of these are:
$$\frac{\sin A}{\sin a} = \frac{\sin B}{\sin b} = \frac{\sin C}{\sin c} \qquad (B)$$
(usually called the *sine formula*)
$$\sin a \cos B = \cos b \sin c - \sin b \cos c \cos A \qquad (C)$$
$$\cos a \cos C = \sin a \cot b - \sin C \cot B \qquad (D)$$
(known as the *four-parts formula*)

Ptolemy had resolved four cases of right-angle spherical triangles, and at first Muslim astronomers dealt with the same problems. They soon went beyond these special cases; al-Battānī for example discovered the basic formula given in (A) above. Already in the tenth century al-Nayrīzī and Abu'l-Wafā' had deduced the sine formula, giving numerous examples of its applications. The most eminent scholar in the field of trigonometry, both plane and spherical, was Naṣīr al-Dīn al-Ṭūsī (d. 1274). His comprehensive treatment of the resolution of spherical triangles was one of a number of studies that makes his work of particular importance in the development of mathematics.

Despite some Muslim astronomers' mastery of spherical trigonometry, caution is necessary when considering results given in Arabic astronomical works. Sometimes it may appear obvious to us that a given problem could only have been solved by using one of the formulae given above, or a formula derived from them, even though the writer has not stated which method he used. The Muslims, however, often derived exact solutions using the construction of Greek mathematics known as the *analemma*, in which the various significant planes involved in a specific problem are either projected or folded into a single working plane. Geometrical solutions can then be derived graphically or the solution can be computed by plane trigonometry. Another possibility is that the solution was derived by using a computational instrument (see next chapter).

3

Astronomy

In its origins and development, Islamic astronomy closely parallels the
genesis of other Islamic sciences in its assimilation of foreign material
and the subsequent amalgamation of the disparate elements of that
material to create a science that was essentially Islamic. Before we
consider the literary and observational activities of Islamic astronomers, which lasted for over a millenium, we should glance briefly at
the traditional astronomy of the Arabian peninsula.

Traditional Arabic astronomy was closely linked to the *anwā'* (sing.
naw'), a word that denotes in the singular the acronycal (i.e. occurring at nightfall) setting of a star or constellation and the heliacal
rising of its opposite. *Anwā'* denotes the whole system based upon
the settings and rising of stars and constellations, and it also appears
in the titles of a number of works that constitute a separate class of
their own.

To estimate the passage of time the early Arabs possessed a primitive system. This consisted basically of two distinct elements. First,
the acronycal setting of a series of stars or constellations marked the
beginning of periods called *naw'*, but within which the duration of the
naw' proper was from one to seven days; the stars themselves were
responsible for rain and were invoked during rain-making ceremonies.
Knowledge of these *anwā'* enabled Beduin trained in the science to
foresee the state of the weather during a given period. Secondly, the
heliacal rising of the same series of stars or constellations, at six-
monthly intervals, marked out the solar year by fixing the number of
periods, probably about twenty-eight. Fragments of folklore that have
survived suggest that this was the basis of the calendar.

Some time before Islam the Arabs learned from the Indians to
distinguish the stations or 'mansions' (*manzila*, pl *manāzil*) of the
moon, numbering twenty-eight. Since the list of these mansions corresponded approximately with their own list of *anwā'*, they proceeded to
combine the two ideas, adjusting their *anwā'* to coincide with the
manāzil, by dividing the solar zodiac into twenty-eight equal parts of
approximately 12° 50' each. Thus the 28 *anwā'*, or *manāzil* are determined by 28 stars or constellations constituting 14 pairs, the acronycal
setting of the one corresponding to the heliacal rising of the other, and
marking the beginning of 27 periods of 13 days and one of 14. These

modifications, which cannot be dated accurately, were definitely completed after the advent of Islam.

This folklore was eventually recorded in the *Kutub al-anwā'*, of which over twenty examples were completed in the ninth and tenth centuries alone, although only four of these survive. One of them, by the great polygraph Ibn Qutayba (d. Baghdad 889), is representative of one type of *anwā'* book, being a collection of knowledge of celestial and meteorological phenomena as found in Arabic sources as folklore, literature and poetry. Another, representative of a second type, is arranged in the form of a calendar containing agricultural, meteorological and astronomical events of significance to farmers; such is the *Calendar of Cordoba*, compiled for a specific year in the tenth century.

A distinctly Islamic flavour was added to this pre-Islamic folk astronomy by the fact that the times of Muslim prayer were defined astronomically, and the direction of Mecca (the *qibla*) was defined geographically. A corpus of literature appeared in which these two subjects were discussed in terms of primitive folk astronomy. This corpus comprises the *Kutub al-mawāqit* and the *Kutub dalā' il al-qibla*, of which the earliest examples are known only quotations in the numerous later works dealing with these subjects in a non-mathematical way. The topics discussed in these works included, for example, the regulation of the daytime prayers by shadow lengths, of the night-time prayers by the lunar mansions and the determination of the *qibla* by the direction of the wind and the risings and settings of the fixed stars. This material has only recently been investigated for the first time. Because of their religious significance these two subjects together with a third – the determination of the visibility of the lunar crescent at the beginning of each Muslim month – are distinct from other aspects of astronomy whose investigations and application have purely secular motivations. There was also a non-folkloric tradition in which these problems were solved by mathematical means; we shall return to this later.

SOURCES OF ISLAMIC ASTRONOMY

The earliest Islamic works relating to mathematical astronomy were based upon Indian and Sasānid works. With very few exceptions these early Islamic works are lost and our knowledge of them has been pieced together from later citations. As early as the eighth century in India and Afghanistan there were compiled a number of Arabic *zīj*s, that is, astronomical handbooks with text and tables. The most important representative of the Indian tradition was the *Zīj al-Sindhind* of al-Khuwārazmī. Only fragments of the original text survive but we have a Latin translation of the revision made by al-Majrītī in Cordoba (c.1000). Indeed, there seems to have been a strong Andalusian predeliction for the Sindhind. The few eastern representatives of the tradition are known mainly from quotations in the works of later astronomers.

Hellenistic astronomical texts were translated into Arabic, the most important being the *Almagest* of Ptolemy, of which several versions were made from both Syriac and Greek in the ninth century. The most authoritative version was that produced by Isḥāq b. Hunayn and corrected by Thābit b. Qurra. During the course of the ninth century Ptolemy's *Hypotheses*, Theon's 'Handy Tables' and the corpus of minor Greek works known as the 'Little Astronomy' were also translated into Arabic, and a number of treatises on the astrolabe were published.

The available original sources enable us to distinguish four main periods of Islamic astronomy: first, a period of assimilation and syncretisation of earlier Hellenistic, Indian and Sasānid mathematical astronomy and pre-Islamic folk astronomy (c.700–c.825); second, a period of vigorous investigation in which the superiority of Ptolemaic astronomy was accepted, and significant contributions were made (c.825–c.1025); third, a period when a distinctly Islamic astronomy flourished and in general continued to progress, if with decreasing vigour (c.1025–c.1450); and finally a period of stagnation in which this traditional Islamic astronomy continued to be practised with enthusiasm but without innovation of any scientific significance (c.1450–c.1900).

Muslim astronomers compiled a remarkably rich corpus of literature, some of which survives in about 10,000 manuscript volumes preserved in the libraries of south-west Asia, North Africa, Europe and the United States. During the past 200 years a very small number of scholars has turned its attention to a fraction of this surviving material, much of which has not even been catalogued. Even so, a reasonably accurate picture of Islamic activity in the field of astronomy can be reconstructed. The most fruitful source of information is to be found in the *zījs*, but also in the writings of Islamic astronomers concerned with one or other branches of the science. For the remainder of this chapter the subject matter has been limited, by reasons of space, to branches of astronomy to which the Muslims made significant contributions.

SPHERICAL ASTRONOMY

Basic Theory

Spherical astronomy is concerned with the apparent motions of objects on the *celestial sphere* caused by the daily rotation of the earth, the annual rotation of the earth around the sun, the rotation of the moon around the earth and the rotation of the planets around the sun. Until the time of Copernicus in the sixteenth century the prevailing astronomical system was geocentric, that is, the earth was considered to be the centre of the universe. For most computing purposes the geocentric theory works perfectly well; certainly for the fixed stars and, with certain adaptations, for the sun, moon and planets. In attempting to explain the irregular motions of the planets, Ptolemy had compiled an elaborate series of geometrical constructions, some of which were objectionable to Muslim astronomers on philosophical or obsevational grounds, or both. In proposing modifications to the Ptolemaic system the Muslims made some notable contributions to theoretical astronomy. This aspect of the subject will be discussed in the next section. For the moment we shall concern ourselves only with those aspects of spherical astronomy that have an application to the solution of practical problems, particularly those that are relevant to Islamic practices.

The advances made by the Muslims in spherical trigonometry, the main mathematical tool for the solution of problems in spherical astronomy, have already been discussed in the previous chapter. A comprehensive treatment of spherical astronomy demands a knowledge of the celestial sphere, but unfortunately we lack the space for an extended discussion of the subject. Most popular handbooks of astronomy will provide the necessary explanations, but for the present we will list the main components of the celestial sphere, in order that those with little knowledge of astronomy may the more easily follow the descriptions in the remainder of this chapter.

Terrestrial co-ordinates can be transferred to the celestial sphere, since we are concerned with directions, not with actual distances. The observer's horizon and his meridian circle, at right angles to it, as determined by his latitude and longitude, are transferred to the celestial sphere, as are the equatorial and polar circles. In the course of a year the sun appears to make a complete circuit of the heavens against the background of the stars. This orbit is called the *ecliptic*, and because of the inclination of the earth's axis it appears to be inclined at an angle of about 23½° to the celestial equator. The stars along the ecliptic are known as the *zodiac*, which is divided into twelve 'signs' each of 30°. (These are the familiar signs listed in newspaper 'horoscopes'.) Twice a year the ecliptic crosses the equator at the equinoxes. The spring or vernal equinox γ is used as a reference point on the celestial sphere. (See Figure 3.1 and 3.2.)

Heavenly bodies are given co-ordinates – *declination* and *Right Ascension* (RA) – analogous to terrestrial latitude and longitude. A

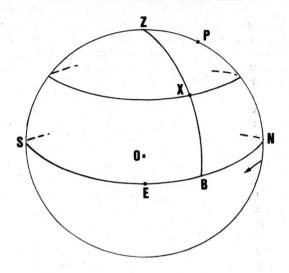

FIGURE 3.1 Celestial sphere 1. NES is the horizon, P is the north pole, PZ is colatitude of the observer. The angle PZX or the arc NB is the *azimuth* of the star.

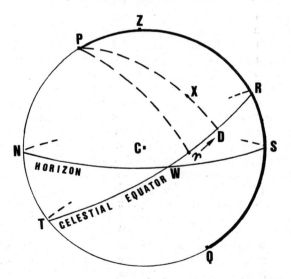

FIGURE 3.2 Celestial sphere 2. the invariable co-ordinates of the star X are its *declination* DX and its *Right Ascension D*.

star's declination is the angular distance of the star from the celestial equator. The RA is the angle between the star's meridian and the meridian of the vernal equinox, measured eastwards from γ. These co-ordinates are invariable for the fixed stars but vary continually for the sun. At a given moment in time the position of a star or the sun is defined by its *hour angle*, that is, the angle made by the plane through the object's meridian and the observer's meridian at this moment. When observing a heavenly body two readings may be taken: its altitude and its *azimuth*, that is, its bearing from the observer's station.

From these observations and the known co-ordinates of the heavenly body, various results can be obtained. For instance, if the time of the observation is known the latitude of the observer can be calculated. Conversely, if the latitude is known the time of the observation can be ascertained. If the observation is made at the instant when the sun or a star is crossing the observer's meridian the subsequent calculations are simplified; otherwise recourse must be had to the appropriate formulae in spherical trigonometry. Because of the inclination of the ecliptic and certain irregularities in the sun's apparent motion, the solar day is not constant, but varies by a small amount from day to day. Hence solar time is measured according to the orbit of a fictitious body, moving at constant apparent speed, called the *mean sun*. Also, the sidereal day, that is the length of time between successive transits of a star over a given meridian, is about four minutes shorter than the solar day. These differences have to be taken into account when calculating results from astronomical observations, but once the necessary rules and formulae have been mastered, the calculations present no especial difficulties.

The computations are, however, usually very tedious, since answers are often required to several places of decimals. The *zījs* usually contain tables of ephemerides for assisting in calculations, as well as trigonometrical tables. Again, most *zījs* also present methods of obtaining results by geometrical constructions. And, as we shall see in a later section, instruments such as astrolabes and equatoria were designed to dispense with calculations altogether, although these could only be used in cases where great accuracy was not required.

Timekeeping

'Ilm al-miqāt (the science of timekeeping) is an essential part of Islamic astronomical practice since the limits for the permitted intervals for the five prayers are defined in terms of the apparent position of the sun in the sky relative to the local horizon. These times vary throughout the year and are dependent upon the local latitude.

In popular practice the daylight prayers were regulated by simple arithmetical shadow schemes of the kind also known to have been used for timekeeping in earlier Hellenistic and Byzantine folk astronomy. A number of different shadow schemes have been located in the Arabic sources. In most cases they are not the result of careful observations. For the noon prayer (zuhr) usually a single digit for the midday shadow of a man of specified height was used. One such scheme, starting with a value for January, is: 9, 7, 5, 3, 2, 1, 1, 2, 4, 5, 8, 10. The corresponding values for the evening ('aṣr) prayer are 7 units more for each month. Somewhat more sophisticated empirical formulae, for instance based upon the observed altitude and the meridian altitude, were proposed by various astronomers.

In practice, at least before the thirteenth century, the regulation of the prayer times was the duty of the muezzin. The muezzins needed to be proficient only in the rudiments of folk astronomy. They had to know the shadows of the zuhr and the 'aṣr for each month, and which lunar mansion was rising at daybreak and setting at nightfall. In the thirteenth century, however, there arose the institution of the muwaqqit, a professional astronomer whose primary responsibility was the regulation of the times of prayer. Simultaneously, there appeared astronomers with the epithet miqātī who specialised in spherical and astronomical timekeeping, but who were not necessarily associated with any religious institution.

The knowledge of spherical astronomy applied to timekeeping did not, of course, originate at this time. In zījs from the ninth century onwards we find accurate methods for determining the time by means of an analemma applied to the celestial sphere. The modern formula for determining the hour angle t can also be derived by these procedures. It is:

$$\cos t = \frac{(\sin h - \sin \delta \sin \phi)}{\cos \delta \cos \gamma}$$

where h is the observed altitude, δ the solar declination and ϕ the local latitude. Though not precisely in this form, the Muslim formula was analogous to it. Since h is observed and ϕ is known, the compilation of tables for timekeeping involved the recording of variations in solar parameters.

In the thirteenth century an astronomer named Shibāb al-Dīn al-Maqsī compiled a set of tables displaying the time since sunrise as a function of solar altitude h and solar longitude λ for the latitude of Cairo, which in the fourteenth century was expanded and developed into a corpus of tables covering some 200 manuscript folios and containing over 30,000 entries. These tables display the altitude and hour angle of the sun relative to prayer times, the solar azimuth for each degree of solar altitude, and other information. A contemporary of al-Maqsī compiled a table of timekeeping which served all latitudes and could be used for timekeeping by the sun or by the stars. The table contained over 250,000 entries.

In the fourteenth century the most valuable work on astronomical timekeeping was done in Syria. Al-Mizzī, after studying in Egypt, returned to Syria and compiled a set of hour angle tables and prayer tables for Damascus modelled upon the Cairo corpus. Ibn al-Shāṭir compiled some prayer tables for an unspecified locality with a latitude of 34°, although his most important achievements were in theoretical astronomy. It was a colleague of al-Mizzī and Ibn al-Shāṭir, Shams al-Dīn al-Khalīlī, who made the most significant advances in *'ilm al-miqāt*. He recomputed the tables of al-Mizzī for the new parameters (local altitude and obliquity of the ecliptic) derived by Ibn al-Shāṭir. His corpus of tables for timekeeping by the sun and for regulating the times of prayer for Damascus was used there until the nineteenth century.

One of the main purposes of water-clocks (see Chapter 7 for details of their construction) was to enable the appointed times for prayer to be announced when the sky was obscured by clouds or by darkness. Astronomical timekeeping was, as it were, 'built in' to water-clocks, since their speed of operation was changed daily to coincide with the lengths of daylight and darkness. The external parts of such a clock, built in the fourteenth century, still exist in one of the upper rooms of the Qarawiyyīn mosque in Fez, Morocco. Prayer times were announced during daylight hours by hoisting a flag on the top of the minaret; at night a fire was lit in a brazier at the top of the minaret so that those outside the city would know the prayer times.

Determination of the qibla

The *qibla* of a given locality is a trigonometric function of the local latitude, the latitude of Mecca and the longitudinal difference from Mecca. The derivation of the *qibla* in terms of these quantities was one of the most complicated of the problems of Islamic spherical astronomy. It was also the most important problem from a purely religious point of view.

In the diagram shown in Figure 3.3 a locality P and Mecca M are shown on the terrestrial surface. The point N represents the north pole and the meridians at P and M are shown as NPA and NMB, where A and B lie on the equator. In mathematical terms the *qibla* at P is defined by the direction of the great circle through P and M. If ϕ and ϕ_m denote the latitudes of the locality and Mecca (i.e. PA and MB) and δl is their longitude difference (=AB), then the angle q is a function of ϕ, ϕ_m

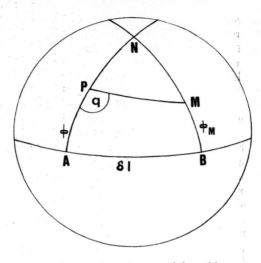

FIGURE 3.3 Determination of the *qibla*.

and δl and can be determined by spherical trigonometry. The modern formula, which can be derived from an application of the spherical cotangent rule to Δ NPM, is:

$$q = \cot^{-1} \frac{\sin \phi \cos \delta l - \cos \phi \tan \phi_m}{\sin \delta l}$$

The exact solutions proposed by the medieval astronomers are less direct but ultimately equivalent to this.

Although the problem of determining the *qibla* is a problem of mathematical geography, it is mathematically equivalent to the astronomical problem of determining the azimuth of a celestial body with given declination for given hour angle, and as such it was usually treated by medieval astronomers.

Several approximate solutions of the problem appeared in *zījs* and in unsophisticated astronomical works from the ninth to the fourteenth century. These *qibla* tables were based upon non-trivial formulae with the trigonometric formulae outlined in words. Exact solutions were devised, either by analemma solutions or by the use of spherical trigonometry. Ḥabash al-Ḥāsib (*c*.850) proposed a solution by analemma, as did Ibn al-Haytham (fl. Cairo *c*.1039), from whose construction a single formula for *q* equivalent to the modern one can be derived directly. Among those to solve the *qibla* problem mathematically were al-Nayrīzī (fl. Baghdad *c*.900) and al-Bīrūnī (d. Ghazna after 1050).

The culmination of Islamic achievements in determining the *qibla*, however, was the work of the astronomer al-Khalīlī (fl. Damascus c.1365), whose work we have already mentioned in connection with mathematical timekeeping. It can easily be shown that the procedures used by al-Khalīlī were equivalent to the formulae of modern spherical trigonometry. He compiled a *qibla* table based upon an accurate formula and displaying q (ϕ, δL) for each degree of ϕ from 10° tp 56° and each degree of δL from 1° to 60°. Al-Khalīlī's table thus contains a total of almost 3,000 entries, and the *qibla* is computed to degrees and minutes. The vast majority of the entries are either correct or are in error by ±1 or ±2 minutes, a remarkable achievement.

In mosques the direction of prayer is indicated by the niche, often beautifully ornamented, called the *mihrab*. The mihrabs were not always exactly oriented. Even though the medieval astronomer might be aware of an exact formula for computing the *qibla*, the accuracy of its determination depended upon the available geographical data. Medieval longitude determinations, based either upon simultaneous observations of lunar eclipses in different localities or on measuring distances between two localities, were generally not very accurate. So, although latitude measurements could be obtained more accurately, medieval mosques may be incorrectly oriented, even though their *mihrabs* were erected in a *qibla* direction by competent mathematicians. Another reason why mosques may be incorrectly aligned is that their *qiblas* were not computed from geographical data at all, but were oriented by tradition.

Crescent Visibility

The third problem of spherical astronomy related to Islamic religious concerns are the predictions of the visibility of the lunar crescent at the beginning of the lunar months. In various Islamic astronomical treatises tables were presented giving the data for making these predictions, based upon a theory related to a single visibility criterion adapted from Indian astronomy. The theory underlying the tables is that visibility can occur if the difference in setting times between the sun and the moon is at least 12 equatorial degrees (or 48 minutes of time). If the interval is less than that the sky will not be dark enough to allow the crescent to appear. (This is purely an empirical parameter.) The difference in setting times depends upon three factors: the longitude of the sun and moon and their differences, the lunar latitude and the local terrestrial latitude. Most tables displayed, as a function of solar or lunar longitude, the differences in longitude between the sun and the moon for which the difference in setting time is 12°. The tables were computed either for a fixed latitude or for a range of latitudes. The tables are to be found mainly in *zijs*, but also in other astronomical publications, from the ninth century to the eighteenth.

41

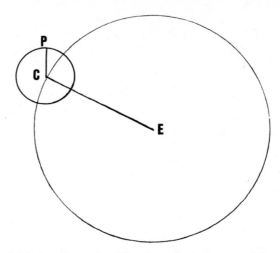

FIGURE 3.4 Epicyclic motion. The planet P moves around the centre
C of the epicycle, which moves in uniform circular motion round
the earth E.

PLANETARY THEORY

The prevailing theory of planetary motion (including the motions of
the sun and moon) was throughout antiquity and the Middle Ages that
of a geocentric universe and of uniform circular motion. In the third
and second centuries BC two models were proposed to explain planetary motion. One was epicyclic motion (Figure 3.4) and the other
eccentric motion (Figure 3.5). The choice between the two depended,
in any particular case, on which of them provided the simpler solution,
that is, the one that was mathematically easier to handle.

In the second century AD Ptolemy introduced several important
modifications in order to attempt to eliminate the inadequacies inherent in the existing system. He also wished to give a satisfactory
explanation of the fact that the planets sometimes appear stationary
against the background of the fixed stars and at times show a retro-
grade movement from east to west. His model of the planets – excluding the moon and Mercury – demonstrates the essential elements of
his system. In Figure 3.6 the planet is imagined as moving on an
epicycle of centre C which moves around a deferent circle of centre F,
eccentric to the earth by the distance EF. The movement is uniform,
not with respect to F but with respect to D (the 'equant'); the angle θ
increases uniformly. The equant is a point on the line from the earth
through the centre of the eccentric circle F and such that EF = ED. The

42

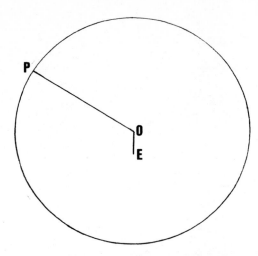

FIGURE 3.5 Eccentric motion. The planet P moves in uniform circular motion round point O, which is eccentric from the earth by distance EO.

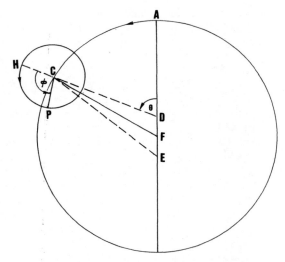

FIGURE 3.6 Ptolemy: planetary model.

line DH turns with uniform angular velocity round D, and the planet's movement on its epicycle is measured from the same line. The planet's longitude depends, therefore, on the two variables θ and φ.

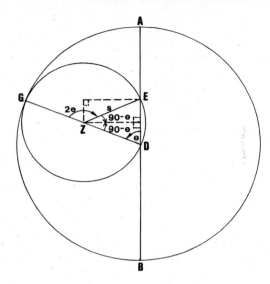

FIGURE 3.7 The Ṭūsī couple.

Ptolemy's planetary theories, as incorporated in the *Almagest*, exercised enormous authority in the Islamic world and in medieval Europe. It had become, clear, however, at least by the time of Ibn al-Haytham (d. *c.*1040), that Ptolemy had been compelled to resort to motions that violated the principles of uniformity and circularity. Ibn al-Haytham identified 16 'difficulties' in Ptolemaic theory, these being irregularities in linear and planetary motions.

The most comprehensive reformation of the Ptolemaic system was undertaken by Naṣīr al-Dīn al-Ṭūsī (1201–74). The most famous of his works, setting forward a comprehensive structure of the universe, was *Al-Tadhkira fī 'ilm al-hay' a* (*Memoir on the science of astronomy*). It was completed at Maragha in 1261, during the time when al-Ṭūsī was the director of the observatory commissioned by the Mongol conqueror of Iran. The *Tadhkira* was highly regarded in the Middle Ages and was the subject of some fifteen commentaries. At least twenty years before writing the *Tadhkira*, however, al-Ṭūsī had written a shorter treatise in which he had resolved the first six of the difficulties enumerated by Ibn al-Haytham. These were all concerned with the irregular motions of the deferents of the moon and planets.

Although al-Ṭūsī's complete system is too lengthy and complex to be discussed here, we shall describe briefly his introduction of a model, in his early treatise, that varies the distance of the epicyclic centre

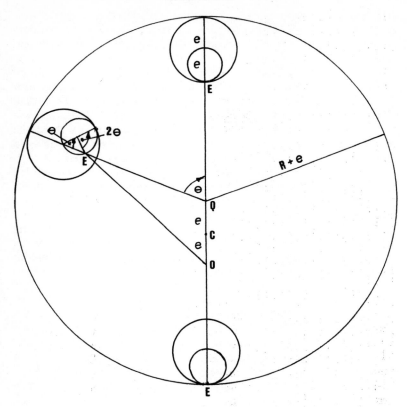

FIGURE 3.8 Ṭūsī: planetary model.

from a given point by having it oscillate in a straight line. The device itself – now known as the 'Ṭūsī couple' – consists of two circles, one having a diameter half that of the other, with the smaller being tangential to the larger (see Figure 3.7). The two circles move in opposite directions, each with a simple uniform rotation, and the smaller circle has a speed of rotation twice that of the larger. it can easily be shown that any point on the smaller circle describes a straight line from A to B on the larger.

A simplified version of the Ṭūsī couple, as applied to the planets, excluding the moon and Mercury, is shown in Figure 3.8. In order for the distance OE from the centre of the world to the epicyclic centre to be R + e at apogee and R – e at perigee so as to conform to the requirements of the Ptolemaic model where R is the radius of the

45

deferent, the epicyclic centre at apogee must be at its closed position at Q while at perigee it must be at its farthest distance. It therefore evidently follows that the inner equator of the deferent in this model has a radius of R + e.

In addition to al-Ṭūsī, other astronomers of the Maragha school proposed modifications to Ptolemy's models, mainly to account for discrepancies between Ptolemy's theoretical constructs and observed phenomena. Prominent among these were Mu'ayyad al-Dīn al-'Urdī (d. 1266) and Ibn al-Shāṭir (d. 1375). Two basic mathematical theorems are very significant in connection with the history of astronomy in general. The first is the Ṭūsī couple, and the second is a theorem of al-'Urdī that allows for the transformation of eccentric models to epicyclic ones. These results are extremely important on account of their relationship to the work of Copernicus. This relationship did not touch upon the Copernican notion of heliocentricity. That key feature of Copernican astronomy entails the reversal of the vector connecting the sun to the earth, while leaving the rest of the mathematical models intact. It is the similarity of the Copernican geocentric versions of those models to those of the Maragha astronomers that has aroused interest.

The relationship depends upon the two basic theorems just mentioned. Copernicus' indebtedness to the Maragha astronomers lies not only in the fact that he uses the same theorems to build his own models, but that he also uses them at the identical points in the models where they were used by the Maragha astronomers. The question naturally arises whether it was possible for Copernicus to have known these two theorems and, if so, through what channels. The only evidence for such a direct transmission is in a Byzantine Greek manuscript which found its way into the Vatican Collection some time after the fall of Constantinople in 1453. On one page of the manuscript there is a clear representation of the Ṭūsī couple together with a lunar model of Ibn al-Shāṭir. On another page there is a representation of Ṭūsī's lunar model as well as a diagram demonstrating the adaptation of the Ṭūsī couple to a configuration of solid bodies. It is significant that these results finally reached Italy – a country where Copernicus resided for a few years – and that Copernicus could read Greek. For the present, however, the direct influence of the results of the Maragha astronomers must remain conjectural. The situation may be clarified when a critical edition of the entire Greek text is produced.

INSTRUMENTS

Our knowledge of astronomical instruments in the Islamic world is derived from two sources: (1) the instruments which survive in various museums and private collections throughout the world and (2) the treatises which are preserved in manuscript form in libraries mainly in Europe and the Near East. No inventory of the surviving instruments has been published, nor is there a comprehensive catalogue of the treatises dealing with instruments. Even so, there is sufficient data, both material and literary, to form the basis of a comprehensive survey. Indeed, complete books have already been written on various types of instruments, and substantial monographs have been written about important individual instruments. In this section we can do more than make a brief survey of the more important types of instruments.

FIGURE 3.9 Persian Celestial Globe, AH 764 (AD 1362). Lewis Evans Collection, Museum of the History of Science, Oxford.

Observational Instruments

Ptolemy's *Almagest* contains descriptions of the celestial globe (of which a mechanically-operated example is known to have been constructed by Archimedes); the armillary sphere; the meridian quadrant; and the parallactic ruler. The first two of these were probably used more for didactic purposes than for observation. The meridian circle was used for taking altitudes of heavenly bodies at transit and the parallactic ruler was a device for measuring the zenith distance of a heavenly body. The Muslims made improvements to these instruments; new scales were added, modified versions were devised and larger instruments were constructed. More details of observational – particularly levelling – instruments are given in Chapter 10.

Celestial Globes

The problems of spherical astronomy can be illustrated by a three-dimensional celestial globe. Today there are known to be 126 extant Islamic celestial globes spanning a period from the eleventh to the nineteenth century. A few of these are made of painted wood or *papier-mâché* on wooden cores but the majority are metallic. The globes were marked with stars and constellations, set into a horizon and meridian ring assembly, the meridian ring usually being rotatable about the north celestial pole. Circles for the ecliptic and the equator were marked on the globes; these circles, together with the meridian and horizon rings, were divided into four quadrants, divided into degrees. By adjusting the meridian ring to coincide with the location of the observer the declinations of stars could be read off from the graduations. The RA of the star could be determined by finding where the great circle passing through the star and the celestial poles intersected the equator. If the globe incorporated a gnomon, this could be used to determine the altitude of the sun.

Astrolabes

The origins of the astrolabe can be firmly placed in the school of Alexandria. It was almost certainly known to Ptolemy and was described by Theon of Alexandria (*c*.350), whose writings are preserved in the treatise of Severus Sebokht, composed in Egypt before 660, i.e. a few years after the Arab occupation of the country. The earliest Arabic treatises are those of Mashā' Allāh (d. *c*.815), 'Alī b. 'Īsa (fl. *c*.830) and Muḥammad b. Mūsā al-Khuwārazmī (d. *c*.835). The earliest Islamic instruments preserved date from the second half of the tenth century.

The astrolabe was the astronomical instrument *par excellence* of the Middle Ages. It is constructed by stereographic projection, whereby points on a sphere are transferred to a plane surface. Figure

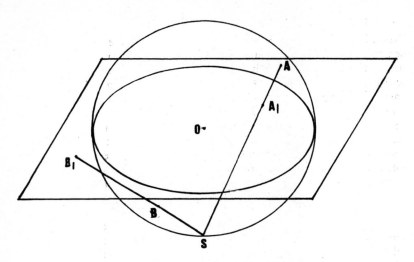

FIGURE 3.10 North stereographic projection.

3.10 shows the principle of North Stereographic Projection. The sphere with centre O and south pole S is bisected centrally by a horizontal plane; points A and B on the sphere are transferred to points A_1 and B_1 on the plane. It can be demonstrated that angular relationships between points, and hence also lines, on the sphere remain unaltered by transfer to the plane.

The essential parts of the instrument are the plate, the body, the rete and the alidade. The plate consists of a metal disc marked out by stereographic projection for the observer's latitude: it shows his meridian and zenith, arcs on circles of equal altitude including the horizon and, radiating from the zenith, lines of azimuth. Around the centre of the plate are circles for the Tropic of Cancer, the Equator and the Tropic of Capricorn, the last named being coincident with the rim of the plate. It is usual to add a crepuscular line for the time of twilight, outside the horizon. There is a hole in the centre of the plate.

The body is also a circular metal plate with a hole in its centre. It is surrounded by a raised annulus, the outside of which is divided into quadrants, each subdivided into degrees. Inside this ring are two semicircles divided into twelve hourly divisions. At the top of the body is an attachment with a hole in it, through which the suspension ring passes. The back of the body can carry various devices, not absolutely essential to the astronomical uses of the instrument. These include the 'shadow squares' for measuring terrestrial objects, as described in Chapter 10, and arcs for the unequal hours.

FIGURE 3.11 Maghribī (Hispano-Moorish) Astrolabe (front). Shawwal,
AH 460 (AD 1068). Lewis Evans Collection, Museum of the History
of Science, Oxford.

The rete, which rotates over the plate, is made of open metalwork,
so that the lines on the plate are visible through it. It is essentially a
star map and has holes (or sometimes gemstones) in it to represent the
major fixed stars, each at its correct RA and declination. An eccentric

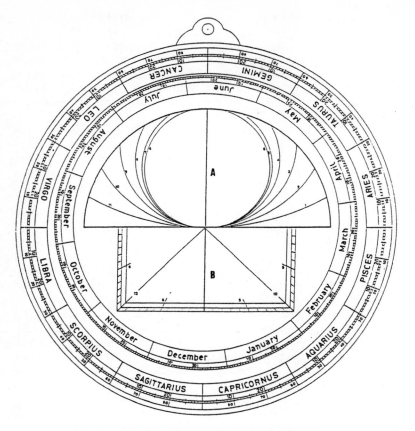

(A) "EQUAL" AND "UNEQUAL" HOURS SCALE

(B) HEIGHTS AND DISTANCES SQUARES

FIGURE 3.12 Layout of back of astrolabe.

ring represents the ecliptic; this is divided into the twelve signs of the Zodiac, each subdivided into 30 degrees. There is a hole in the centre of the rete. The alidade usually carries sights. In most cases an alidade is also provided for the back of the astrolabe. The instrument is assembled by placing the plate on the body inside the annulus, then placing the rete over the plate, then the alidade over the rete. The other alidade, if one is provided, is placed in position on the back. A pin is then passed through all the parts, and secured behind the rear alidade by a cotter.

A number of problems can be solved directly by the astrolabe, without recourse to calculation. To take but two examples:

1. To find the time of sunrise on June 22 (June 22 = 12 Gemini). The rete is rotated until the point 12 Gemini on the edge of the Zodiac circle comes up to touch the eastern horizon line on the plate below. The rete is held in this position and the alidade is laid across the point. The time is read off where the end of the alidade nearest 12 Gemini crosses the hour scale.

2. To find the time of rising of a fixed star and its bearing as it rises on (say) February 13 (February 13 = 25 Aquarius). The rete is rotated until the point representing the star is on the horizon line. With the rete in this position the alidade is laid across 25 Aquarius; the time is read off from the hour scale and the aximuth under the point representing the star.

These results, and many others, can be obtained in a few seconds, whereas considerably longer times would be needed to obtain them by calculation. Moreover, the use of the astrolabe can be mastered quite quickly by anyone with a rudimentary knowledge of spherical astronomy. Its one major disadvantage is that its use is confined to a single location. This disadvantage could be partly overcome by having a set of plates for different locations, but various astronomers proposed more general solutions. The most comprehensive of these was provided by the eleventh-century Andalusian astronomer al-Zarqall who devised a single instrument applicable to all latitudes. This later became famous in Europe under the name of Saphaea (a corruption of the Arabic word for 'plate'). Nevertheless, the ordinary planispheric astrolabe retained its popularity throughout the Middle Ages and until the eighteenth century. Knowledge of the instrument entered Europe from the Islamic world early in the eleventh century. Almost certainly the route of its transmission was from Andalusia via the abbey of Ripoll in Catalonia.

A unique example of an astrolabe fitted with a geared mechanism survives from thirteenth-century Iran. A similar mechanism, in fact a geared calendar, was described by al-Bīrūnī in the eleventh century. This consisted of 8 gear-wheels of various sizes meshing inside a thin, circular, metal box. On the lid of the box was a lever that was moved daily, causing pointers for the sun and moon to move, indicating the passage of those two bodies through the Zodiac. There was also a circular aperture that displayed the moon in its correct phase for the day. Similar devices are described in earlier Arabic treatises. Recently, the fragments of another geared calendar, made in the Byzantine Empire about AD 500 were acquired by the Science Museum, London. Further research is required before the relationship of these instruments to astrolabes and other instruments can be established.

Sundials

The most ancient sundial extant dates to the fifteenth century BC but the simple vertical gnomon (the style used to cast a shadow) was certainly even more ancient. The Muslims inherited the sundail from their Hellenistic predecessors – presumably they found sundials in the territories they occupied in the seventh and eighth centuries. Muslim astronomers made several notable improvements to the theory and construction of sundials. As is the case with astrolabes, one of the distinctive Muslim contributions was the preparation of tables to eliminate computations on the part of craftsmen. For example, al-Khuwārazmī, working in Baghdad early in the ninth century, compiled tables displaying, for ten different latitudes, values of the following functions for each seasonal hour at the solstices: the solar altitude, the solar azimuth and the length of the shadow cast by a gnomon of unit length. The shadow lengths and azimuths constitute the polar co-ordinates of the points of intersection of the solstitial shadow traces with the lines representing the seasonal hours, and with these the construction of the sundial is reduced to a task for a mason or metal-worker.

In Baghdad in the tenth century, tables were compiled to facilitate marking the curves on vertical sundials inclined at any angle to the meridian for any latitude. Later sets of tables for vertical sundials display ninety subtables for each degree of inclination to the local meridian. Such tables would have been very useful to the astronomers who constructed sundials on the walls of so many of the mosques in medieval Cairo or Damascus. A sundial made in Damascus in the fourteenth century to adorn the main minaret of the Umayyad Mosque displays time with respect to sunrise, midday and sunset, as well as with respect to the times of afternoon prayer. It is the most sophisticated sundial known from the medieval period.

Quadrants

Several varieties of quadrant whose purposes were computational were invented in the Islamic world in medieval times. As is the case with other Islamic instruments and tabulations, they were intended to remove the need for complex calculations. The sine quadrant was developed in Baghdad in the ninth century and remained popular for a millenium. It was a kind of astronomer's slide-rule. With such a device, bearing markings similar to modern graph-paper, together with a cord attached at the centre of the quadrant and carrying a movable bead, one can solve numerically the most complicated problems of medieval trigonometry, such as the *qibla* problem. New kinds of trigonometric grids were invented in Syria in the fourteenth century as alternatives to the sine quadrant.

The horary quadrant bears either a series of markings for the seasonal hours, which are twelve divisions of the hours of daylight, or for the equinoctal hours. In the first case the markings serve all latitudes, in the second they serve one specific latitude. When one edge of the quadrant is aligned towards the sun, a bead on a plumb-line attached at the centre of the quadrant indicates the time of day.

The time and place of the invention of the almucantar quadrant are unknown, but it was described in an Egyptian manuscript of the twelfth century. The basic idea is simple: since the markings on a standard astrolabe are symmetrical with respect to the meridian, one uses just half of such a plate engraved on a quadrant. The rete is replaced by a cord attached to the centre of the quadrant, and this carries a bead that can be moved to represent the position of the sun or a fixed star, either of which can be found from markings for the ecliptic and star positions which are now included on the quadrant itself.

Equatoria

The equatorium is an Islamic invention originating in Andalusia. No medieval equatoria survive, but we have several treatises on their use, the first three being by Andalusian astronomers and dating from the period 1015–1115. The equatorium is a mechanical device for finding the positions of the sun, moon and planets without calculation and using instead what is essentially a geometric model to represent the celestial body's mean and anomalistic position. To use Ptolemy's models for this purpose, one simply takes the values of the mean longitude and the anomaly from the mean-motion tables standard in the astronomical handbooks and feeds them into the instrument, which then displays the true position of the celestial body.

OBSERVATORIES

The first systematic observations in Islam took place under the patronage of the caliph al-Ma'mūn. One of the first undertakings that he sponsored was the careful measurement of a meridian degree in the Syrian desert and on the Iraqi plain. Astronomical observation also took place in Damascus and Baghdad, probably not in observatories properly speaking, but in premises temporarily assigned to the purpose. Observations were also carried out in small private observatories. Solar parameters were established and observations of the sun, moon and planets were undertaken.

In the tenth century the Buwayhid dynasty encouraged the undertaking of extensive works. These included the construction of a large-scale instrument with which observations were made in 950. The prince 'Aḍud al-Dawla (d. 983) patronised, in Isfahan, 'Abd al-Raḥmān al-Ṣūfī whose observations resulted in a systematic revision of Ptolemy's catalogue of stars. Simultaneously Ibn al-A'lam made planetary observations which were recorded in his famous zīj. The work was continued under Sharaf al-Dawla who had an observatory constructed in the royal palace gardens in Baghdad where some large-scale instruments were used. The Buwayhid example awakened the desire to emulate them among members of other dynasties, and observations continued in the following century in Iran and Afghanistan.

From the tenth century observational activity began further west. Of particular note are the observations carried out by the famous astronomer Ibn Yūnus (d. 1009) in Egypt at the close of the tenth century. He describes his activities in the introduction to his zīj: he does not seem to have operated from a permanent establishment, but to have obtained his excellent results with essentially portable instruments. A remarkable series of observations by al-Zarqall with the assistance of several collaborators took place first at Toledo then at Cordoba over a period of twenty-five years. He made observations of the moon and fixed stars, yet there is no proof of the existence of an organised institution.

The observatory as an institution lasting for a considerable period seems to have been an eastern development in the late Middle Ages. The most obvious antecedent is the observatory founded by Malik Shāh (1071–92), probably in Isfahan. Here 'Umar al-Khayyām, in conjunction with collaborators, completed a zīj and effected the reform of the Persian solar calendar.

The most influential observatory, however, was founded by Hülagü Khan (d. 1265) at the suggestion of Naṣīr al-Dīn al-Ṭūsī at Maragha in Adharbayjān. It contained several buildings, including a residence for Hülegü, a mosque and a rich library. Hülagü's motives seem to have been largely astrological but, as mentioned in a previous section, it was at Maragha that the most famous astronomers of the age participated in the observatory's work, which, as we have seen, resulted in important modifications to the Ptolemaic system. Altogether, the observatory's activities spanned a period of over fifty-five years.

No observatory of the size of Maragha appeared until the foundation of the Samarqand observatory in 1420 by the prince Ulugh Beg, himself a mathematicisn and astronomer of note. The observatory, situated on a hill near the town, was equipped with huge instruments such as a large meridian axis, remains of which were excavated in 1908. For a period of about thirty years a group of leading astronomers carried out systematic observations. It was there that the zīj of Ulugh

Beg was prepared. In the pre-modern period the only other observatory of note was founded at Istanbul in 1575 by Taqī al-Dīn b. Ma'rūf. It was said to have been a large establishment on the lines of Maragha and Samarqand, but it was destroyed by order of the Sultan in 1580.

ASTROLOGY

The original purpose of astrology was to inform the individual of the course of his life on the basis of the positions of the planets and of the zodiacal signs at the moment of his birth or conception. From this science, called genethialogy, were developed the fundamental techniques of astrology, which were later applied to a variety of other problems. The main subdivisions that developed after genethialogy are general, catarchic and interrogatory.

General astrology studies the relationship of the significant celestial moments (for example, the times of the occurrences of vernal equinoxes or planetary conjunctions) to social groups, nations or all humanity.

Catarchic (pertaining to beginnings or sources) astrology determines whether or not a chosen moment is astrologically conducive to the success of a course of action begun in it. Basically in conflict with a rigorous interpretation of genethialogy, it allows the individual or group to act at astrologically favourable times and thereby to escape any failures predictable from his (or its) nativity.

Interrogatory astrology provides answers to a client's queries based on the situation of the heavens at the moment of his posing the question. This astrological consulting service is even more remote from determinism than is catarchic astrology; it is thereby closer to divination by omens and insists upon the ritual purification and preparation of the astrologer.

Astrology entered Islam in the eighth and ninth centuries in three simultaneous streams – Hellenistic, Indian and Sasānid. Arabic translations from Greek and Syriac represented the Hellenistic science, from Sanskrit the Indian version and from Pahlavi the Sasānid combination of the two. Hellenistic astrology may, however, be considered as providing the essentials of the science, since it was transmitted to India in the second and third centuries AD and despite modifications retained its basic characteristics. Broadly speaking, the science that had been practised in Egypt since about 100 BC was the science that was inherited by Islam. This depended upon the division of the zodiac into twelve signs, subdivided into 'decans' of 10° each. Various arcs of the zodiac were either primarily or secondarily subject to each planet, whose strength and influence in a nativity depended partially on its position relative to those arcs and to those of the other planets.

56

The casting of a horoscope for a given spot on the surface of the earth at a given time depended upon determining the exact degree of the zodiac at that moment together with the latitudes and longitudes of the seven planets at that time. Since according to the celestial configurations each planet's 'strength' and 'weakness' varied, any horoscope could yield an enormous number of predictions. An astrologer had therefore to rely on his knowledge of the client's social, economic and ethnic background to guide him in avoiding error and attaining credibility. Penalties for incorrect predictions could be severe – even fatal.

There were a number of practising astrologers in the courts of the early 'Abbāsid caliphs in eighth-century Baghdad. Most of them were of Iranian origin. Four astrologers – three Iranians and an Arab – were responsible for casting the catarchic horoscope for the foundation of Baghdad. The most influential of the four was Mashā' allāh b. Atharī, a Persian Jew from Basra who died about 815. He is credited with about nineteen works, a few of which survive in Arabic or Latin.

In the ninth century astrology continued to be influential, although ninth-century translators worked far more industriously in the field of astronomy than in that of astrology. The most impressive astrologer at this time was Abu Ma'shar al-Balkhī, who died in Iraq in 886, almost a centenarian. He formulated the standard expression of Islamic astrological doctrines, creating a synthesis of Indian, Iranian, Greek and Ṣabian astrology. Of his known works, *al-Madhkal al-kabīr* (*The Great Introduction to Astrology*) is of particular importance since it was twice translated into Latin and had a great influence in Christian Europe. It contains an exposition of the theory of the tides and it can be said that medieval Europe learned the laws of the ebb and flow of the sea from it.

After the ninth century few astrological treatises were composed in Islam, and these were either elementary handbooks or vast compendia based upon the work of earlier authorities, although the great scientist al-Bīrūnī wrote many treatises dealing with specific points of astrology. Under attack from the theologians for denying divine intervention and man's free will, astrology rapidly declined in its appeal to Muslim intellectuals after the Mongol invasions of the thirteenth century. By this time, however, its influence had been transmitted to India, the Latin West and Byzantium. Moreover, the requirements for casting horoscopes almost certainly led to developments in astronomy, notably in the construction of instruments.

4

Physics

There have always been two kinds of physics – speculative and experimental. Since the scientific revolution in seventeenth-century Europe the two approaches have tended to converge, and to become complementary to each other. In the Middle Ages, however, because of the immense authority of Aristotle, the speculative approach was the more highly regarded among scholars. Although Aristotle used the experimental technique of dissection to extend the range of his observation of animals, in physics he adopted an approach in which speculation reigned unchallenged and observation played a negligible role. Those who followed this path in the Middle Ages – for example Ibn Sīnā and Ibn Rushd in Islam, St Thomas Aquinas in Latin Christendom – attempted to reconcile Aristotle's views with theological and cosmological dogmas. Such philosophers might on occasions hold widely different views from Aristotle's, but their differences were based upon logical and theoretical grounds, not upon observation and experiment. Reverence for the authority of Aristotle was such that his influence had a stultifying effect upon creative thought. The freeing of scientific thought from Aristotelian bonds was to prove an immensely difficult task for scientists over many hundreds of years. Nevertheless, in the Islamic world there were a number of great scientists who did take the experimental path, and in doing so achieved highly significant results in physical investigations.

The students of the physical sciences in Islam were far fewer than the students of mathematics, astronomy, alchemy and medicine. Of the subjects usually considered as constituting the substance of classical physics – electricity and magnetism, heat, sound, optics, solid and fluid mechanics – only the last two were given much attention by Arabic writers. In the fields of statics and optics, however, the Islamic contribution was very important, and can best be appreciated by a consideration of the achievements of a few great scientists. Before doing this, we shall discuss briefly the work done on other subjects, where there is anything of significance to report.

References to magnetic phenomena are to be found here and there in the works of Arabic scientists and geographers. It was known that an electric charge could be induced in amber or musk by rubbing them. Several reports say that in the mountains near Āmid in Mesopotamia there was a cleft in a rock; if a sword was drawn repeatedly through this cleft it became magnetised and would attract nails and other small objects made of iron. The invention of the floating magnetic needle as applied to the ship's compass is probably due to the Chinese, but it was certainly in use by Muslim mariners early in the twelfth century.

Heat was not studied at all as a scientific subject, since it can only be considered quantitatively with the aid of temperature scales and thermometers. Also, although we have a comment from al-Bīrūnī showing that he realised that the speed of light was immensely greater than the speed of sound, the study of sound was in general confined to the theory of music. Abu Yusūf al-Kindī is the earliest Arab writer on music whose works have come down to us; they contain a notation for the determination of pitch. Abu Naṣr Muḥammad al-Fārābī wrote an important treatise on music, indicating that he had some knowledge of mensural music and recognised the major third and the minor third as consonances. The musical part of the *Kitāb al-Shifā'* by Ibn Sīnā marked much progress on al-Fārābī's treatise, itself far ahead of Western knowledge on the subject. It deals with doubling with the octave and doubling with the fourth and fifth, this being a great step towards the harmonic system.

MECHANICS

In Hellenistic times a number of scholars devoted some of their attention to mechanics, both solid and fluid. These included Archimedes (d. 212 BC), Philo of Byzantium (*c.*230 BC), Hero of Alexandria (fl. 60 AD), Menelaus (*c.*100 AD) and Pappus of Alexandria (early fourth century AD). The works of these men were well-known to the Muslims, the most important being the various treatises of Archimedes on statics and hydrostatics. Also important is the *Mechanics* of Hero, which has survived in an excellent Arabic translation made by Qustā b. Lūqā in the ninth century. Its contents comprise: movement of a known weight with a known force by means of gears; geometrical problems; movement on an inclined plane; distribution of loads over a number of supports; the five simple machines and their uses, singly and in combination; mechanical advantage; centres of gravity of various figures; lifting machines; presses. The *Mechanics* was probably intended as a textbook for architects and craftsmen, for which purpose it was eminently suitable. The Arabic translation may have been used in a similar way. At all events, there is no close reproduction of is subject matter by a Muslim writer, although all the matters it contains, and others, were dealt with discretely by Muslim scientists.

One of the earliest scholars to deal with physics in the Islamic world was the renowned translator and scientist Thābit b. Qurrā (d. 901). Among his numerous works on scientific subjects were several on statics, on the theory of moments and one on the steelyard. A work of considerable interest, written towards the close of the tenth century by Abu 'Abd Allah al Khuwārazmī, is called *Mafātiḥ al-Ulum* (*The Keys of the Sciences*). This is essentially an encyclopaedia of the sciences and its eighth treatise deals with mechanics. It is divided into two sections, the first of which is entitled 'On the movement of weights by a smaller force and the machines used for that purpose'. It is thus clearly inspired by Hero, but the section in the *Mafātiḥ* is much shorter than the parallel passage in the *Mechanics*. Al-Khuwārazmī limits himself, in the entry for each device, to a discussion of the etymology of the device's name, together with a brief description of its construction and purpose. Each entry is confined to a few sentences. In this section the subjects dealt with include the lever, fulcrum, pulley, wedge and screw. (The second section of the eighth treatise deals with the components used in ingenious devices and other machines; we shall have occasion to refer to these later.)

The main interest of Arabic writers on mechanics, as far as we know from the current state of research, seems to have been in the question of weighing, in the widest sense. Thus the great scientist al-Bīrūnī (d. *c*.1050) is known to have compiled an accurate table of specific gravities. The equally renowned astronomer and mathematician, 'Umar al-Khayyām (d. 1123) discussed the problem of determining the quantities of two constituent metals in an alloy. The most important and comprehensive work on mechanics in the Middle Ages, from any cultural area, was *Kitāb Mizān al-Ḥikma* (*The book of the Balance of Wisdom*), completed in 1121 by Abu'l-Fatḥ al-Khāzinī. The value of the work is enhanced by the fact that al-Khāzinī gives a history of statics and hydrostatics, with commentaries on the works of his predecessors, including Archimedes, Euclid, Menelaus, Pappus, al-Bīrūnī and 'Umar al-Khayyām. Although he acknowledges the work of these scholars, there is no doubt that he made significant contributions of his own.

The work is divided into eight treatises, as follows;

1. Theories of centres of gravity according to various Greek and Arabic scholars
2. Further discussion on centres of gravity; mechanism of the steelyard
3. Comparative densities of various metals and precious stones, according to al-Bīrūnī
4. Balances designed by various Greek and Arabic scholars
5. The water-balance of 'Umar al-Khayyām – its adjustment, testing and use
6. The Comprehensive Balance; determination of the constituents of alloys

7.   Weights of coinage
8.   The steelyard clepsydra

The comprehensive nature of al-Khāzinī's work is clear from the foregoing list, as is his scrupulous acknowledgement of the work of his predecessors. The first treatise (maqāla) gives a number of theories, from Greek and Arabic writers, on the fundamental formulae for weighing. For the most part there is nothing new in this; al-Khāzinī repeats the vagueness of the Greeks in failing to differentiate clearly between force, mass and weight. What is remarkable, however, is his treatment of gravitation – excluding heavenly bodies – as a universal force. Like the Greeks, he considered this force as attracting all bodies towards the centre of the earth, and that this attraction depended upon the mass of the body. Al-Khāzinī was also aware of the weight of the air and of the decrease in its density the higher one goes.

Most of the remainder of the work is concerned with hydrostatics, in particular the determination of specific gravities by application of the Archimedean principle of flotation. The equipment required to obtain accurate results is described in some detail. The first description is concerned with the determination of the specific gravities of liquids, using the aerometer (i.e. hydrometer) of Pappus. This instrument is a copper tube about 25 cm long by 4 cm in diameter. Both ends are closed; at the lower end a conical lead weight resting on the base ensures that the tube floats vertically when placed in a liquid. Two scales are engraved vertically on the tube, one with its numbers increasing upwards, to indicate the volume submerged in liquids of different densities, the other with its numbers increasing downwards, to show the specific gravities corresponding to those submerged values. The principle of the instrument is simply that a given body will float in a liquid to a depth proportional to the specific gravity of the liquid. It will therefore sink further in a light liquid than in a dense one, the volumes submerged being in inverse proportion to the specific gravity of the liquid.

Figure 4.1 shows the divisions of the instrument. The ascending scale is divided into divisions from 50 to 110, water corresponding to division 100. (The lower section from 0 to 50 and the upper section from 110 to 120 serve no purpose.) The descending scale was generated by dividing the values of each division on the ascending scale into 100, to obtain a specific gravity in numbers and sixtieths. To obtain the specific gravity of a liquid one simply read off the numbers on the second scale corresponding to the number at the liquid surface on the first scale, interpolating if necessary. For example, if we take the line on the first scale marked '88' we find that the corresponding number on the second scale is 113 and 38 sixtieths – or 113.6333 in decimal

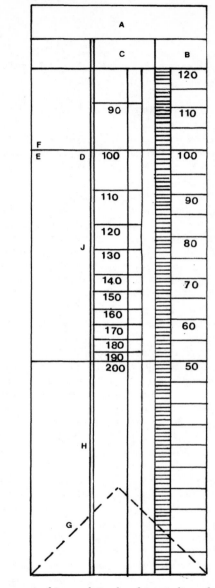

Note: Subdivisions
omitted from
Scale C

FIGURE 4.1 Pappus' aerometer. Arabic words in the places indicated read as follows; A. Picture of the instrument for measuring liquids of Pappus the Greek. B. Ascending line of numbers. C. Descending

TABLE 4.1   Scale on Pappus' aerometer.

Line of Numbers	Parts	Sixtieths	Line of Numbers	Parts	Sixtieths
110	90	54	80	125	0
109	91	45	79	127	35
108	92	35	78	128	12
107	93	27	77	129	53
106	94	21	76	131	35
105	95	14	75	133	20
104	96	9	74	135	8
103	97	5	73	137	0
102	98	2	72	138	54
101	99	1	71	140	51
100	100	0	70	142	51
99	101	1	69	144	56
98	102	2	68	147	3
97	103	6	67	149	15
96	104	10	66	151	30
95	105	15	65	153	51
94	106	23	64	156	15
93	107	31	63	158	44
92	108	42	62	161	17
91	109	54	61	163	56
90	111	7	60	166	40
89	112	21	59	169	30
88	113	38	58	172	25
87	114	57	57	175	26
86	116	17	56	178	34
85	117	39	55	181	49
84	119	3	54	185	11
83	120	29	53	188	40
82	121	57	52	192	18
81	123	28	51	196	5
			50	200	0

numbers for measuring. D. Equator of equilibrium. E. The heavier side. F. The lighter side. G. Cone made of lead. H. The relation of distance to distance, successively, from the base is, by inverse ratio, as the numbers of the second distance to the numbers of the first distance. J. Different part [=numbers] required, determining the weight of the liquid.

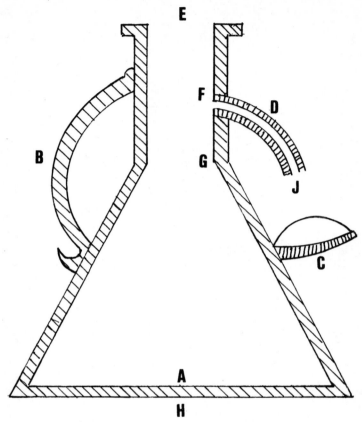

FIGURE 4.2   Al-Bīrūnī's conical instrument. Arabic words in the
places indicated read as follows: A. Picture of the conical instrument of Abu'l-Rayḥān [al-Bīrūnī]. B. Its handle. C. Place of the
[weigh-] scale. D. Pipe like a water conduit. E. Mouth of the vessel.
F. The hole. G. Its neck. H. Its base. J. End of the pipe.

notation. The specific gravity of a liquid which reads 88 on the other
scale should be 100/88 or 113.6363. The error is therefore very small.
In both cases, of course, one multiplies by 100 in order to bring the
figures to the base of the specific gravity of water. (See Table 4.1.)

The limits of the instrument are 50 to 110, which at the time were
more than sufficient for all possible cases. The Muslims were then
acquainted with the specific gravities of seventeen liquids, excluding
water, which as we have seen they took as their unit, and mercury,

which they classed among the metals and not among the liquids. In this series the heaviest liquid was in their opinion honey with a specific gravity of 1.406, hence falling between 71 and 72 on the first scale of the instrument. The lightest was oil of sesame, having a specific gravity of 0.915, which corresponded on the instrument to the interval between 108 and 109.

The remainder of the work (apart from the eighth treatise) is mainly devoted to the determination of the specific gravities of metals, precious stones and alloys. This work had obvious commercial connotations in determining the purity of various substances and in the detection of frauds.

The first instrument described by al-Khāzinī he attributes to al-Bīrūnī. Indeed, he calls it 'The conical instrument of Abu'l-Rayḥān [al-Bīrūnī].' Its purpose is clear from Figure 4.2. The vessel was filled with water up to the lower rim of hole F. When a specimen was lowered into it the water ran out through tube D into the weigh-scale C. the specimen having been weighed in air giving value of W_1, if the displaced water weighed W_2, then the specific gravity of the substance was W_1/W_2.

Al-Bīrūnī took considerable care to ensure that his results were as accurate as possible. The neck of the vessel was made narrow, since its bore obviously affected the sensitivity of the instrument. The diameter was the width of the little finger; al-Bīrūnī would have preferred to have made it even narrower, but this would have caused difficulties in inserting and extracting the specimens. There were also problems with the outlet tube, since surface tension caused some of the water to remain in the tube. It was therefore made in the shape of the arc of a circle and was pierced with small holes. It was then found that the water flowed readily through it, no more remaining in the tube than just enough to moisten its inner surface.

Using this instrument, al-Khāzinī, following al-Bīrūnī, made repeated trials with several metals. A similar procedure was followed with a number of gemstones. He also measured the specific gravities of other substances such as clay, salt, amber, pitch, etc., noting whether the substances floated or sank in water.

In all, al-Khāzinī records the specific gravities of fifty substances: nine metals, ten precious stones, thirteen non-precious solids and eighteen liquids, including water. In most cases al-Khāzinī acknowledges that he is simply reproducing the results obtained by al-Bīrūnī. The accuracy of the results is impressive, particularly when we consider the difficulties they must have met with in graduating the instruments. Moreover, it was not easy to manufacture glass or metal vessels of uniform wall thickness and internal dimension, although the results provide indirect evidence that the vessels were indeed made to close specifications. The following table gives a list of some of the commoner substances investigated by al-Bīrūnī/al-Khāzinī, with modern values given for the sake of comparison:

TABLE 4.2   Specific gravities recorded by al-Khāzinī.

Substances	Specific gravities according to al-khāzinī	Modern values
Gold	19.05 (cast)	19.26–19.3
Mercury	13.56	13.56
Lead	11.32	11.39–11.445
Silver	10.30	10.43–10.47
Copper	8.66 (cast)	8.67–8.73
Brass	8.57	8.45–8.60
Iron	7.74 (forged)	7.60–7.79
Tin	7.32	7.29
Emerald	2.75	2.68–2.77
Fine pearl	2.60	2.68
Cornelian	2.56	2.62
Coral	2.56	2.69
Pure salt	2.19	2.07–2.17
Pitch	1.04 (white)	1.07
Sweet water	1.00	1.00
Hot water	0.958 (boiling)	0.960
Ice	0.965	0.916–0.927
Sea water	1.04	1.029–1.04
Wine-vinegar	1.027	1.013–1.08
Wine	1.022(various kinds)	0.992–1.04
Olive oil	0.92	0.918–0.919
Cow's milk	1.11	1.02–1.04
Hen's egg	1.035	1.09
Honey	1.406	1.45
Blood of a man in good health	1.033	1.053

The tabulation of specific gravities was conceived much earlier by the Muslims than by the Europeans. Serious attention was first paid to the subject in Europe during the seventeenth century, culminating in the work of Robert Boyle (d. 1691). He determined the specific gravity of mercury, for example, by two different methods giving values of 13.76 and 13.357. Both are less exact than the value recorded by

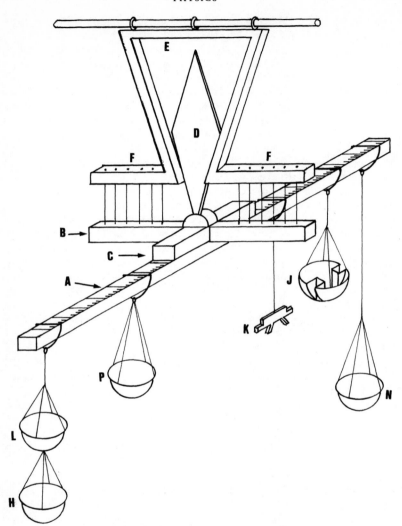

FIGURE 4.3 Al-Khāzinī's 'Balance of Wisdom'.

al-Khāzinī, most of whose results, as can be seen, were fairly accurate.

The remainder of al-Khāzinī's book is devoted to the description of various balances, beginning with a balance attributed to Archimedes, proceeding through balances developed by Muslim scholars and concluding with an exhaustive description of the balance which

67

al-Khāzinī calls 'The Balance of Wisdom' or, more explicitly, 'The Comprehensive Balance'. This balance had first been developed by a certain Muẓaffar b. Ismāʿīl, a native of Harāt (in modern Afghanistan) and an immediate predecessor of al-Khāzinī. He added a further two scales to the three already in common use, but further refinements were introduced by al-Khāzinī himself. The design was a carefully constructed weighing machine capable of the most accurate measurements, and represents the culmination of Muslim achievement in this branch of applied physics. We shall therefore give a description of its construction and applications in some detail. Even so, we shall be compelled to abbreviate al-Khāzinī's specifications somewhat, since they are given with great minuteness.

Figure 4.3 is a reconstruction of the balance in its complete assembly. The beam A was made of iron or brass. Its cross-section was a square with sides of about 8 cm; its length was 2 metres. Soldered to the beam in the centre was a stiffening piece C and at the same point the cross-piece B was fitted. The tongue D, about 50 cm long, was provided with a tapered tang that passed through holes in the cross-piece and the beam, being secured below the latter by a knob. The tongue was surrounded by a single metal fitting as shown, consisting of two 'shears' connected at the top by the cross-piece E, while at the bottom were two cross-pieces F parallel with a cross-piece B. Rings soldered to the top of E allowed it to be connected to a beam. In cross-pieces F there were narrow holes exactly in line with similar holes in B. These were connected by threads; this arrangement avoided the friction of an axle, which would have been considerable in a machine of this weight.

The various scales, as designated by al-Khāzinī, were as follows:

L   air-bowl for the end
N   second air-bowl for the end
H   third, or water-bowl
J   fourth, or winged bowl
K   movable running weight (rummāna)
P   fifth or movable bowl

Bowl H, which was specified as having a conical shape, was suspended from the underside of bowl L. Otherwise all the bowls (i.e. scales) and the rummāna were suspended from the beam by very delicate steel rings which fitted into notches on the upper surface of the beam. Bowl L and bowl N (hence also bowl H) were immovable longitudinally. The special shape of bowl J was to allow it to be brought close to the adjoining scales.

The beam was graduated from end to end. In addition, small silver discs were inserted into the beam at various points. The position of

each of these discs represented the specific gravity of a given substance. Thus if a substance was weighed in the air, the disc would
automatically indicate its weight in water.

Al-Khāzinī attained an extraordinary degree of accuracy with this
balance. This was the result of the length of the beam, the special
method of suspension, the fact that the centre of gravity and the axis of
oscillation were very close to each other and of the obviously very
accurate construction of the whole. Al-Khāzinī's tells us that he
attained an accuracy of about 1:60,000.

Al-Khāzinī used his scales for the most varied purposes. First, for
ordinary weighing then for all purposes connected with the taking of
specific gravities, examining the composition of alloys, changing of
dirhams to *dinars* and countless other business transactions. In all
these processes the scales were moved about until equilibrium was
attained; the desired magnitudes could in many cases be read at once
on the divisions of the beam.

Although al-Khāzinī describes many of these various procedures, he
devotes particular attention to determining the proportions of two
constituents in an alloy. The basic formula for resolving this problem
is derived as follows:

let a body M of weight W and specific weight S be composed of
two metals A and B of specific weights S_1 and S_2. Let the weight
of substance B in the alloy be x. Then:

$$\frac{W}{S} = \frac{W - x}{S_1} + \frac{x}{S_2}$$

whence

$$x = \frac{W(S - S_1)}{S_2 - S_1} \cdot \frac{S_2}{S}$$

Several different procedures for making the examination are described by al-Khāzinī. These procedures all involved weighing samples
of the two substances and the alloy in both air and water. When the
'air-weight' of a sample had been obtained by weighing it in scale N, it
was transferred to scale H, which was immersed in water in a tank.
The scales were then moved until equilibrium was again reached, so
giving the 'water-weight' of the sample. Al-Khāzinī states clearly that
he was aware of the variation of the density of water due both to the
temperature and to the nature of the water itself, e.g. the quantity and
nature of salts and other solids dissolved in it. He therefore recom-
mends that water from a particular source be used as a standard and
also that the temperature of the water when observations were made
be taken into account. Unfortunately, he does not tell us how the
temperature was estimated.

To reiterate: the 'Balance of Wisdom' represents the culmination of centuries of developments, both Greek and Islamic, in the science of weighing, the determination of specific gravities, and so on. Because al-Khāzinī was so conscientious in acknowledging and describing the work of his predecessors, his book provides us with a valuable record of their contributions, many of which would otherwise have been unknown to us. It is not possible to isolate al-Khāzinī's own innovations but it is clear that these were not negligible. And we can be sure, from his own accounts, that he was most scrupulous in the preparation of his equipment and materials, and in the carrying out of the numerous applications of his balances. His book is one of the finest examples, from the medieval period, of rigorous attention to scientific accuracy.

There are no treatises in Arabic on the theories of fluid mechanics, that is to say, the physical formulae underlying hydrostatic and aerostatic phenomena, nor of the principles of liquid flow through channels or pipes. These mathematical bases had not yet been formulated. For example, although we have mentioned that al-Khāzinī understood that the air had weight, throughout the Middle Ages the idea of 'nature abhorring a vacuum' persisted, and it was assumed that if air was evacuated from a vessel, air from outside rushed in to take its place.

On the other hand, the Muslims' skills in empirical fluid mechanics, from their use of different types of siphons and valves in ingenious devices to their design of complex irrigation schemes, were frequently most impressive. These skills will be demonstrated in the appropriate chapters, as an integral part of the descriptions of the various machines and constructions.

OPTICS

In Greek optics there were two diametrically opposed views: (a) *intromission* – 'something' entering the eyes representative of the object, and (b) *emission* – vision occurring when rays emanate from the eyes and are intercepted by visual objects.

The main arguments for the first theory are first found in Aristotle. His account of the facts surrounding vision was rudimentary and could not produce the detailed explanations required by complex optical phenomena. Consequently, he had to resort to emission theory in attempts to explain, for example, the halo and the rainbow.

In his *Optics* Euclid accepted the emission theory and was able to construct a total geometrisation of the visual process. His theories of course fell short of a full explanation of vision since they ignored the physical, physiological and psychological elements of visual phenomena. Ptolemy, in his *Optics*, did not depart essentially from the emission theory although he also discussed luminous radiation. He attempted to harmonise the geometric with the physical approach. He also introduced into the study of optics the experimental method. This was a valuable innovation, but ultimately it failed because its use was limited to supporting conclusions already arrived at; sometimes experimental results were even manipulated to safeguard these conclusions.

The first Arabic writer to concern himself with optics was the philosopher Abū Yūsuf al-Kindī (d. c.861) who followed Theon of Alexandria (late fourth century AD) in discussing the rectilinear propagation of light and the formation of shadows. Although al-Kindī followed the emission theory, he also gave a precise description of the principle of radiation and in doing so – ironically – formulated the basis of a new conceptual scheme that would eventually supplant the emission theory.

The foregoing brief introduction summarises the first 1,300 years of optics. It will be apparent that by the tenth century AD the subject was a confused tangle of uncertainties and contradictions. Although relieved from time to time by real insights, there had been too many defects in the various writings on the subject to allow a coherent picture to emerge. The preference for the speculative as against the empirical approach, the tendency of experiments, when they were made, to be used in support of pre-conceived theories and the predominance of the mathematical as opposed to the physical, physiological and psychological aspects of the subject, all tended to perpetuate the confusion. Above all, perhaps, the oscillation – sometimes the mind of the same scholar – between the emission and intromission theories, rendered the emergence of an integrated, coherent explanation of vision impossible. The situation was transformed when the study of optics was put on a sound footing by one of the greatest, perhaps the greatest, physicist of medieval times.

Abū 'Alī al-Ḥasan b. al-Haytham was born in Baṣra in about 965 and died in Egypt in 1039. About one hundred works are credited to him by the Arab biographers, of which some fifty-five are extant; all of these deal exclusively with mathematics, astronomy and optics.

The work which has made Ibn al-Haytham's name live through the centuries in his *Kitāb al-Manāẓir (Book of Optics)*. The book illustrates a conception of optics as primarily a theory of vision, one that differs radically from the visual-ray hypothesis which had been maintained by the mathematical tradition from Euclid to al-Kindī. To this explanation of vision Ibn al-Haytham also introduced a new methodology. He was thus enabled to formulate problems that would either not have made sense from the standpoint of the visual-ray theory or had been ignored by philosophers aiming primarily to give an account of what vision is rather than an explanation of how it takes place.

One of the chief characteristics that distinguishes Ibn al-Haytham's work from that of his predecessors is his rejection of the axiomatic approach in which postulates were assumed to be self-evident and any experiments were designed solely to reinforce the axioms. In contradistinction Ibn al-Haytham was concerned predominantly with the origin of first principles and their justification. He regarded this as the first step in a truly scientific investigation. He was acutely aware of the fallibility of sense-perception and it is scarcely an exaggeration to say that his efforts to circumvent this fallibility in gaining knowledge about the world was the generating force of his method.

Ibn al-Haytham's theories of perception and cognition are fully defined and elaborated in Book 2 of *Kitāb al-Manāẓir*. Here only a brief summary of these principles can be given, bearing in mind that such a précis must inevitably subject Ibn al-Haytham's chain of reasoning to a certain amount of distortion. It is important, nevertheless, to have at least a general appreciation of his ideas on perception, since these influenced the way in which he investigated the phenomenon of vision.

The first mode of sense-perception is 'perception by mere sensation' in which the viewer's percept of an object is determined only by external stimuli; he receives an awareness, through colour and light of 'something' within his field of vision. This initiates the second phase, of 'perception by recognition': the 'something' that has registered on the brain in the first mode is subjected to 'comparison' with the characteristics of objects known to the viewer and recalled by him. Thus the viewer might become aware that the 'something' was a horse because it showed the properties of horses previously perceived and registered in the memory. In other words a distinguishing faculty is brought into play. The time-span between the two modes may be very short, so short as to seem instantaneous. Nevertheless, there is a lapse of time between the initial sensation and the final recognition. In this brief span the distinguishing faculty, by noticing one or two aspects in the object, may receive sufficient information for comparison and hence recognition to take place.

The third mode of perception involves the situation where the 'distinguishing faculty' cannot compare to a corresponding specific concept, either because of the lack of previous perceptions or because of failure to recall any of those perceptions. But even when the distinguishing faculty is confronted with an object with which it can find no corresponding specific concept, it can still partially identify the object by certain 'criteria of perception'. In other words, the experience and knowledge of the viewer assist in identification. In al-Haytham uses as an example the estimation of distance, the aptitude for which is acquired by habit; land surveyors, for example, are more adept at judging distances than others.

To these three modes of perception Ibn al-Haytham adds what he calls 'attentive perception'. This means essentially the induction of an object by close examination. To induct an object is to probe its parts, moving one's visual attention from one part to the next, while at the same time remaining aware of the relationship between each part, the object itself and all the other parts of its totality. By such exhaustive examinations Ibn al-Haytham believes that knowledge can be derived from sense-perception.

The most important feature of Ibn al-Haytham's methodology is that, since in his view knowledge is based upon sense-perception, investigations must be carried out, not mere contemplation. He lists the conditions for vision to occur as follows;

1   The visual object must lie on straight lines from its surface to the 'surface of vision'.

2   The object must be luminous. It can be self-luminous or, if opaque, it can be illuminated by external sources. Light can also reach the observer by reflection from polished surfaces or by refraction between two media of different transparencies.

3   It must also be of a certain size, which is found to vary with the relative strength of eyesight.

4   It must be at a certain distance from the eye, which distance, however, is found to vary with size, luminosity and other properties of the object and of the eye.

How these properties interrelate is treated fully in the book, which also subjects the conditions to experimental tests. The first postulate, the rectilinearity of light, is proved by a simple yet rigorous experiment. Ibn al-Haytham's approach differs from Ptolemy's. He is testing a hypothesis and employs great care in the conduct of his experiments. The difference can best be seen when comparing the conclusions derived by the two men from the 'same' experiment. Ptolemy's contains an assumed element not yielded by the evidence; Ibn al-Haytham's conclusion reflects only the evidence. Indeed, he was quite prepared to modify or even reject a hypothesis if it conflicted with experimental results. He took great care in the construction and assembly of the equipment for his experiments, and made the radical innovation of including dimensions as an integral part of his specifications – an essential element in any serious experiment. Even so, the practice is not to be found in earlier works on optics. Ibn al-Haytham's experiments, apart from verifying the conditions for vision were also applied to the problems of reflection and refraction. One of the results of his methodology was the development of precision instrumentation. Although not alone in this field – astronomers and surveyors, for example, made notable advances in the construction of accurate instruments – Ibn al-Haytham's contribution undoubtedly led to significant improvements in instrument design.

The results of his experiments are too lengthy to be described here. His investigations of reflection from a number of surfaces with indifferent profiles, led to a fundamental reappraisal of the basic scientific laws. Indeed, the laws of reflection, as universal laws about light, were first given proper experimental demonstration by Ibn al-Haytham. He dealt with refraction in a number of qualitative experiments but also attempted to work out the correlation between the angle of incidence and the angle of refraction. He arrived at some empirical results, which are true only within certain limits and under certain conditions. He did not, however, discover Snell's Law (the sine of the angle of incidence equals the sine of the angle of refraction multiplied by the Refractive Index).

Ibn al-Haytham, as we have seen, postulated that vision was caused by radiations from luminous objects reaching the eye. He attempted, therefore, to harmonise the various factors concerned with the visual perception of objects – physical, physiological and psychological – in order to explain how the images are 'translated' by the viewer. In describing the interaction between the light and the various layers of the visual organ he alternates between physical and physiological explanations. After passage through the eye and along the optical nerve the light reaches what Ibn al-Haytham calls the 'final sensor' in the anterior part of the brain, where image perception occurs. His theories on this aspect of vision seem somewhat confused and contradictory; further research is required before they are fully understood and expounded.

Despite the importance and influence of *Kitāb al-Manāẓir*, it should be stressed that Ibn al-Haytham wrote a number of other treatises on optics in which he gave the results of his studies into discrete elements of the science. He wrote substantial treatises, for example, on the burning sphere, on burning mirrors of various shapes, and on the formations of shadows. He discovered spherical aberration, expounded for the first time the use of the *camera obscura* in the observation of solar eclipses, and wrote treatises on the halo and the rainbow. He established that astronomical twilight began and ended when the sun reached 19° and, proceeding from there, he fixed the height of the atmosphere at 52,000 paces.

Having said this, however, the fact remains that *Kitāb al-Manāẓir* is by far the most influential of Ibn al-Haytham's works. 'because of its highly-sophisticated character, combining physical mathematical, experimental, physiological and psychological considerations in a methodically-integrated manner, the influence of Ibn al-Haytham's book upon later writers on optics, both in the Muslim world and (through a medieval Latin translation) in the West, can hardly be exaggerated' (A.I. Sabra in *Encyclopaedia of Islam*, VI, 377).

5

Chemistry

The Arabic word *Al-kīmiyā* can apply to chemistry or to alchemy, but it would be an unrewarding task to attempt to make a clear distinction between the two. A more meaningful division is between scholarly investigations into the behaviour of substances when subjected to various processes, and industrial chemistry which is concerned solely with the manufacture of economically valuable products. The first we shall designate as Alchemy and the second as Industrial Chemistry.

ALCHEMY

Despite the attention given to alchemy by modern scholars, many obscurities still hamper the serious student of the subject. These obscurities include the actual definition of the term 'alchemy', its origins in East and West, the authorship of many of the extant texts, the methods used by the alchemists, and the identification of many of their materials. Much of the obscurity of the subject is also due to its esoteric nature and the consequent use made by many of its practitioners of analogy, allusion and cryptic utterances. Indeed, the very nature of an occult system precludes any clear, rational presentation of its tenets. Alchemistic authors often imply that they preserve the secrets of alchemy by the use of allegory and simile in order to keep unqualified persons at a distance. Another technique was the dispersion of esoteric instruction among technical writings, so that only the initiated would grasp the meaning of the apparently irrelevant interpolations. Moreover, it was held that true alchemy could only be passed on from a master to a pupil, not learned from books. Another difficulty, particularly for the student of Islamic alchemy, is the large mass of manuscript material that has yet to be edited and studied.

Despite these difficulties – and they are formidable – it is possible to attempt a general survey of Islamic alchemy. Much of the difficulty in alchemical writings arises from its occult, esoteric aspects, 'the art of the the transformation of the soul'. This speculative alchemy has an important place in the development of man's religions, philosophical and psychological thinking; it cannot be neglected if one wishes to write a holistic account of alchemy. Our concern, however, is with the more mundane side of the subject, namely its considerable influence on the development of modern chemistry. From this restricted viewpoint there is sufficient information in our sources to enable us to describe the main equipment, materials and processes used by the alchemists. First, however, it may be of service to set down the three broad categories into which alchemy may be divided, and which were established by Joseph Needham (see Bibliography).

Aurifiction

There are a number of artisanal crafts, predating the rise of alchemy, which demand varying degrees of empirical knowledge. These include the manufacture of perfumes, glass, ceramics, inks, pigments and dyes. More relevant to our present subject were the arts used by jewellers and smiths to imitate genuine substances such as gold, silver, gems and pearls. The term 'aurifiction' applies to methods used for simulating gold. This could be achieved by 'diluting' gold with other metals; by making gold-like alloys with copper, tin, zinc, nickel, etc.; by the surface-enrichment of such alloys containing gold; by amalgamation gilding; or by the deposition of surface films of appropriate tints produced by exposure of the metal to the vapours of sulphur, mercury or arsenic, or volatile compounds containing these elements. The deception of the client was not essential, for he might be quite content with an artifact of gold-like appearance. The artisan, however, would have been well aware that his product would not stand up to the ancient test of cupellation. In this test gold (or silver), with or without other metals, is heated with lead in a vessel made of bone-ash, a crucible or a shallow hearth, set in an oxidising furnace with a reverbatory heat-flow. Lead monoxide (litharge) is formed, as well as the oxides of any other base metals, and these separate with any other impurities, soaking into the porous ash and being blown off by the fumes, until a cake or globule of the precious metal remains. Cupellation does not separate gold and silver, but this could be achieved by the ancient method known as 'dry parting' or 'cementation'. This process could also be used for the surface-enrichment of a gold-containing alloy by the withdrawal of copper and silver from the external layers, so that an object thus treated would give a positive result to the touchstone, as the Hellenistic artisans certainly knew.

Aurifaction

Aurifaction, the attempt to produce gold (or silver) from base metals, is commonly regarded as synonymous with alchemy. It is not possible here to discuss in any depth the ideas that led to the growth of alchemical thought. Some attempt must be made, however, to mention the most important concepts. Aristotle, though not an alchemist, formulated theories that are widely thought to be the basis of much alchemical thought. As is well known, he taught that all substances are composed of four elements: fire, air, water and earth, which are distinguished from one another by their 'qualities', these being the fluid (or moist), the dry, the hot and the cold. Each element possesses two of these, as follows:

Fire – hot and dry
Air – hot and fluid
Water – cold and fluid
Earth – cold and dry

None of the four elements is unchangeable; they pass into one another through the medium of that quality which they possess in common; thus fire can become air through the medium of heat; air can become water through the medium of fluidity, and so on. Since each element can be transformed into any of the others, it follows that any kind of substance can be transformed into any other kind by so treating it that the proportions of its elements are changed to accord with the proportions of the elements in the other substance. The many hundreds of recipes given by the alchemists nearly all revert to this basic concept. One or more substances were subjected to chemical treatments such as roasting, amalgamation or calcination, and a substance known as the 'philosophers stone' or the 'elixir' was applied to the resultant product. The preparation of this substance, and its application to the materials to be transmuted, could involve elaborate chemical processing. Sometimes the operations were carried out under auspicious planetary influences. If everything had been carried out correctly, then pure gold would be produced.

Macrobiotics

The concept of linking alchemy and medicine is without doubt of Chinese origin. The main ideas of macrobiotics include the conviction of the possibility of a chemically induced longevity, hope in a similar conservation of youth, speculation on what the achievement of a perfect balance of qualities might be able to accomplish, the enlargement of the life-extension idea to life-donation or artificial generation systems, and the uninhibited application of elixir chemicals in the medical treatment of diseases.

Attempts to transmute base materials into gold, or to prolong life by chemical means were, of course, bound to fail. Other early scientific work was also often based upon false premises. Valuable work was done in pneumatics, for example, before it was realised that aerostatic effects were produced by the weight of air. It is a little strange, therefore, that alchemists have been singled out for more than their fair share of ridicule, since many of them were serious seekers after truth, using the best theoretical assumptions that were known in their time. The ridicule may be partly explained by the fact that over the centuries many charlatans professed to be alchemists with the sole object of deluding the unwary and so enriching themselves. Nevertheless, even serious alchemists must share part of the blame for the dubious status of their profession. They were either ignorant of, or chose to ignore, the assaying methods such as cupellation that were well known to the artisans. In other fields, for example machine technology, there was fruitful co-operation between scientists and craftsmen; if a scientist ignored the advice of craftsmen then the machines he designed simply would not work. There is no simple answer to the failure of alchemists to seek practical advice.

History of Islamic Alchemy

In the West alchemy came into being in Hellenistic Egypt. The writings of the Hellenistic alchemists themselves have survived only in a number of fragmentary manuscripts, many of which carry the names of legendary or celebrated figures such as Hermes, Isis, Moses and Cleopatra. The oldest of these writings is probably the pseudo-Democritus, which can be dated to the early years of the first century AD. The other writings were composed later – from the second to the fourth centuries AD. An important figure was Zosimus of Panopolis who around AD 300 wrote an encyclopaedia of alchemy, parts of which have survived.

A considerable number of Greek writings were translated into Arabic. Indeed, it is clear from references in the works of Islamic alchemists and biographers that many more Greek works were known to the Muslims than have come down to us. There is no doubt, therefore, that Hellenistic alchemy was a major influence on its Islamic counterpart. We must be careful, however, not to assume that the only sources of Islamic alchemy were Greek, simply because the written transmissions were from the Greek pseudographs. The whole course of Hellenistic proto-chemistry was primarily metallurgical, while Islamic joined with Chinese alchemy in the profoundly medical nature of its preoccupations. Macrobiotic ideas appear in the Jabirian writings and in the works of other Arabic alchemical writers, and it seems almost certain that they were imported from China, where the characteristic form of Chinese alchemy had existed since the fourth century BC. No translations of Chinese works are known from the early centuries of Islam, but the two cultures had commercial relations from the eighth century onwards and non-literary transmissions could have occurred in alchemical matters as we know they did in other fields: for example, in paper-making and in techniques of siege warfare.

For the beginnings of Islamic alchemy we have only the reports of a legendary nature in the works of later alchemists. Although there may have been other early Muslim scholars who were interested in the subject, undoubtedly the most important name in early Islamic alchemy was that of Jābir b. Ḥayyān, long familiar to Western readers under the name of Geber, the medieval rendering of the Arabic name. A large number of books have been attributed to Jābir, who is said to have lived from 721 to 815. The very existence of such a man has been queried, and few scholars now accept that all the books attributed to him were from a single hand. The most credible conclusion of modern research is that the Jabirian corpus was composed by a group of Ismāʿīlī scholars at the close of the ninth and the early decades of the tenth century. It is also possible, though conjectural, that Jābir was a historical personage who may have initiated the serious study of alchemy in Islam.

The Jabirian corpus contains in its various parts virtually all that was known of alchemy at the time. Very little was added to this sum of knowledge later, except for practical advancement in the way of equipment and processes. All that can be mentioned here are some of the ideas that distinguish Jābir from his Hellenistic predecessors. The first of these is the quicksilver/sulphur theory. In quicksilver, it was held, water and earth are present, sulphur contains fire and air and thus these substances together hold the four elements. When the particles of sulphur and quicksilver are mixed and enter into a close compound, the heat generates a process of maturation and cooking which results in the various kinds of metals. If the quicksilver is clean and the sulphur pure, if the quantities stand in ideal relation to one another, and if the heat has the right degree, pure gold comes into being. If before maturation coldness enters then silver is produced; if dryness, then red copper. The more disturbing factors enter, the more low-grade the metals become. The alchemist, then, exerts himself to imitate nature. He tries to discover how much quicksilver and how much sulphur are contained in gold and how great the heat must be to bring about the maturation process If he succeeds in establishing these conditions, he is able to synthesise gold.

Although the above theory appears for the first time in the Jabirian corpus, it does not differ in essence from the methods used by the Hellenistic alchemists. Two other theories, however, do represent a radical departure from the principles and practices of earlier times. The theory of the 'balance' was a highly speculative one, in which the alchemist attempted to assess the equilibrium of 'natures' (heat, dryness, coldness and fluidity) in any given substance. An elaborate system of numerology was used in conjunction with the Arabic

FIGURE 5.1 The Imam Ja'far-i-Ṣadiq (d. 768) sees the famous
alchemist Jābir b. Ḥayyān. British Library MS Or 11837, f. 29v.

alphabet of twenty-eight letters to estimate the proportions of the natures in a substance. The 'balance' was determined by giving numerical values to each letter of the alphabet and assigning these values to the letters in the name of the substance, whereupon the proportions of the natures in the substance could be calculated. These being known according to the theory they could then be adjusted to produce another substance, usually gold, whose balance was known. This system, of which the foregoing is only an outline, undoubtedly had esoteric significance.

The idea of an elixir that could be used as a medicine or as a life-giving force appears for the first time in the West in the writings of Jābir. As mentioned earlier, the idea was probably diffused from China. The elixir, which could be prepared from animal, vegetable or mineral substances, could be used to prolong life or given as a medicine to desperately sick people. Even more startling is the so-called Science of Generation, concerned with the asexual generation of plants, animals and even men, as well as the production of ores and minerals in nature and in the laboratory, including the generation of noble metals from the base ones. The transmutation of base metals into gold by means of an elixir is therefore but one specialised application of the theory.

The other great name in early Islamic alchemy is that of Abū Bakr Muḥammad b. Zakariyyā' al-Rāzī. He is, of course, justly famous as a medical practitioner and teacher, but he also turned his attention to philosophy, logic, metaphysics, poetry, music and alchemy. He wrote a number of alchemical books, some of which have survived, including his major work on the subject, *Kitāb al-asrār* (*The Book of Secrets*). From this work we receive the impression of a powerful mind, much more interested in practical chemistry than in theoretical alchemy. Thus, although he was a contemporary of the later Jabirian authors, his views are very different from theirs. He did not accept Jābir's theory of the 'balance', does not discuss the elixir of life and does not speculate about the esoteric meaning of alchemy. He believed, with the Hellenistic writers, that all substances are composed of the four elements and that therefore the transmutation of metals is possible. The object of alchemy was to effect this transformation by means of elixirs, and also to 'improve' valueless stones such as quartz and even glass with similar elixirs and so convert them into emeralds, rubies, sapphires and the like. Al-Rāzī followed Jābir in assuming that the proximate constituents of metals were quicksilver and sulphur, but sometimes he suggests a third constituent of a salty nature – an idea that occurs very frequently in later alchemical literature. Elixirs were of varying powers, ranging from those which could covert only 100 times their own weight of base metal into gold to those that were effective 20,000 times. Most of our knowledge about materials, equipment and processes used in Islamic proto-chemistry comes to us from *Kitāb al-asrār*

Although alchemical books continued to be written in Islam into the fifteenth century and beyond, not much of real importance was added to the works of 'Jābir' and al-Rāzī, either on the esoteric or the practical side of the subject. One of the more interesting was a book written in Spain early in the eleventh century by an author known as the pseudo-Majrītī. One of his books contains very precise and intelligible instructions for the purification of gold and silver by cupellation and in other ways, serving to show that contemporary alchemy knew the discipline of the laboratory. Also, the author of the book describes an experiment, on the preparation of what is now called mercuric oxide, carried out on a quantitative basis. Very seldom in alchemical literature do we find even the slightest suggestion that pursuing the changes in weight that occur during a chemical reaction might lead to significant results; a procedure that, first methodically applied by Joseph Black in the middle of the eighteenth century, has for 200 years been a guiding principle in the science of chemistry. The very many books of Aydamir al-Jildakī, an Egyptian who died in 1342, are important not so much for their technical content but because he quotes extensively from the works of other Muslim alchemists. In many cases the original works from which the quotations were made are still in existence, and examination of them shows that al-Jildakī was a careful copyist; we may therefore with fair confidence accept as genuine other passages of which no earlier provenance is known.

Substances, Equipment and Processes

Al-Rāzī's *Book of Secrets* foreshadows a laboratory manual and deals with substances, equipment and processes. From the lists he gives of material and apparatus it is evident that his own laboratory was very well equipped. His store-cupboard contained not only specimens of all metals then known, but pyrites, malachite, lapis lazuli, gypsum, haematite, turquoise, galena, stibnite, alum, green vitriol, natron, borax, common salt, potash, cinnabar, white lead, red lead, litharge, ferric oxide, cupric oxide, verdigris and vinegar. He drew up a scheme for the classification of all substances used in alchemy; here for the first time we meet with the now familiar division of substances into animal, vegetable and mineral.

The types of equipment mentioned in *The Book of Secrets* is obviously quite a comprehensive list of the apparatus in general use in alchemical laboratories, apparatus that was the result of centuries of development by Hellenistic and Islamic scientists and artisans. The tools and simpler devices included bellows, shears, hammers, files, pestles and mortars, ladles, funnels, sieves, filters, dishes, beakers, bottles, phials, flasks, cauldrons, blacksmiths' hearths, and lamps for imparting a gentle heat .

The more complex pieces of equipment, many of which are still in use today, included:

1.. Crucible (butāqa)
2. Decensory (but-bar-but), literally 'a crucible on a crucible', the upper one having its bottom perforated with holes.
3. Cucurbit or retort for distillation (qarʿ) and the head of a still with a delivery tube (anbīq, Latin alembic)
4. Closed vessel with a lid in which reactions can occur (uthāl, Latin aludel)
5. Various types of furnace or stove
   (a) large baker's oven (tannūr, Latin athannor)
   (b) brazier or chafing dish
   (c) a stove with perforated sides, half filled with charcoal and mounted on three legs, and in which a receptacle containing substances to be calcined (roasted) or brought in combination, was placed
6. Sand-bath on which a vessel could be heated by a fire underneath
7. Water-bath

The chemical processes described or mentioned by al-Rāzī include distillation, calcination, solution, evaporation, crystallisation, sublimation, filtration, amalgamation and ceration, the last-named being a process for converting substances into pasty or fusible solids. Most of these operations were used in attempts at transmutation, which according to al-Rāzī were conducted as follows. First, the substances to be employed had to be purified by distillation, calcination, amalgamation or other appropriate treatment. Having freed the crude materials from their impurities, the next step was to reduce them to an easily fusible condition by means of ceration, which should result in a product that readily melted, without any emission of fumes, when dropped upon a heated metal plate. After ceration, the product was to be further disintegrated by the process of solution, which included dissolving in 'sharp waters'; these were not generally acid liquids but alkaline and ammoniacal, though lemon juice and sour milk, which are weakly acidic, were sometimes employed. The solutions of the various substances, suitably chosen for the amount of 'bodies', 'spirits', etc., they were supposed to possess, were then brought together. The combined solutions were finally subjected to the process of coagulation or solidification, and if the experiment were successful the resulting substance would be an elixir. In view of al-Rāzī's methodical approach and his insistence upon the necessity for practical work, he has been considered, rightly, as one of the main founders of modern chemistry.

The distinction between Alchemy and Industrial Chemistry reflects modern ideas of categorisation. Various Muslim alchemists included in their works recipes for products that had industrial or military uses while, on the other hand, there was feed-back from artisanal practices and discoveries in the esoteric world of alchemy. Nevertheless, the distinction is valid within limits, provided these reservations are borne in mind.

Alcohol

The number of references to distillation in the works of Muslim authors makes it probable that the preparation of alcohol was known in Islam before it reached Europe. Al-Kindī (d. c.866) in his *Book of Perfume Chemistry and Distillation*, after describing distilling apparatus, adds: 'In this way one can distil wine using a water-bath, and it comes out the same colour as rose-water'. The addition of sulphur to the distilled wine is found in a work of al-Fārābī (d. 950). Abu'l-Qāsim al-Zahrāwī, known in the West as Abulcasis (d. c.1013), described the distillation of vinegar in an apparatus similar to that used for rose-water, adding that wine could be distilled in the same way. Ibn Bādīs (d. 1061) described how silver filings pulverised with distilled wine could provide a means of writing in silver.

Perfumes

In the Islamic world the distillation of rose-water as well as other perfumes and the scented oils in plants and flowers – the 'essential oils' – became a flourishing industry. An important centre for the manufacture of these scents was Damascus, and there were important distilleries in Jūr and Sabūr in Iran and Kūfa in Iraq. The industry's products were exported within the Islamic world and as far as India and China.

Al-Kindī's treatise, mentioned above, is the only one known to have survived from the earlier centuries of Islam; it contained 107 methods and recipes. The stills he used were fairly simple. One, for example, was of the retort type, with no annular rim but set in a water-bath above the stove; in another the still was provided with an annular ring and placed in a stove gently heated by charcoal. By the time of Ibn al-Ishbīlī in the twelfth century we find the use of mass ovens containing anything between sixteen and twenty-five cucurbits. Such an oven

FIGURE 5.2 Caste of druggists or perfumiers, N. India. British Library
MS Add. 27255, f. 340v.

was described by al-Dimashqī (d. 1327) for the distillation of flowers to make rose-water. In this case heat was provided by steam; the oven's fire was regulated by openings in the furnace itself and the cucurbits, which stood on mats, were placed in circles over a pan of water which produced the steam. Such circles of cucurbits, fitting on top of one another, might reach one and a half times the height of a man. The necks and mouths of the cucurbits emerged from the steam to the outside where there were alembics, which thus had their necessary cooling surfaces in the open air; receivers were attached to collect the distillates. Al-Dimashqī also described another industrial installation for rose-water, but using a hot-air oven instead of a steam one.

As well as the rose-water and essential oils produced by distillation, the industry included the manufacture of a number of other preparations, for example, amber and musk and the perfumes derived from them.

Petroleum

Petroleum was an important product in Islamic economic life long before it attained its present global significance. Crude petroleum (naft) was extracted and distilled extensively; it had both military and domestic uses.

Crude oil was usually called 'black naft' and the distillates 'white naft', even though some of the crude oils were colourless in their natural state. We have a number of descriptions of the distillation process in Arabic writings, such as that in al-Rāzī's Book of Secrets. From this we learn that the crude oil was first mixed with white clay or sal ammoniac into 'a dough like a thick soup' and then distilled. The light distillates, i.e. the white naft, were used by him to 'soften or loosen' some solid substances, such as certain gems and minerals. Moreover in his chemical and medical work al-Rāzī made use of oil lamps (naffāṭa) for gently heating chemicals; the fuel for these was either vegetable oils or petroleum.

The oilfields at Baku were developed on a commercial scale by the Muslims at an early date; it is reported that in 885 the caliph al-Mu'tamid granted the revenues of the naft springs to the inhabitants of Darband. There are several accounts of Baku oil. For example the geographer al-Mas'ūdī, after visiting the wells in 915, wrote that 'vessels carrying trade sail to Baku which is the oilfield for white naft and other kinds'. In the thirteenth century wells were dug at Baku to get down to the source of the naft; it was at this time that Marco Polo reported that a hundred shiploads might be taken from it at one time. Other sources record crude oil production in Iraq where there were seepages on the eastern bank of the Tigris along the road to Mosul.

Muslim travellers reported that it was produced on a large scale and was exported. Other Arabic reports give information on crude oil production at Sinai in Egypt and Khuzistan in Iran.

Besides crude petroleum and its distillates, asphalts were also abundant. Particularly in Iraq *qīr* (pitch) and *zift* (pitch or asphalt) were produced and exported, having been known and used in this region by earlier civilisations, though their use was extended in Islamic times. They became familiar in building construction, especially for baths, and in shipbuilding, while they were also adopted as ingredients in the recipes for many incendiary weapons.

Acids

Clearly the discovery of inorganic acids is of great importance in the history of chemistry. They were the products of the distillation of alum, sal ammoniac (chloride of ammonia), saltpetre (potassium nitrate) and common salt in various proportions, as well as vitriol. Vitriol was a term used in early times for hydrated sulphate crystals; in later times it became synonymous with sulphuric acid. The various acids were produced during alchemical experiments, but they were of course valuable agents in a number of industrial processes.

A description of the manufacture of nitric acid appears in one of the manuscripts in the Jabirian corpus called *Ṣandūq al-ḥikma* (*The Chest of Wisdom*). It reads as follows:

> Take five parts of pure flowers of nitre, three parts of Cyprus vitriol and two parts of Yemen alum. Powder them well, separately, until are like dust and place them in a flask; plug the latter with palm fibre and attach a glass receiver to it. Then invert the apparatus and heat the upper portion (i.e. the flask containing the mixture) with a gentle fire. There will flow down by reason of the heat an oil like cow's butter.

Analogous instructions appear in the Latin work *Summa Perfectionis* by 'Geber'.

Sulphuric acid was first described in Islamic literature in the Jabirian writings. It can be made by distilling vitriol or alum, or by the combustion of sulphur. In one of his recipes al-Rāzī called it 'water of distilled alum', and he used it as one of the reagents which he prepared beforehand and kept for use in his alchemical work. In the tenth century al-Masʿūdī, who was a geographer and a historian, not a chemist, described a few chemical reactions, among them the reaction of al-qālī water (see below) with *zāj* or vitriol water (sulphuric acid). He noted too the red colour that resulted, and commented on the dangers that could come from 'subliming vapours and vitriolic fumes and other mineral exhalations'.

In an Arabic manuscript written in the Syriac script but with additions made probably in the thirteenth century, the preparation of sulphuric acid is also described. It runs: 'take three parts of vitriol (*zāj*) and three parts of sulphur, pulverise them them well and distil them on a dry fire. A yellow water distils'. Similar distillation recipes for sulphuric acid are given more than once and it is clear that this acid was often prepared and stored for future use, as al-Rāzī did. The author of the Syriac text calls the acid 'water of vitriol and sulphur', and in other Arabic manuscripts it is also sometimes called *rūḥ al-zāj* (spirit of *zāj*).

Hydrochloric acid was known as *rūḥ al-milḥ* (spirit of salt). Al-Rāzī gives the following recipe:

> Take equal parts of sweet salt, bitter salt, Tabarzad salt, Indian salt, salt of *al-qālī* and salt of urine. After adding an equal weight of good crystallised sal ammoniac, dissolve by moisture and distil the mixture. This will distil over to give a strong water which will cleave stone instantly.

In other Arabic manuscripts there are recipes in which sal ammoniac and vitriol are distilled together .

Besides the mineral acids there were some organic acids such as vinegar which were produced in large quantities, while vinegar itself was also distilled to give acetic acid. Silicic acid (a compound of silicon, oxygen and hydrogen) which can be used to make substances that are insoluble in water was another familiar product; it was obtained from bamboo.

Alkalis

Soda and potash were in great demand for making glass, glazes and soap. Natron and plant ash were the sources. Natron is crude sodium carbonate; it was found in its natural state in Egypt in the Western Desert and was exported widely. It was from the Arabic *natrun* that the European variation 'natron' was derived and hence the symbol 'Na' for sodium.

Al-qālī was obtained from the fused ashes of a low, woody shrub found in Syria and variously called *ashnan, ushnan* and *shinan*. It is of the family Chenopodiaceae and has the botanical name *salsola soda*, while chemically it is about 80 per cent potassium carbonate with some 20 per cent sodium carbonate. The ashes of wood, especially oak, were also utilised. Al-Rāzi described the concentration and purification of *al-qālī* and of oak ashes to give pure potassium carbonate and sodium carbonate. Abu Manṣūr Muwaffaq in the tenth century, however, was the first to make a clear distinction between sodium carbonate (soda) and potassium, which are similar in many respects.

FIGURE 5.3 Caste of limeburners, N. India. Kiln is shown. British Library MS Add. 27255, f. 348v.

Caustic soda or sodium hydroxide was never produced on a commercial scale, but it is of historical interest to note that al-Rāzī knew how to prepare it. His recipe ran as follows:

Taken one *mann* [about 1 kg] of white *al-qālī* and an equal quantity of lime and pour over it [i.e. the mixture] seven times its amount of water and boil it until it is reduced to one half. Purify it [by filtration and decantation] ten times. Then place it in thin evaporating cups and hang it in heated beakers. Return what separates out [to the cup], raise it [the cup] gradually and protect from dust whatever drops from the cups into the beaker and coagulate it into a salt.

Lime (*kils*) was abundant. Used in soap-making, as a building material and for military purposes, it was produced by burning limestone marble. When slaked with water it was known as *nūra*.

6

Machines

Water-raising machines were (and are) used for a number of purposes, of which the most important was that of crop irrigation. They were also used for supplying water for private and communal purposes, for pumping flood water from mines and bilge water from ships. Our information on these machines comes from both archaeological and literary sources. Also, since several types are still in use today, their operation can be understood by examining working machines. It might be argued that the machines could have altered drastically over the centuries, but this is not the case. Descriptions given in the works of medieval Arabic writers tally closely with the design of machines constructed in the recent past.

Two devices date back to Antiquity. The well-windlass is the system whereby a rotable wooden cylinder is erected over the mouth of the well. A rope with a bucket attached to its free end is caused to wind and unwind around the cylinder by a man turning a crank. Another early method was the *shādūf*. This was illustrated as early as 2500 BC in Akkadian reliefs and about 2000 BC in Egypt. It has remained in use to the present day and its application is world-wide, so that it is one of the most successful machines ever invented. Its success is due to its simplicity and its efficiency. It can easily be constructed by the village carpenter using local materials, and for low lifts it delivers substantial quantities of water. It consists of a long wooden pole suspended at a fulcrum to a wooden beam supported by columns of wood, stone or brick. At the end of the short arm of the lever is a counterweight made of stone or, in alluvial areas where stone is not available, of clay. The bucket is suspended to the other end by a rope. The operator lowers the bucket into the water and allows it to fill. It is then raised by the action of the counterweight and its contents are discharged into an irrigation ditch or a head tank.

Several machines were developed in Egypt in Hellenistic times. The screw or water-snail was probably invented by Archimedes whose name, of course, it carries. It consists of a central wooden cylinder, the rotor, into the ends of which are fitted spigots that rotate in metal bearings. A helix of laminated timber or sheet metal is wound around the rotor and this is enclosed by a wooden casing bound with iron hoops. All joints are caulked with pitch to minimise leakage. In Roman times the screw was operated by a treadmill, but by a manually

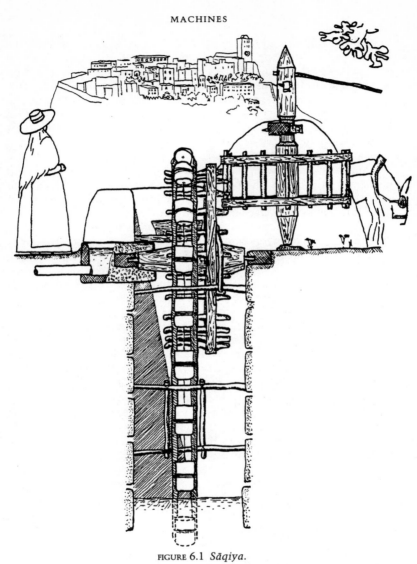

FIGURE 6.1 *Sāqiya.*

operated crank in more recent times. The lower end of the screw dips into the water source, the upper end discharges into an irrigation ditch. The angle of the screw determines its output. The machine has not retained its popularity: it was still in common use in Upper Egypt and other parts of the Arab world in 1965, but had already disappeared from the Delta region.

Another machine is the tympanum or drum. As described by the Roman writer Vitruvius in the first century BC, the machine consisted of a wooden axle with iron pegs protruding from its ends. The pegs were housed in iron journals that were supported on stanchions. Two large timber discs made up from planks were mounted on the axle, and the space between them was divided into eight segments by wooden boards. The perimeter was closed by wooden boards, there being a slot in each segment to receive the water. Circular holes were cut around the axle in one face of the drum, one to each segment. The whole machine was coated with tar. The water discharged into a small tank connected to a channel through which the water flowed to the fields or to a drainage area. In Roman times the tympanum was operated by a treadmill but in the Arab world, in recent times, it was sometimes operated by an animal through gears, in a similar manner to the *sāqiya*.

The *sāqiya*, also invented in Hellenistic Egypt, is a more important machine than any of those mentioned so far (Figure 6.1) The following is the description of the basic constructional details of a Spanish *sāqiya*, which was still in use in 1955 but was in ruins a few years later. (See Bibliography for the indispensable work by Thorkild Schiøler.)

The draught animal, a donkey in this case but often an ox or a camel in the Middle East, wears on its shoulders and neck a collar harness that transmits the power through two traces to a double-tree fastened to the drawbar. The drawbar passes through a hole in the upright shaft. This shaft carries the lantern pinion, which is a type of gear-wheel consisting of two wooden discs separated by pins, the spaces between the pins being entered by the cogs of a vertical gear. This vertical gear has cogs on one side of its disc and these protrude from the other side to form the wheel that carries the chain-of-pots, or potgarland. The component is therefore known as the potgarland wheel. It is erected directly over the well or other water source. The pots fill with water at the bottom of their travel and discharge at the top into a head tank or irrigation channel.

In order to prevent the wheel from going into reverse, the machine is provided with a pawl mechanism, which acts on the cogs of the potgarland wheel. To appreciate the vital function of the pawl it is only necessary to remember that the draught animal is subjected to a constant pull both when moving and when standing still. The pull is exerted by the part of the potgarland wheel carrying the pots. The pawl is activated in two cases – when the animal is to be unharnessed and in the event of the harness or the traces breaking. Without the pawl the machine would turn backwards at great speed and, after one revolution, the drawbar would hit the animal on the head. At the same time,

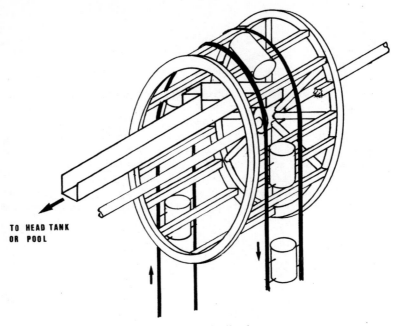

TO HEAD TANK
OR POOL

FIGURE 6.2 Sindī wheel.

many of the pins of the lantern pinion would break and the pots smash.

In some machines, the vertical gear-wheel was separate from the potgarland wheel, which was a special wheel called by the Arabic engineer al-Jazarī, writing in 1206, a 'Sindī' wheel. This implies that this was an improvement to the *sāqiya* introduced in the province of Sind, in the north-east of the Indian subcontinent. The addition of this wheel helped to avoid the 'splash-back' of water into the well. (See Figure 6.2.)

The *sāqiya* was in widespread use throughout the Islamic world in the Middle Ages. It was also diffused to the east and eventually to the New World. Like the *shādūf* it has retained its popularity in some parts of the world to the present day. It can be repaired on the spot without the necessity of importing fitters and spare parts from outside, a vital point when an interruption of the water supply to the fields for even twenty-four hours can be literally a matter of life or death.

One of the problems in water-raising engineering is that of raising large quantities of water through a small lift. The problem can be solved by using a spiral scoop-wheel (Figure 6.3), which raises water to the ground level with a high degree of efficiency. This machine is very

<small>FIGURE</small> 6.3 Spiral scoop-wheel.

popular in Egypt nowadays, and engineers at a research laboratory near Cairo have been trying to improve the shape of the scoop in order to achieve maximum output. Although it appears very modern in design, this is not the case, since a twelfth-century miniature from Baghdad shows a spiral scoop-wheel driven by two oxen. The transmission of power is the same as that employed with the standard *sāqiya*.

The *noria* is perhaps the most significant of the traditional water-raising machines. Being driven by water, it is self-acting and requires the presence of neither man nor animal for its operation. Essentially it is a

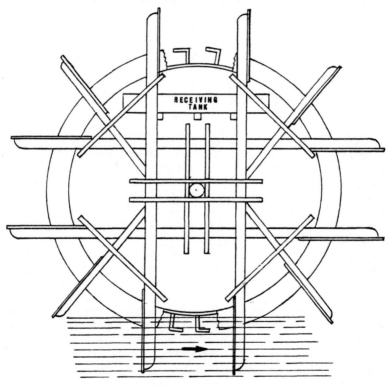

<small>FIGURE</small> 6.4 Noria.

96

large wheel constructed of timber. At intervals paddles project outside the rim of the wheel, the rim being divided into compartments (Figure 6.4). The noria is provided with an iron axle and this is housed in bearings which are installed on columns over a running stream. As the wheel is rotated by the impact of the water on the paddles, the compartments fill with water at the bottom of their travel and discharge their contents at the top, usually into an aqueduct. Instead of compartments, pots similar to those of a *sāqiya* may be lashed to the rim of the wheel.

The origin of the noria is uncertain. It was described by Vitruvius, and was therefore known in the Roman world by the first century BC. At about the same period, however, it was also in use in China. There is a possibility, therefore, that it was invented somewhere in the highlands of southwest Asia, perhaps in northern Syria or Iran, and was diffused to the east and the west from its area of origin.

At all events, there is ample evidence for the widespread use of the noria in medieval Islam. The first mention that we have refers to the excavation of a canal in the Basra region in the second half of the seventh century. Only when the excavator had built norias on the banks of the canal was he able to found a village nearby, suggesting that the community would not have been viable without this means of raising water on to the fields. Norias were also used in combination with dams, in order to provide an increased head of water for driving the machines. We do not need to rely only on literary sources, however, for information about norias. The large wheels at Ḥama, on the river Orontes in Syria, still exist, although they are no longer in use. The largest has a diameter of about 20 metres and its rim is divided into 120 compartments. The large noria at Murcia in Spain is still in operation, as are norias in various parts of the world, where they are often able to compete successfully with modern pumps.

Al-Jazarī completed his great book on machines in 1206 in Diyar Bakr, at which time he had been twenty-five years in the service of the ruling family of Artuqid princes. Most of the devices he describes are water-clocks and various types of automata; we shall be discussing this aspect of his work in the next chapter. There was obviously a demand from al-Jazarī's masters for devices that would provide amusement and aesthetic pleasure, but it is also highly likely that his responsibilities included the design and construction of public works. In this capacity he would have appreciated the need for improving the efficiency of water-raising methods, and have attempted to devise means to this end. Apart from their potential as practical machines, his designs have the added significance of incorporating techniques and components that are of importance in the development of machine technology.

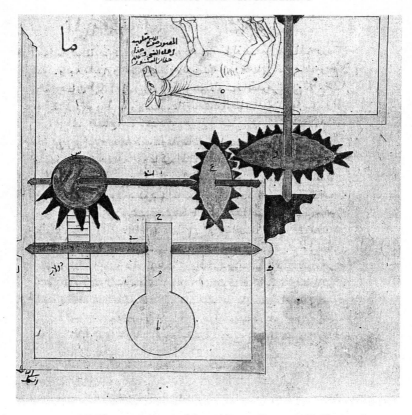

FIGURE 6.5 Water-raising machine, al-Jazarī Category V, Chapter 1.
Bodleian Library MS Greaves 27, f. 99v
(animal drawn inverted in error).

The first machine is shown in Figure 6.5. Two strong stanchions
were erected in a pool, and two axles, one vertically over the other,
rotated in journals housed in these stanchions. A flume-beam swape (a
large scoop attached to a channel) with a capacity of about fifteen
litres, and a lantern-pinion were fixed to the lower axle. On the upper
axle there were two gear-wheels, one of them having teeth on only a
quarter of its perimeter (i.e. a segmental gear), the other being a normal
gear-wheel. The segmental gear meshed with the lantern-pinion and
the other one with a horizontal gear-wheel, the vertical axle of which
passed through the floor of the operating room. On its upper end was a
drawbar, to which a donkey was tethered. As the donkey walked in a
circular path, the upper horizontal gear-wheel was turned and the

98

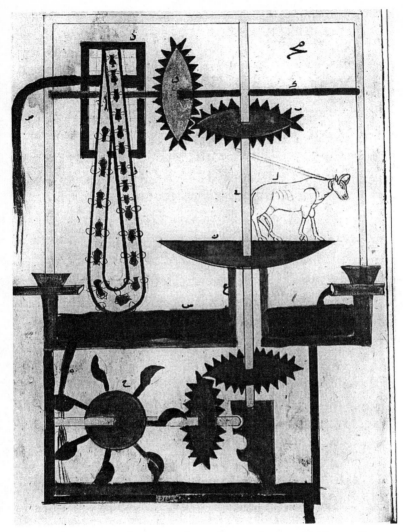

FIGURE 6.6 Water-raising machine, al-Jazarī Category V, Chapter 3.
Bodleian Library MS Greaves 27, f. 101r.

teeth of the segmental gear-wheel entered the bars of the lantern-pinion. The scoop was therefore raised and the water ran through the channel and discharged into an irrigation channel. When the teeth disengaged from the lantern-pinion the scoop fell back into the water

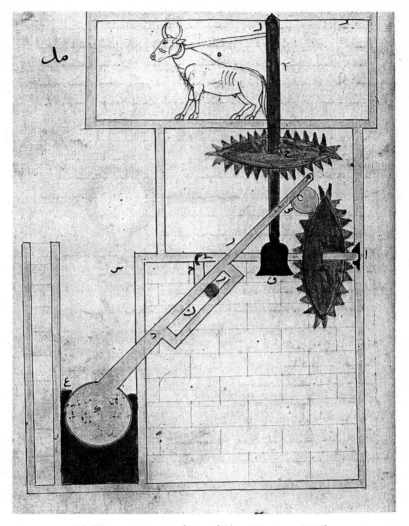

FIGURE 6.7 Water-raising machine, al-Jazarī Category V, Chapter 4.
Bodleian Library MS Greaves 27, f. 103r.

and was refilled in time for the next rotation. The segmental gear is an interesting part of this machine. A similar wheel first appeared in Europe in Giovanni de' Dondi's astronomical clock, completed about 1365. This type of gear was, however, known in Islam by the eleventh century, when a Spanish Muslim called al-Murādī used it in some of

100

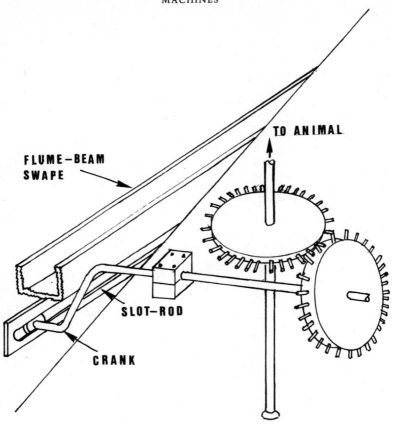

FIGURE 6.8 Line drawing of part of Figure 6.7.

his devices (see next chapter). The second of al-Jazarī's machines is a quadrupled version of the first, having four swapes, four lantern-pinions and four segmental gears.

The third machine is a miniature water-driven *sāqiya*, erected as an attraction by an ornamental pool. The actual drive is concealed and a model cow simulates the motive power. The discharge is through a 'Sindī' wheel shown at the top left in Figure 6.6. The water-driven *sāqiya* was an everyday machine in medieval Islam. One of these, which can still be seen, was built on the river Yazīd in Damascus about 1254 to serve the needs of a hospital.

Al-Jazarī's fourth machine again has a donkey in a raised chamber tethered to a drawbar and turning a vertical axle, as in the first two machines. On this axle, below the chamber, is a gear-wheel meshing at

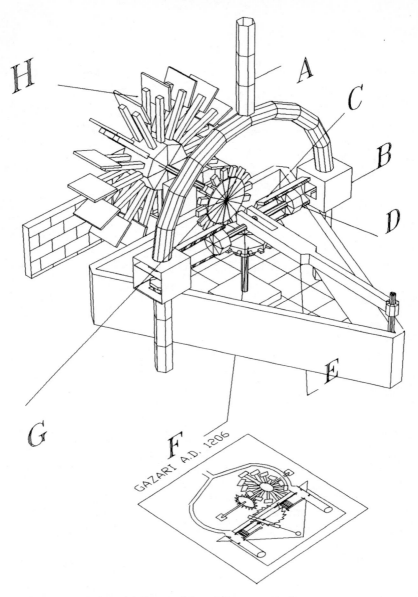

FIGURE 6.9 Pump, al-Jazarī Category V, Chapter 5 (computerised view).

102

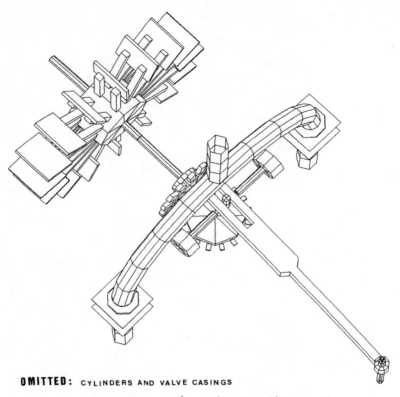

OMITTED: CYLINDERS AND VALVE CASINGS

FIGURE 6.10 Pump, al-Jazarī Category V, Chapter 5
(another computerised view).

right angles with a second wheel, mounted on a horizontal axle which
has a crank fitted to it. The free end of the crank enters a slot-rod under
the channel of a flume-beam swape, the scoop of which is in a pool. As
the donkey walks in a circle the horizontal axle is turned by the gears,
and the action of the end of the crank in the slot-rod raises and lowers
the swape. (See Figures 6.7 and 6.8.) This is the earliest evidence we
have for the crank as part of a machine, although manually operated
cranks had been in use for centuries.

The fifth machine is of considerable importance in the development of machine technology. It is a piston pump with two alternative
means of propulsion. The first of these is a horizontal vaned wheel
turned by a running stream. The axle of this wheel enters the machine
itself direct, without any gearing. In the second version a paddle wheel

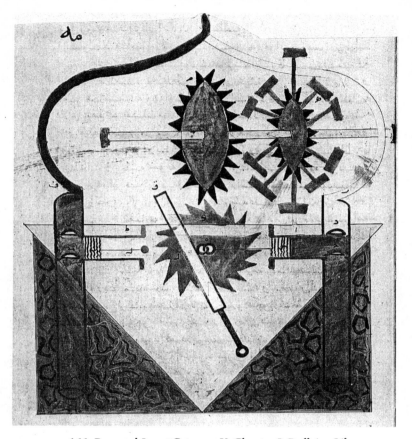

FIGURE 6.11 Pump, al-Jazarī Category V, Chapter 5. Bodleian Library
MS Greaves 27, f. 105r.

was mounted on a horizontal axle over a stream. Al-Jazarī devotes
most of the chapter to this version. To assist in understanding the
operation of the pump three illustrations have been provided. Figures
6.9 and 6.10 were obtained from the computer by my friend Dr
Thorkild Schiøler of Copenhagen, while figure 6.11 is a slightly modified version of the illustration in one of the manuscripts of al-Jazarī's
work. The first two are of the greatest help in explaining how the
machine works, but there are a couple of minor points on which cross-
reference to al-Jazarī's drawing and textual description is necessary.
Identifying letters have been added to the components on Figure 6.9.

The paddle wheel is H; on the extension of its axle gear-wheel G is mounted and this meshes with the horizontal gear-wheel F which has a vertical peg on its upper surface. This peg enters the slot-rod E which is pivoted at the end of the triangular box in which the pump is housed. Connecting rods attached to the sides of the slot-rod carry the pistons D on their ends, and these enter the cylinders C. At the end of each cylinder is valve-box B; the suction pipes descend into the water from the underside of the box and the delivery pipes emerge from its top. The mouths of both pipes are fitted with non-return clack-valves for suction and delivery. The delivery pipes were brought together above the machine to form a single pipe A which could deliver the water with great force to a height of about fourteen metres.

The action of the pump was as follows; as the paddle wheel rotated it turned the vertical gear-wheel which in turn caused the horizontal gear-wheel to rotate. The slot-rod oscillated – one piston was on its suction stroke as the other was on its delivery stroke. There are some minor points that require clarifying. The cylinders were made of smooth copper and were circular in cross-section. The pistons were each made of two copper discs with a gap between them which was packed with hemp. The delivery pipes, as is usual in pumps, were of a smaller bore than the suction pipes. Finally the connecting rods were attached to the sides of the slot-rod with ring-and-staple joints.

This pump is remarkable for three reasons. First, it is an early example of the conversion of rotary to reciprocating motion, in this case by means of a slot-rod. Secondly, it is also one of the earliest machines to embody the double-acting principle. And thirdly, it is the first known case of a pump with true suction pipes. In Greek and Roman pumps the cylinders had stood vertically in the water which had entered them through plate-valves fixed to the centre of their bases.

WATER-MILLS

There are three basic types of water-wheel. The vertical undershot wheel is a paddle wheel which is installed on a vertical axle over a running stream (Figure 6.12.a). Its power derives almost entirely from the velocity of the water and it is therefore affected by seasonal changes in the rate of flow of the stream over which it is erected. Furthermore, the water level may fall, leaving the paddles partly or totally out of the water. Despite these drawbacks and its relatively low efficiency the undershot wheel retained its popularity over many centuries. This may be due partly to the simplicity of its construction and partly to special measures that can be taken to improve its performance (see below).

105

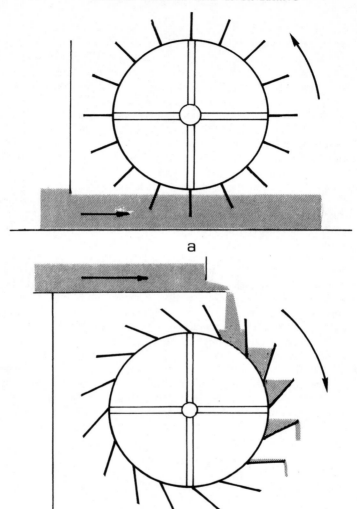

a

b

FIGURE 6.12 (a) Undershot wheel. (b) Overshot wheel.

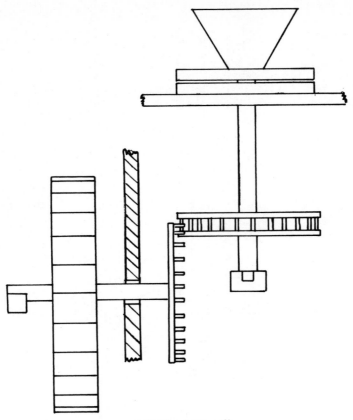

FIGURE 6.13 Vitruvian mill.

The overshot wheel is also vertical on a horizontal axle. Its rim is divided into bucket-like compartments into which the water discharges from above, usually from an artificial channel or 'leat' (see Figure 6.12b). Its efficiency can be high, perhaps three times that of the undershot wheel. Due to the necessary hydraulic works, however, the capital costs of installing it can be considerably higher.

When used for corn milling both types of vertical wheel require a pair of gears to transmit the power to the millstones. A vertical toothed wheel is mounted on the end of the water-wheel's axle inside the mill-house. This engages a lantern pinion, whose vertical axle goes through the floor to the milling room; it passes through the lower, fixed millstone and is fixed to the upper, rotating stone. The corn is fed into the concavity of the upper stone from a hopper (see Figure 6.13).

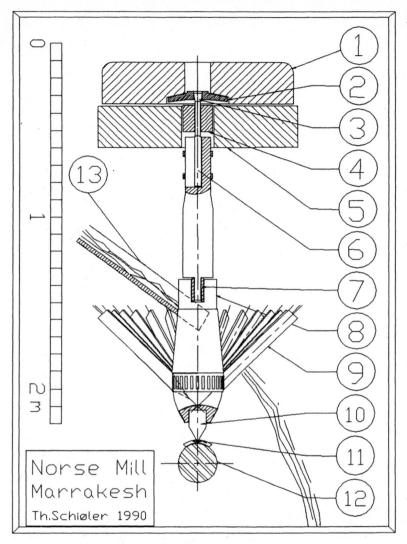

FIGURE 6.14a Marrakesh mill. 1. Runner stone with 'eye' for supply of the grain. 2. The rynd, an iron bearer set into the stone across the eye. 3. Flattened part of the spindle fitting into the rynd. 4. Neck journal. 5. Bedstone. 6 and 7. Joint in the spindle. 8. Hub shaft for the rotor. 9. Turbine vanes. 10. Iron pivot. 11. Iron footstep bearing. 12. Cross-section of the bridge tree. 13. Wooden chute which guides the water on to the blades.

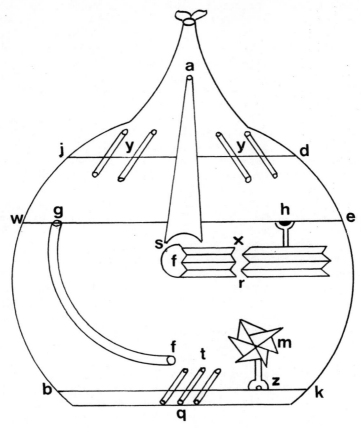

FIGURE 6.14b Horizontal wheel in Banū Mūsà's fountain. A circle of
vertical jets of water, t, turn the vaned wheel m, which operates a
worm-and-pinion gear.

The third type of wheel is horizontal and can be subdivided into two
types. The first of these is a wheel with curved or slanted vanes fitted
to a central wooden rotor. It is mounted at the bottom of a vertical
shaft and water from an orifice fitted to the bottom of a water tower is
directed on to the vanes, the flow being therefore mainly tangential
(see Figure 6.14a). The second type is made by cutting along the radii of
a metal disc, then bending the segments to form curved vanes, rather
like those of a modern air fan. This wheel, also fixed to the lower end
of a vertical axle, is installed inside a cylinder, into which the water
cascades from above, turning the wheel mainly by axial flow.

The locations and dating of the origins of the different types of water-wheel is still open to question. The undershot wheel was described by Vitruvious in the first century BC and the overshot wheel is depicted on a mural in the Roman catacombs dated to the third century AD. Both types were therefore in use long before the advent of Islam. Evidence for the early existence of the horizontal wheel is scanty. Indeed, the first unequivocal description of it occurs in a collection of Irish tracts dating to the eight century AD. There is, however, evidence for its existence in China and the Middle East by the first century AD, and there is little doubt that it was known by the time of the seventh-century Arab conquests. There are no direct references to horizontal wheels in the Arabic sources. The records we have of mills with horizontal wheels, in medieval and modern times, both in Europe and in the Middle East, indicate that they were almost always of the tangential flow type. There is, however, an interesting device in the works of the Banū Mūsà (c. 850 AD) in which a miniature axial-flow wheel is used. It is usually safe to assume, when a component is incorporated in an ingenious device, that it was already in use in utilitarian machines. It is possible, therefore, that the axial-flow wheel was used as a power source in Islam, but there is no certain evidence for its practical application before the invention of the so-called 'tub-wheel' in sixteenth-century Europe. It would be good to know more about the origins of horizontal wheels in general, because they are the direct ancestors of modern turbines.

There is plenty of evidence to show that the Muslims considered that corn-milling using water power was an essential part of economic life. Muslim geographers, when looking at a stream, would sometimes say that it would turn so many mills, as if they were estimating, as it were, the 'mill power' of the stream. It is possible to mention only a few of the many references to mills in the works of Muslim writers from the ninth century onwards. At Nīshāpūr in Khurāsān there were seventy mills on the river near the city; Bukhārā was noted for the number of its mills driven by undershot wheels and there were may mills in the Caspian province of Tabaristan. In the Iranian province of Fars the mills were owned by the State, and there were many mills in all the other Iranian provinces. The use of water power was widespread in North Africa, notably at Fez and Tlemcen. In tenth-century Palermo, then under Muslim rule, the banks of the river below the city were lined with mills. There are many references to mills in the Iberian peninsula, for example at Jaen and at Merida.

The Muslims used various methods for increasing the rate of flow of the water which operated mills, and so increasing the power and the productivity. One such method was to install the water-wheels between the piers of bridges to take advantage of the increased rate of flow caused by the partial damming of the river. Dams were also constructed to provide additional power for mills and water-raising machines, such as the dam built in the ninth century over the river Kūr in Iran. At Cordoba in Spain, below the Roman bridge, there was a large dam below which there were three millhouses each of which contained four mills. The foundations of the dam can still be seen and the millhouses are intact, although they no longer contain any machinery.

The ship-mill was widely used in the Islamic world as a means of taking advantage of the faster current in midstream, and of avoiding the problems caused to fixed mills by the lowering of the water-level in the dry season. Mills of this type are reported from Murcia and Zaragoza in Spain, from Tblisi in Georgia and from a number of other places. The most impressive of them, however, were in Upper Mesopotamia, which was the granary for Baghdad. In a work written in 988, the geographer Ibn Ḥawqal reports that the ship-mills on the Tigris at Mosul had no equal anywhere. They were very large, made of teak and iron, and they were in very fast current, moored to the bank by iron chains. There were similar mills at other places on the Tigris and on the Euphrates. Each mill had two pairs of stones and each pair ground in the day and night fifty donkey-loads. If we take a donkey-load as 100 kg, then the output of one of these mills in twenty four hours was ten tonnes, sufficient for about 25,000 people. At this time the population of Baghdad has been estimated at 1.5 million, making this kind of large-scale milling operation absolutely essential. Long after the time of Ibn Ḥawqal, Upper Mesopotamia continued as a large supplier of flour to Iraq. In about 1183 the traveller Ibn Jubayr saw the ship-mills across the river Khābūr, 'forming, as it were, a dam'. Further evidence of the Muslims' eagerness to harness every available source of water power is provided by their use of tidal mills. In the tenth century in Basra, for example, there were mills that were operated by the ebb-tide. This is at least a century before the first report of a similar application in Europe.

It has been suggested by some historians of technology that the Muslims were slow to exploit water power, but as we have seen that is far from being the case. It is usual to cite the figure of 5,624, given in the Domesday Book as the number of mills in England in the eleventh century, as evidence for the European commitment to the use of water power. It is not suggested that there was no such commitment, but it should be borne in mind that the population of England at the time was of the order of one million, so that on average less than 200 people were provided for by each mill. The mills must therefore have been small, low-powered units and it seems likely that many of them were powered by horizontal water-wheels.

The quality of millstones was an important consideration for Muslim millers (as indeed it was for their European counterparts). They must be hard but of homogeneous texture, so that pieces of grit do not become detached and mixed with the flour. The stone from certain localities was therefore particularly prized for milling purposes. In the area of Majjana, in modern Tunisia, for example, stones from the nearby mountains were considered highly suitable for grinding. It was said that they could last a man's lifetime without dressing or other treatment, due to their solidity and the fineness of their grains. The black stone of al-Jazīra – i.e. upper Mesopotamia – was called 'the stone of the mills'. It was the stone used for the mills that supplied Iraq with flour; a stone made from this material cost about fifty dinars. Stone for the mills of Khurāsān was mined from the hills near the city of Harāt.

Water power was important for industrial uses, in addition to that of grinding corn. In AD 751, after the battle of Atlak, Chinese prisoners of war introduced the industry of paper-making to the city of Samarqand. The paper was made from linen, flax or hemp rags after the Chinese method. Soon afterwards paper-mills after the pattern of those in Samarqand were established in Baghdad, the Yemen, Egypt, Syria, North Africa and Spain. It is known that the Chinese were using water power for industrial purposes by the first century AD, and there is abundant evidence that water-powered trip-hammers were used in China by the third century. It is therefore probable that the early paper-mills in Islam used trip hammers operated by vertical undershot water-wheels to pound the raw materials. In this system a number of cams are attached to the extended horizontal axle of the wheel. As the axle rotates, the cams bear down in succession on the pivoted lever-arms of the trip-hammers; when the cam moves away the hammer falls on to the material. In a treatise written between 1041 and 1049, the great scientist al-Bīrūnī gives a description of the processing of gold ores. He states clearly that the ores were pounded with water-driven trip hammers 'as is the case in Samarqand with the pounding of flax for paper'. This is further evidence of the use of water power in paper-mills, and although it does not prove conclusively that this system was in operation in Samarqand in the eighth century, when the paper-mills were established, this seems highly likely. Al Bīrūnī's remarks also indicate that the application of water power to other industries had begun no later than the early eleventh century, a conclusion that is supported by other reports. Writing in 1107, Ibn al-Balkhī calls a newly-restored dam on the river Kūr in Iran by the name of Band-i-Qassār, meaning 'Fuller's Dam', an indication that its impounded water provided power for fulling mills. In a recent survey in the Jordan valley the remains of thirty-two water-powered sugar-mills, dating to the Ayyūbid- Mamlūk period, were discovered. Writing in the first half of the twelfth century, the historian Ibn al-'Asākir mentions the use of water power for sawing timber. Also, in some of al-Jazarī's devices, such as water-clocks, there are small water-wheels with cams on their axles which are used to activate automata. These were probably copied from the similar mechanisms in industrial mills.

The question of the diffusion of industrial milling is not easily resolved. The first fulling-mill in Europe may have appeared in Italy by 983, and there were certainly fulling-mills and mills used in forges in the eleventh century. Industrial mills appeared in Christian Spain, notably in Catalonia, during the twelfth century. There are frequent references to fulling-mills in Catalonia from 1150 on, and towards the end of the century water power was applied to the Catalan forges. Paper-mills also appear in Catalan documentation during the 1150s and although there is no hard evidence that the mills themselves were of Islamic origin, there is no reason to believe that they were not, inasmuch as the rest of the technology of paper-making was identical with Islamic methods.

While it is probable that the Catalan adoption of industrial milling was inspired by Islamic examples in the Iberian peninsula, it is by no means certain that developments in northern Europe had similar derivations. As far as we can tell from the present state of evidence, the adoption of industrial milling in Islam and northern Europe were roughly simultaneous. Although the Samarqand paper-mills predate any installations in Europe, it has been conjectured that milling may have been applied to industrial purposes in the later Roman Empire. The possibility of separate developments in Islam and Europe cannot be ruled out.

WINDMILLS

The first reference we have to windmills occurs in the writings of the geographer al-Iṣṭakhrī, who mentions the windmills of Seistan (the western part of modern Afghanistan). Al-Iṣṭakhrī's book was completed about 951, but in one of al-Mas'ūdī's books, written a few years later, he relates the story of a Persian who claimed to the caliph 'Umar I that he was able to build a windmill. The story is somewhat unreliable, because there are tendencies in some of the historians of the ninth and tenth centuries to invent traditions that show the Persians in a better light than the Arabs. But while we must accept al-Iṣṭakhrī as our first reliable witness, he was probably describing a tradition which had existed for some time before his report. The earliest

113

description of the Seistan mills is given by the Syrian geographer al-Dimashqī, who died in 1327. He tells us that they were supported on substructures built for the purpose, or on the towers of castles or on the tops of hills. These mills were quite unlike the European types, which had vertical sails and a horizontal axle. Part of the superstructure, both in post-mills and in tower-mills, could be rotated so that the sails were at right angles to the wind direction. There were usually two pairs of sails.

The Seistan mills, on the other hand, had vertical axles and horizontal sails. According to al-Dimashqī's account, and the rather poor illustrations in the manuscripts, the building consisted of two chambers, the lower one housing the sails and the upper one the millstones. The main vertical axle was of iron and projecting from it were twelve or twenty-four crossbars, between which either six or twelve sails of coarse cloth were stretched. The axle was pointed at the lower end and rotated in a bearing embedded in the stone base of the mill. Four vents were left in the walls to direct the wind on to the sails. They were, says al-Dimashqī, like the loopholes in a fortress, except that they were reversed, with the narrower opening towards the inside, in order to increase the speed of the wind on the sails. There was a hole in the floor between the two chambers through which the axle passed, after which it passed through the lower fixed millstone – the bed-stone – and entered the circular cavity in the centre of the moving or runner-stone. A hopper was suspended above the centre of the runner-stone from which the corn trickled into the cavity in the runner-stone and then into the gap between the two stones where it was ground. Hoppers could be fixed as well as suspended.

There are, unfortunately, a number of dubious statements in al-Dimashqī's report. In the first place, it seems most odd that he locates the millstones *above* the rotor. This arrangement would have entailed a great deal of labour in carrying the grain up to the first floor and the flour down again, not to mention the extra costs in building access stairways and doors. It is worthy of note that when Chinese embassies visited Samarqand in 1219 and Harāt in 1414, the millstones were on the ground floor. Moreover, they are always in that location in modern mills in eastern Persia and Afghanistan. Secondly, it states on the illustration that the main axle is made of iron, which would have added greatly to the weight of the machinery and also made it difficult to attach the crossbars for holding the sails. And thirdly, there is the question of the apertures for the wind. In modern mills in the region there is a narrow vertical slit facing the prevailing wind – NW in Khurāsān, NNE in Seistan – and a wide opening on the opposite side of the building. Admittedly, al-Dimashqī says that the prevailing wind in Seistan varied from NW to NE, but this does not explain where the

FIGURE 6.15 Persian windmills at Khaf (Khurasan), 1977; viewed from the north.

four openings were located. There is no evidence that al-Dimashqī had ever visited Central Asia or that he had had any technical training. It seems likely that he obtained his information from a traveller and that this information became garbled when it was put down on paper.

There has been a high rate of attrition of the traditional horizontal mills in recent years, the result partly of the growing use of diesel engines and partly the recent disastrous war in Afghanistan. Fortunately, a number of mills in the region were examined before they fell into disuse and became dilapidated. We therefore have both written and photographic records of these machines from as recently as 1977 (see Bibliography). Today, as far as can be ascertained, only a few remain in remote areas, maintained by aging men with a respect for the old traditions. When these have gone, as they certainly will, our debt to researchers such as Michael Harverson who recorded their results in permanent form will be even greater than it is now.

Typically, Persian mills are built in banks, rather like a terrace of houses, with one wall being common to two mills except the outer two. Each mill is about twenty feet high; it is surrounded on three sides by walls of mud brick, the NW wall having a slit about two feet wide for its full height. The rotor consists of a vertical wooden axle to which the sails are fixed. There are generally seven or eight of these, made of wooden slats or matted reeds (see Figure 6.15). The mills are designed to make use of the '120-day wind', which blows strongly for that period from a single direction. Afghan mills have certain constructional differences from their Persian counterparts, but the basic design is very similar.

Beneath the mill the axle enters the millstones where the method of construction allows the corn to be fed into the aperture in the runner-stone and allows a gap to be maintained between the two stones. Also in the mill house is a fixed hopper, bins and shelves, a winnowing floor, corn bins and a sitting space. Entry is through a single door.

There is no evidence for the use of windmills in Europe before the end of the twelfth century. Once they were introduced they spread with great rapidity over the plains of northern Europe. Their construction, however, was completely different from that of the mills of Islam. They had, as already noted, vertical sails and a horizontal axle. They also had a set of gears. It has been credibly suggested that they were invented by analogy with the water-mills with vertical wheels. At all events, there is no reason to suppose that they were inspired by the Islamic mills, although it is possible that the idea of using wind as a source of power came to Europe from Islam. There was no reverse transmission; the European type of windmill was not used in Islam.

116

There are stories that the Crusaders built this type of mill in some of their castles. In Syria, for example, the great Crusader castle of Krak des Chevaliers, completed in 1240 and still largely intact, is said to have had a windmill on its walls. Such stories have no foundation in fact and are almost certainly later inventions.

The machines used for missile throwing in classical times depended upon the resilience of wood or twisted fibres for their propulsive force. Their missiles were fairly light – fifty pounds at the most – and had a flat trajectory. They were probably more effective as field artillery than in assaults on fortifications. In medieval times two more powerful machines operated by the rotation of beams, superseded the classical types. These were the trebuchets. One, the traction trebuchet, which was operated by teams of men pulling on ropes, was in use in the early Middle Ages. The second more powerful counterweight trebuchet was not introduced until late in the twelfth century.

The Traction Trebuchet

There is abundant evidence to show that this machine was known in China in Antiquity and in the early centuries of the Christian era. Its transmission westwards probably began in the seventh century AD passing to the Turks of Central Asia and reaching the Islamic world by the late seventh century, together with Khurāsānī or Soghdian artficers. One can test the probability of this hypothesis by referring to the Arab historians, although the vocabulary in itself is of no assistance. The words *manjanīq* and *arrāda* are used to describe missile-throwing siege machines but the terms seem to have been interchangeable, with *manjanīq* the commoner of the two. The word *manjanīq*, however, when it occurs in the descriptions of sieges, could apply to any type of machine: the classical types, the traction trebuchet and, later, the counterweight machine.

But although we cannot derive any information from the terminology by itself, there is nevertheless sufficient information in the Arabic chronicles to give an indication of the type of machine being used. At the siege of Mecca in 683 there was a *manjanīq* called *The Mother of the Hair*. This description may well have been derived from the appearance of the ropes hanging down from the end of the beam. A poet added his own description: 'swishing its tail like a foaming camel stallion'. At the siege of Daybul, in Sind, in AD 708, the Muslims had a siege machine called *The Bride*. It was operated by 500 men and was under the control of a skilled operator who took charge of the aiming and shooting. In Khurāsān in AD 710 there was a machine called *The*

Straddle-legged. There was a battery of machines at the siege of Baghdad in AD 865: a team of men to pull on the ropes and let fly the missiles was assigned to every *manjanīq* and *arrāda*. These reports, and other similar ones, leave no room for doubting that the missile throwers in use in Islam in the early centuries were traction trebuchets.

Descriptions of the traction machine occur in the works of Chinese, Islamic and European medieval writers, the first named providing the most detailed reports, from which we learn that the machine consisted essentially of a beam, resting on a fulcrum, which was supported on a timber tower. This tower was often provided with wheels to assist in the emplacement and aiming of the weapon. The beam itself might be a single spar, or several such spars bound together to form a composite beam. The trebuchets of the Sung period (960–1280) usually had from 1 to 10 spars in the beam but machines with 13 or even 15 were not unknown. The spars were from 5.6 to 8.4 metres long, with diameters at the extremities of 12.5 and 7 centimetres. At the narrower end was a copper 'nest', attached to the spar by iron wire, thus forming a sling. The missile, which could weigh from 2 to 130 pounds, was placed in the nest. At the other end of the beam there was a special attachment to which the ropes were attached, from 40 to 125 in number, between 12.40 metres and 15.50 metres in length and 16 millimetres in thickness. The team of men who pulled on these ropes to discharge the missile could range in number from 40 to 250 or more. The beam was divided into two arms by the axle – a long arm and a short arm – in the ratio 5:1 or 6:1 for the light machines, 2:1 or 3:1 for the heavy machines. The range of the missiles varied from 85 to 133 yards.

The Muslim sources do not differ radically in their specifications from the Chinese account, except that they usually seem to have known of a beam with only one spar. This may be due to the greater availability of bamboo in China; a beam made of several spars of a heavier wood could not have been made to rotate rapidly enough. The best information comes in a treatise written for Saladin by a certain Murḍā b. ʿAlī. The figures that he gives for the ranges and missile weight tally closely with those given in the Chinese sources. The fulcrum divided the beam in the ratio 6:1. the sling was a cubit in length. The best effects were obtained if the beam was flexible, not rigid, and the best wood was said to be cherry. Murḍā b. ʿAlī assigns an important role to the *rāmī* or 'shooter'. This man held the pouch containing the missile and pulled it against his chest with all his force. It was important that he held the sling at the correct angle, otherwise the angle of discharge would be incorrect. Presumably he let go of the pouch at the moment before the crew pulled hard on the ropes. The

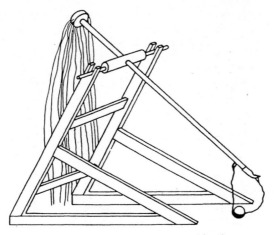

FIGURE 6.16 Traction trebuchet.

traction trebuchet had several disadvantages: the missiles were not very heavy, the ranges not long and the operating crew were vulnerable to counterattack from missiles and sorties. On the other hand it could be fabricated from materials obtained locally, it was easy to handle and must have had a fairly rapid rate of shooting (see Figure 6.16).

The Counterweight Trebuchet

The counterweight trebuchet appears to have been invented somewhere in the Mediterranean area in the late twelfth century and to have spread outward very rapidly from its point of origin into northern Europe and western Islam. But the exact provenance of the invention, whether in Europe or in Islam, is not yet resolved. There are a number of reports on the use of the machine in Islam in the thirteenth century. Counterweight trebuchets were used, for example, in the siege of Ḥims in Syria in 1248-9, and they were used in great numbers by the Muslims at the siege of Acre in 1291. The machine entered East Asia from Islam. Two Muslim engineers, 'Alā' al-Dīn and Ismā'īl, are honoured by a biography in the official history of the Yuan dynasty. They constructed the machines for Kubilai at the siege of Fan-chhêng towards the end of 1272. The counterweight trebuchet acquired the name of 'the Muslim *phao*'.

References to the design and performance of this machine are not infrequent and many illustrations of it occur in medieval and later works. Some of the drawings in these works are highly fanciful and the machines as depicted would have been useless. Perhaps the best

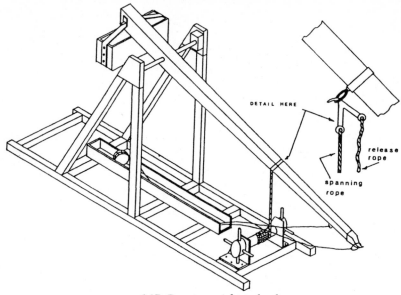

DETAIL HERE

release
rope

spanning
rope

FIGURE 6.17 Counterweight trebuchet.

drawing is in *Bellifortis* by Conrad Kyeser, written about 1405. This shows a trebuchet of workmanlike appearance, with a closed box at the end of the shorter arm to carry the counterweight. The machine is constructed of timber apart from some iron fittings. The beam is supported on an axle that rests between triangular towers. The drawing is dimensioned, the total length of the beam being 54 feet, with a short arm of 8 feet and a long arm of 46 feet, giving a ratio of 5.75:1. The sling, carrying a round stone, rests in a wooden channel in the base, the channel being horizontal and in the same vertical plane as the beam; the sling is as long as the complete beam (Figure 6.17).

The missiles could be very heavy. During the fourteenth-century siege of Tlemcen the trebuchets were capable of bombarding the town with balls made of marble, some of which have been found there, the largest with a circumference of 2 metres and weighing 230 kilograms. At the siege of Ḥims in 1248, a *manjanīq* was erected which could throw a stone weighing 140 Syrian *raṭls*. A Syrian *raṭl* was about 4 pounds in weight, hence the missile weighed about 560 pounds or 304 kg. On average, however, missiles were probably somewhat lighter, weighing 200–300 pounds, 90–136 kg. We do not have any reliable information about the masses of the counterweights; from a combination of remarks in the sources and a dynamic analysis, we can assume loads of 5 to 15 tonnes.

120

For some reason, European historians of technology and military affairs have paid far more attention to the counterweight trebuchet than to the traction type, even though the latter was in use in Islam for about seven hundred years while the counterweight machine had an effective life of only about two hundred years in all areas. Modern writers, in fact, have sometimes refused to believe that the traction machine ever existed, despite overwhelming evidence – textual and iconographic – in Chinese, Arabic and European sources. This neglect seems to be due in large measure to a faulty grasp of dynamics. A well-known author on ballistic weapons dismissed the traction machine as a fantasy because 'however many men pulled at the arm of a trebuchet they could not apply nearly the force that would be conveyed by the terrestrial gravitation of a heavy weight'. But of course it is not only the force that matters, but also the resistance.

The counterweight machine is essentially a compound pendulum. The weight not only provides the propulsive force but it is also part of the Inertia system of the machine and so contributes to the resistance. Nor can the power of the machine be increased in a linear relationship simply by increasing the counterweight. The beam must be strengthened to accommodate the extra weight, and this increases the Inertia of the beam. Moreover, the extra weight itself adds to the Inertia and acts as a decelerator. In fact, the counterweight trebuchet will only work at all by incorporating a very long sling, to act as a very light extension to the throwing arm. In the traction trebuchet, on the other hand, the propulsion is due to an outside source of energy, namely the impulsive torque applied by the pulling team. The beam can therefore be quite light, 'whippy' as an Arabic source specifies, and a short sling is essential. A detailed dynamic analyses of the two machines is unfortunately too complex to be discussed here.

Both types of trebuchet were superseded by the cannon in the last decades of the fourteenth and the first decades of the fifteenth centuries. The cannon had the advantages of a more rapid rate of fire, higher missile velocity, greater range and accuracy. Against this must be set the fact that the trebuchet could often be fabricated from materials near the beleaguered strong point, whereas the cannon foundry might be many miles away. In the early years the founding of cannons was a hit-or-miss business, and often costly in both lives and materials. Moreover, the higher velocity of the cannonball was partly offset by the greater weight of the trebuchet missile. For a long time after the introduction of the cannon the trebuchet must have remained the superior weapon in some types of siege warfare. Convenience, and perhaps questions of prestige, rather than military effectiveness, gave victory to the cannon before its due time.

Fine Technology

Fine Technology is the kind of engineering that is concerned with delicate mechanisms and sophisticated controls. Before modern times the category comprised clocks, trick vessels, automata, fountains and a few miscellaneous devices. Some of these machines – water-clocks for example – served practical purposes, whereas others were designed for amusement or aesthetic pleasure. The apparent triviality of many of these constructions should not, however, be allowed to obscure the fact that a number of the ideas, components and techniques embodied in them were to be of great significance in the development of machine technology. Indeed, the influence of fine technology upon the Industrial Revolution was certainly more important, from a purely technical point of view, than that of the utilitarian machines discussed in the previous chapter. Moreover, the construction of moving simulacra of humans, animals and the heavens was an important factor in inducing mankind to regard the universe in mechanistic terms.

Unlike the utilitarian machines, very little archaeological evidence exists in the case of fine technology, whose constructions were almost always too fragile to survive the passage of time. We therefore have to rely very largely upon literary and iconographic sources for our information on the construction and operation of these machines. As we shall see in the course of this chapter, however, there is sufficient supporting evidence to show that they were practicable devices that were actually manufactured, not simply the paper constructions of theoretical scholars. The Islamic engineers who devoted some of their attention to fine technology had predecessors whose works were available to them. There is no evidence that Chinese or Indian treatises were among the documents that were transmitted to the Muslims; their sources lay in the Hellenistic culture of the Near East.

Our earliest information about the origins of fine technology occurs in the writings of Vitruvius, who attributes the invention of the organ and the monumental water-clock to an Egyptian engineer named Ctesibius, who worked in Alexandria around 300 BC. Treatises from two important writers have survived from the Hellenistic period. The *Pneumatics* of Philo of Byzantinium (fl. *c.*230 BC) exists only in a number of Arabic versions, all of which contain Islamic additions to Philo's original text. Nevertheless, the bulk of the machines, mostly trick vessels, can be positively attributed to Philo. From Hero of Alexandria (fl. mid-first century AD) we have a number of surviving works of which the *Pneumatics* and the *Automata* are directly concerned with fine technology. Another treatise, *On the Construction of Water-clocks*, carries the name of Archimedes (d. 212 BC) and this also exists only in Arabic versions. The first two chapters are probably from the hand of Archimedes, whereas the remainder are probably Hellenistic, Byzantine and Islamic additions. The chapters attributed to the great scientist are important since they describe sophisticated water machinery which, as we shall see, was incorporated by Muslim engineers in their water-clocks. The tradition for building monumental water-clocks continued in Byzantium and Sasānid Iran and was still thriving in Damascus when the Umayyads assumed power there in 660.

ISLAMIC SOURCES FOR FINE TECHNOLOGY

The first substantial evidence for the development of fine technology in Islam is provided by the Banū Mūsà's *Book of Ingenious Devices*, written in Baghdad about the middle of the ninth century. Although these three brothers undoubtedly took the works of Philo and Hero as their starting point, their work exhibits a greater mastery over physical media than does that of either of their Greek predecessors. They were the first Islamic engineers to demonstrate a preoccupation with 'in-line' automatic controls. In many ways they were ahead of their time, and none of their successors attempted to improve upon their results in the construction of trick vessels. Their work was well known and appreciated in the Islamic world. The great fourteenth-century historian Ibn Khaldūn says of their work: 'there exists a book on mechanics that mentions every astonishing remarkable and nice mechanical contrivance. It is often difficult to understand, because the geometrical proofs occurring in it are difficult. People have copies of it. They ascribed it to the Banū Shākir' (Mūsà b. Shākir was the brothers' father). In addition to this major work, there is also a treatise by the Banū Mūsà on an automatic fluting machine that exhibits the same mastery over control techniques that is so evident in the *Book of Ingenious Devices*.

The tenth century scientific encyclopaedia *Mafātiḥ al-'Ulūm* by Abu 'Abd Allah al-Khuwārazmī has already been mentioned in connection with theoretical mechanics. It also contains a very valuable section on the components used by the 'makers of wonderful vessels'. This does not confine itself to terminology, but gives brief descriptions of the manufacture of the various components.

One of the most important works on fine technology was not discovered until the 1970s. It was written in Muslim Spain in the eleventh century by a certain al-Murādī. Unfortunately, the only

123

known manuscript copy is so badly defaced that it is impossible to derive from it precisely how any of the machines was constructed. Enough remains, however, for us to make an assessment of its significance. Most of the devices were water-clocks but there were also five automata machines driven by water-wheels. Al-Murādī's devices contain several important elements, perhaps the most significant being his use of complex gear-trains.

There is a long treatise, written by Riḍwān b. al-Saʿātī (The Clockmaker) in 1203 describing the repairs carried out to the water-clock built by his father at the Jayrūn gate in Damascus about 1160. Riḍwān was not an engineer and his descriptions are long-winded and repetitive. Because of his lack of technical skills, however, he sometimes provides us with details that an engineer would take for granted; for example, his description of the manufacture of copper pipes.

One of the most important works on engineering from any cultural area before the Renaissance was the machine book of Ibn al-Razzāz al-Jazarī, written in Diyar Bakr in 1206. We know nothing of his life except what he tells us in the introduction to his work, namely that at the time of writing his book he had been for twenty-five years in the service of the Artuqid princes of Diyar Bakr. The book is a summary of most of the accumulated knowledge of mechanical engineering up to this time, with improvements and innovations due to al-Jazarī himself. The importance of the book lies partly in the machines, components and ideas that are described in it. Of equal importance is the fact that al-Jazarī composed the book with the declared intention of enabling later craftsmen to reconstruct his machines. For each of the fifty machines the manufacture, construction and assembly are scrupulously described, giving us a wealth of information about the methods of mechanical engineers in the Islamic world. The work is divided into six categories: Clocks, Trick vessels, Liquid dispensers and phlebotomy measuring instruments, Fountains and musical automata, Water-raising machines, Miscellaneous. Water-raising machines have already been dealt with in the previous chapter; examples from the remainder of the work will be discussed in due course.

The last important work that we shall consider was not written in Arabic but in Castilian. Called the *Libros del Saber de Astronomia*, it was compiled in 1277 under the direction of Alfonso X of Castile. It was a collection of translations and paraphrases made from Arabic origins with the declared intention of making Arabic knowledge available to the Christian world. The section that concerns us is at the end of the work and includes descriptions of three timepieces.

There are a number of references to fine technology scattered among the works of Arabic geographers, travellers and historians.

FIGURE 7.1 Face of water-clock, al-Jazarī Category I, Chapter 1.
Bodleian Library MS Greaves 27, f. 4r.

Some of the mentions are fanciful but there are several sober statements, all of which, as it happens, are concerned with water-clocks.
For instance, two large water-clocks were built on the banks of the
river Tagus at Toledo about 1080 by the famous astronomer al-Zarqall.
These not only told the time of day but also indicated the phase of the
moon. There are the remains of two monumental water-clocks built in
the fourteenth century at Fez, Morocco. One of them was described by
a contemporary historian of the city of Fez. These literary and archaeological attestations confirm the tradition for building monumental
water-clocks in the Islamic world. Moreover, several of al-Jazarīs's
devices, including a water-clock, a phlebotomy measuring instrument
and the slot-rod pump have been reconstructed by modern craftsmen
using al-Jazarī's instructions and specifications. The first two were full
size, the third one quarter scale; all worked perfectly.

CLOCKS

Water-clocks of varying degrees of complexity are described in the
treatises, especially those of Riḍwān and al-Jazarī. The clock built by
Riḍwān's father is similar to al-Jazarī's first clock, but it was less
accurate and its construction made it prone to damage. Perhaps the
most important statement in his treatise is his attribution of the water
machinery to Archimedes. The same attribution is made by al-Jazarī,
whose machinery is basically similar to that of Riḍwān's clock, except
for improvements that make it more accurate.

The monumental water-clock described in the first chapter of al-
Jazarī's book includes almost all the techniques and methods which
had traditionally been used in this type of timepiece. The face of the
clock is shown in Figure 7.1 The working face consisted of a screen of
bronze or wood about 225cm high by 135cm broad, set in the centre of
the front wall of a wooden roofless house which contained the machinery. At the top of the screen was a Zodiac circle made of beaten copper
about 120cm in diameter. Since only half of this disc was visible at a
given time the total height of the clock was about 285cm. The rim of
the Zodiac circle was divided into the twelve signs. Inside these signs
were glass roundels representing the sun and the moon. Each could be
moved daily to its correct position in the Zodiac. Below the Zodiac
circle, at the top of the screen, was row of double leaved doors beneath
which was a row of single leaved doors. In front of these, projecting on
a rod from a slit in the screen, was a small silver crescent. Below the
second set of doors was a semicircle, its convexity uppermost, in
which were set 12 roundels of clear glass. At either side of this
semicircle was a brass falcon in a niche; below each falcon was a vase
in which a cymbal was suspended. Finally, on a platform at the bottom

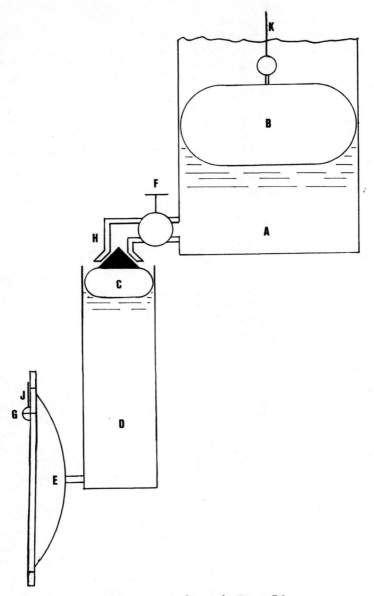

FIGURE 7.2 Water-machinery for Figure 7.1.

of the clock were the figures of five musicians: two drummers, two trumpeters and a cymbalist.

The operation was as follows: at daybreak (or nightfall) the Zodiac circle began to rotate at constant speed, one sign setting below the 'horizon' (the top of the screen) as another rose. The crescent moved steadily in front of the lower row of doors. At the end of an hour it was between the first two doors, whereupon the leaves of the first of the upper doors opened to reveal a standing figure, while the lower door rotated to show a different colour. The falcons leant forward, spread their wings, and each discharged a ball from its beak on to the cymbal in the vase. The first of the roundels in the semicircle had become completely illuminated. At the end of the day the Zodiac circle had turned through 180⁰, the upper doors had all opened, the lower doors had all revolved and all the roundels were illuminated. The musicians played at the sixth, ninth and twelfth hours.

All the automata except the musicians were operated by the steady descent of the large float B in the reservoir A (see Figure 7.2). The reservoir, made of beaten copper, was about 150cm high by 30cm in diameter; great care was taken to ensure that it was of uniform cross-section throughout. The string K passed through a system of pulleys and operated the jackwork by means of various mechanisms. The rate of descent of the float was kept constant by means of the float-chamber D. A bronze tube led out from the bottom of the reservoir, its end bent down to form the seat H of a conical valve, whose plug was soldered to the top of the small float C on the float-chamber. When tap F was opened water ran into the float-chamber and the water rose, closing the valve momentarily. When water discharged from the outlet at the bottom of the float chamber the valve opened momentarily, only to close momentarily when water flowed in from the reservoir. When the present writer observed this action on a full-scale facsimile of the clock, no change in level in the float-chamber could be detected with the naked eye. This was a brilliant concept, the first known example of feed-back control. There seems no reason to doubt the attribution of its invention to Archimedes, as made by both Riḍwān and al-Jazarī.

The device to the left of the float-chamber in Figure 7.2 is a flow regulator. This clock, as with many early clocks, operated on 'unequal' hours: the hours of daylight and darkness were divided by twelve to give 'hours' that varied in length from day to day throughout the year. The rate of discharge therefore had to be varied daily, and this was achieved by varying the distance of the orifice below the water level in the float-chamber daily. The flow regulator consisted of a dished plate with a flat rim. A flat circular plate carrying the orifice G was rotatable within the rim, with which it was a co-planar. A system of pipes and

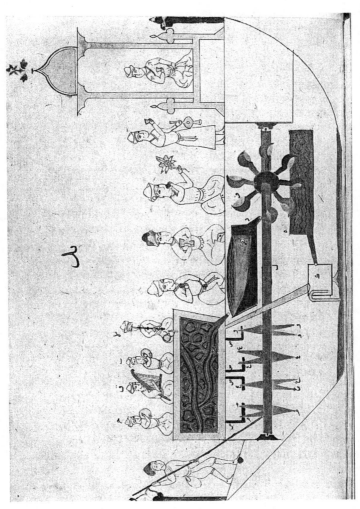

FIGURE 7.3 Cams operated by a water-wheel to activate musicians. From an ornamental boat with automata, al-Jazari Category II, Chapter 4. Similar systems are used in all al-Jazari's clocks. Bodleian Library MS Greaves 27, f. 61r.

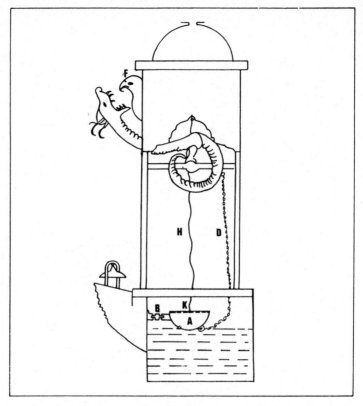

FIGURE 7.4 Water-machinery, al-Jazarī water-clock Category I,
Chapter 3.

channels inside the dished part of the plate ensured that the flow to the
orifice, a drilled piece of onyx, was not interrupted when the plate was
rotated. Al-Jazarī described how he had found all the earlier flow
regulators to be inaccurate and how he graduated the instrument
empirically until it was accurate. The rim was divided into unequal
sections for each pair of signs having the same lengths of days. The
signs were subdivided into degrees. A pointer J enabled the operator to
set the orifice to the correct degree for any day or night of the year.

The musicians were operated by the sudden release of water collected from the outflow. The orifice discharged into a special tank,
which overflowed once it was full. At the end of six hours, a mechanism caused the plug of this tank to be pulled out, whereupon the
water ran over a scoop-wheel that had cams on its extended axle.

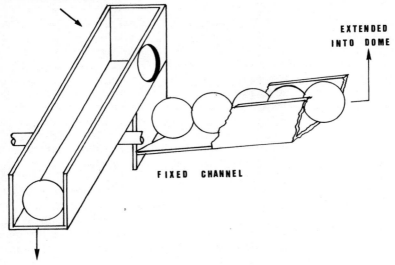

FIGURE 7.5 Ball release, al-Jazarī water-clocks Category I, Chapters 3 and 4.

These cams operated concealed extensions to the arms of the percussion players who therefore struck their instruments for a while (see Figure 7.3). This system was used several times by al-Jazarī; it was probably a miniature version of the system of trip-hammers used in the paper, fulling, metalworking and other industries. From a tank beneath the scoop wheel the water ran into an air-vessel the air from which was expelled through a mechanical whistle to simulate the sound of the trumpeters. The water from the air-vessel was evacuated, when it neared the top of the vessel, by a bent-tube siphon.

Two of al-Jazarī's water-clocks (Chapters 3 and 4) have automata very similar to that of the clock just described, but their water machinery is quite different. Similar machinery does not appear in any other known treatise, and may have been al-Jazarī's own invention. It is important for the ideas that it embodies. In Figure 7.4 a bowl A with a graduated orifice in its underside rested on the surface of a tank concealed in the hull of a boat or in the belly of an elephant. Columns supported a 'castle' (a metal box on top of which was a removable dome). At the side of the castle was the head F of a falcon. A transom was fixed centrally across the columns and a brass serpent was

131

attached to an axle in the centre of the transom. At the outset its head was close to the head of the falcon; its tail was formed into a circle and was, in effect, a pulley. The bowl was attached to the side of the tank by the links B. A rod K was soldered across its diameter and a wire H attached to a hole in the centre of this rod led up to the ball-release concealed in the castle (see Figure 7.5). A light chain D was attached to the curvature of the bowl and to a staple in the tail of the serpent.

At the start of an hour (of sixty minutes, not an 'unequal' hour) the empty bowl was resting on the surface of the water. It sank gradually until it suddenly submerged completely, whereupon wire H pulled the end of the ball-release, a ball ran into the falcon's head and out of its beak into the serpent's mouth. The serpent's head sank, due to the weight of the ball and at the end of its travel it dropped the ball on to a cymbal. At this juncture the bowl tilted due to the combined action of links B and chain D, emptied its contents, and settled back on the surface of the water. Meanwhile the head of the serpent had risen to its original position and the cycle restarted. The magazine for the balls extended into the dome. It was therefore simple to remove the dome to replenish the magazine, and it was never necessary to stop the clock. Nor was any external water supply needed – the level in the tank remained constant. This is one of the earliest known examples of a closed loop system.

Another important clock for the history of horology occurs in the *Libros del Saber*. This consisted of a large drum made of walnut or jujube wood, tightly assembled, and sealed with wax or resin. The interior of the drum was divided into twelve compartments, with small holes between the compartments through which mercury flowed. Enough mercury was enclosed to fill just half the compartments. The drum was mounted on the same axle as a large wheel powered by a weightdrive wound around the wheel. Also on the axle was a pinion with six teeth that meshed with 36 oaken teeth on the rim of an astrolabe dial. The mercury drum and pinion made a complete revolution every four hours and the astrolabe dial made a complete revolution in 24 hours.

This type of timepiece had been known in Islam since the eleventh century – at least 200 years before the first appearance of a weightdriven clock in the West. The *Libros del Saber* were translated into Italian in 1341, but it was not until 1598 that a similar clock was described by Attilio Parisio. The clock aroused some interest, and it became widely known through the publication of commentaries on Parisio's work that were written during the seventeenth century. Compartmented cylinder clocks became popular as cheap and quite reliable timepieces in the eighteenth and nineteenth centuries,

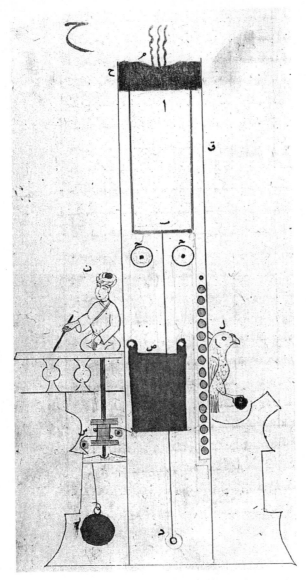

FIGURE 7.6 Candle-clock, al-Jazarī Category I, Chapter 8.
Bodleian Library MS Greaves 27, f. 50r.

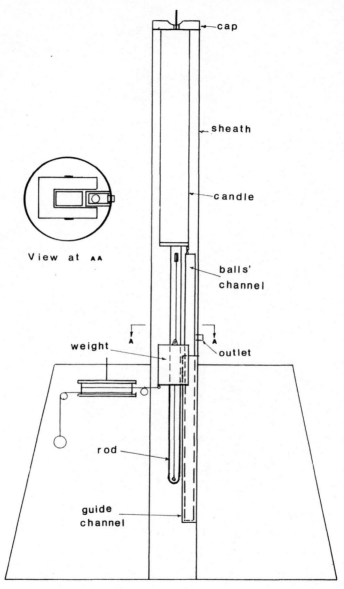

FIGURE 7.7 Line drawing of Figure 7.6.

especially in agricultural areas. They differed somewhat from the clock described in the *Libros del Saber* in that the medium was water instead of mercury and the drum itself revolved slowly down two cords, with hour scales marked on columns at the side. No direct influence from the *Libros del Saber* – and hence from Islamic clocks – upon these later European timepieces can be proved, but such influence is a distinct possibility. And although the compartmented cylinder clock is no longer in use, the idea of a weight drive was, of course, an important factor in the development of the mechanical clock.

Al-Jazarī, in four chapters of his first Category, described candle-clocks which are, on a smaller scale, as impressive from an engineering point of view as the water-clocks. Figures 7.6 and 7.7 show the second of these (Figure 7.7 shows a reconstruction of the machinery only, with the automata omitted). The candle was closely specified by size and weight, including even the weight of the wick. The sheath was partly exposed, partly concealed inside the hollow pedestal. The cap for the sheath, against which the end of the candle rested, was machined on a lathe to be truly flat and was fitted to the top of the sheath by a bayonet fitting; the wick protruded through a hole in the cap. A metal dish was pushed on to the bottom of the candle; a channel containing fourteen metal balls was suspended from one side of this dish. Soldered to its centre was a long vertical rod. A lead weight with a wide channel in it enclosed the rod. Strings from holes at the top of the weight passed over two small pulleys fixed to the side of the sheath, and were then brought down through the channel in the weight and were tied to a hole at the bottom of the rod. A ring at the bottom of the weight was connected through a slit in the side of the sheath to a pulley system inside the pedestal. The end of the axle was squared off and entered a hole in the underside of the figure of a scribe whose pen was poised over a graduated scale. (This system was used several times by al-Jazarī in his clocks.) When the candle was lit and burned gradually away the dish on its end was forced upwards by the action of the weight. Every hour a ball reached the outlet pipe and ran out of the falcon's head. The pen of the scribe marked the passage or time in four minute intervals. The wax collected in the hollow in the centre of the top of the cap, from where it was removed regularly. Earlier designs were criticised by al-Jazarī, mainly because the wax ran into the sheath and over the machinery, rendering it useless. Oddly enough, there is a candle-clock described in the *Libros del Saber* which would have suffered from precisely this defect. Indeed, both the water-clock and the candle-clock described in the *Libros* are cruder than those of al-Jazarī, even though they were described some eighty years later.

135

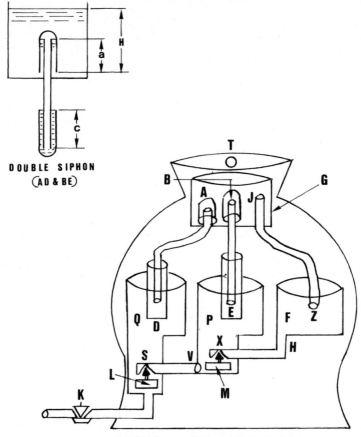

FIGURE 7.8 Trick vessel, Banū Mūsà, Model 44.

TRICK VESSELS

About eighty of the 100 devices described by the Banū Mūsà are trick vessels of various kinds. They exhibit a bewildering variety of effects. To quote but three of their own descriptions of these:

> Model 34. A flask from which only a known quantity of wine can be poured each time it is tilted.
>
> Model 39. A jar with a tap: it is first filled with wine, but water discharges, not wine, as long as the water is poured into the top of the jar.
>
> Model 75. A trough that always replenishes itself when men draw water from it or when animals drink from it.

136

Although the original inspiration for their work came from the Hellenistic engineers and indeed several of their Models are exact copies of devices appearing in the works of Philo or Hero, most of their work shows notable advances on that of their Greek predecessors. These advances were mainly in the field of automatic controls: the masterly use of small variations in hydrostatic and aerostatic pressures and the incorporation of self-operating conical valves in flow systems. The conical valve, so important a component in modern machine technology, was not used by Philo or Hero. It was, of course, an integral part of the feed-back control system in al-Jazarī's first clock. If the attribution of the invention of this system to Archimedes is correct, it seems to have been the only application of conical valves before they were used with such confidence by the Banū Mūsà, Not until al-Jazarī's book do we get a description of their manufacture. Both seat and plug were cast together from bronze in the same mould, then ground together with emery powder until a watertight fit was achieved.

The best way to gain some appreciation of the Banū Mūsà methods in the space available to us is to examine three of their devices in some detail. These are not the most complicated of their devices, but between them they show most of the mechanisms used in *The Book of Ingenious Devices*.

The first is a jar from which three different liquids are extracted in succession. Figure 7.8 is a tracing from the Topkapi manuscript (A3474) in which the original Arabic letters have been replaced by Roman ones. A hole T allows the liquids to be poured in. Below this is a small tank in which are the ends of pipes AD, BE and JZ, which terminate in the tanks Q, P and F respectively. A is lower than B which is lower than J. Both AD and BE are fitted with caps at each end – in other words they are double concentric siphons. Their action is such that once inpouring through them is stopped they will accept no more liquid (unless the head of liquid above them is much greater than is possible in this vessel). A pipe HX connects tank F to tank P; on the end is a conical valve, its plug soldered to the top of the small float M. Similarly, pipe VS connects tank P to tank Q; on end S is a conical valve, its plug soldered to the small float L. The outlet pipe from the jar leads out from the bottom of tank Q. On it, outside the jar, is tap K.

The first liquid was poured in. It ran through the double concentric AD and into tank Q; presumably the amount poured was a known quantity, sufficient almost to fill tank Q. The second liquid was then poured in, and since the first route was now closed, it flowed through concentric siphon BE into tank P. The third liquid ran through pipe JZ into tank F. Tap K was now opened and the first liquid discharged from

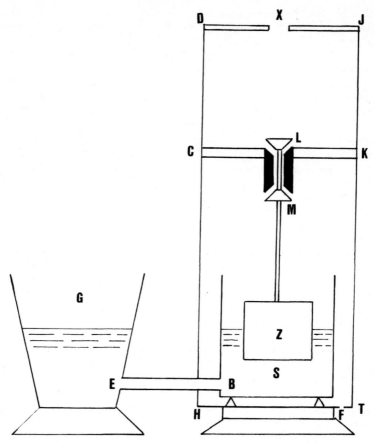

FIGURE 7.9 Constant level device, Banū Mūsà, Model 77.

tank Q; when this tank was almost empty float L descended, the valve opened and tank P evacuated through route VSLK. Float M descended and the third liquid flowed out along route HXMVSLK.

The next device consisted of a large container DJHT, with a filler hole at X. It was divided laterally by a partition CK. In the centre of this partition was a hole to which the double seat of a conical valve was soldered. In the lower chamber of the container was a tank S which was connected to tank G, which was outside the container, by pipe BE. Inside tank S was a float Z to the top of which a valve rod was soldered. This rod carried two valve plugs, M and L, the first entering the lower

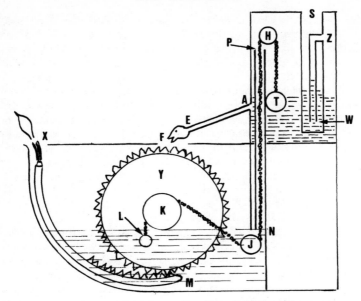

FIGURE 7.10 Lamp, Banū Mūsà, Model 97.

valve seat, the second the upper seat. There was a small air-hole F in
the bottom of the container (Figure 7.9).

Water was poured in at X. It ran into the upper chamber of the
container and through the open valves into tank S and from there into
tank G. When the water reached a level near the tops of G and S, valve
M closed. Inpouring was continued until the reservoir DJCK was
almost full. When anyone took a moderate amount of water from tank
G, the float dropped, valve M opened and tanks G and S were replen-
ished up to the original levels. If, however, someone who knew the
secret of the device extracted a large amount from tank G, then the
float dropped far enough to close valve L, and no further replenishment
could taken place. The purpose of this device was amusement and
mystification. Nevertheless, it embodies one of the earliest fail-safe
mechanisms.

Finally, Figure 7.10 is a reconstruction of a self-feeding, self-trimming lamp. The oil is poured into the wide pipe at the left. It runs
down pipe S and up the narrow pipe WZ into the reservoir. This system
ensures that air cannot enter the reservoir by this route. A float T rests
on the surface of the oil in the reservoir. From it a light chain passes
over pulley H and down the long pipe that goes into the body of the
lamp. The chain then passes under pulley J, over pulley K and is tied to

139

the lead weight L. On the same axle as this pulley is the large gear-wheel Y. This meshes with the rack M, the end of carries the wick X. From the side of the upper reservoir the narrow pipe AE leads out slantwise. Its lower end, in the shape of a bird's head F, terminates just above a hole in the cover of the lamp. The oil is poured in, rising in the reservoir and discharging into the lamp down pipe AE until the level in the lamp reaches the end of the long vertical pipe PN. Air is now cut off and no further flow can take place. The wick is now lit and as the level in the lamp falls momentarily the end of the pipe is exposed and oil enters the lamp whereupon the flow ceases momentarily, and so on. As the level in the reservoir falls, float T descends and gear-wheel Y turns, thus extruding the wick. The system of feed-back control using an occluded orifice is also used in the water-clock described in the *Libros del Saber*. Though not as sophisticated as the feed-back control used by al-Jazarī, it is equally effective.

A thorough perusal of all the Banū Mūsà's devices is an exhausting task. The principles and method of operation of each device has to be understood, and this is not always easy from the often skimpy descriptions given in the text. Also, the fact that many of the devices are very similar is not conducive to retaining one's attention over long periods. A close study of their work is, however, rewarding because of the wide variety of techniques that they employ. We have examined only three of their devices, but in these we have met the following mechanisms: artificially induced air-locks (in the double concentric siphons); automatically-operating conical valves; a fail-safe mechanism embodying a double-acting conical valve; feed-back control using pneumatic means. We may consider that their technical brilliance was wasted upon the triviality of their constructions. If we think like this, however, we should also consider the banality of some of the end results of modern electronic engineering.

The Banū Mūsà had no real successors in their chosen field. Al-Jazarī did devote one of his Categories to trick vessels, but these are simpler than those of the Banū Mūsà. He preferred to use direct hydraulic and mechanical forces rather than the small pressure variations handled with such delicacy by the brothers. There are, for example, no double concentric siphons in his devices.

AUTOMATA

It is not always possible to consider automata in isolation. As we have already seen, water-clocks usually incorporated a whole array of automata – celestial and biological – as time signals. But there was also a tradition for making machines whose main purpose was the display of moving automata. A number of al-Jazarī's devices are of this nature, but the most interesting of the automata machines occur in the treatise of al-Murādī. His machines, including the water-clocks, are notable for their sheer size and power. This feature distinguishes the work sharply from that of the Banū Mūsà, with its emphasis upon delicate mechanisms and controls, and from those machines of al-Jazarī which embody similar concepts. In al-Murādī's work there are no conical valves, delay systems, feed-back controls, or use of small variations in atmospheric pressure; all the ideas, in fact, that had until recently been regarded as typical of Islamic mechanical technology. The element of intermittent operation is not of course absent from al-Murādī's work – indeed it is of the utmost significance – but it is achieved by different means. Delicacy is replaced by ruggedness: we have ropes instead of strings or light chains; large wheels up to about 72cm in diameter; spanning weights of at least 3kg; with other weights and dimensions in proportion. Gearing is important, and in addition to the special gears discussed below we find all the usual types: parallel meshing, meshing at right angles, worm-and-pinion.

Al-Murādī's water-clocks, which occupy the bulk of his work, can be neglected. They are crude compared with those of al-Jazarī and even the clock described by Riḍwān. It is the first five machines, designed to display automata, that are of considerable interest in the history of technology. Figure 7.11 is the illustration of Model 5, which is the most complex of these machines. Its purpose was to cause a set of doors, set in a row, to open at successive intervals, revealing jackwork figures. These doors were on one side of a boxlike structure that contained the working parts. The prime mover was a water-wheel, mounted in a stream outside the box – in Figure 7.11 this is represented by the two concentric circles to the left of the illustration. The use of a full-size water-wheel is significant. It had previously been assumed that the use of a water-wheel to drive Su Sung's monumental clock in China was the first known example of this application of water power, and that the idea may have been transmitted from China to Islam. Su Sung, however, was working some decades later than al-Murādī, and it is therefore quite possible that transmission took place in the reverse direction.

The water-wheel was mounted on an axle that passed into the box and rested in bearings fixed to its walls. The main central gear-wheel was on this axle. This wheel had 64 teeth on half its perimeter,and meshed with two outer gear-wheels, each of which had 32 teeth around its complete perimeter, and a diameter equal to one quarter of the diameter of the large wheel. Each of the smaller wheels therefore made two rotations for one rotation of the large wheel. The description of the wheels inside the main wheel is badly defaced. The description

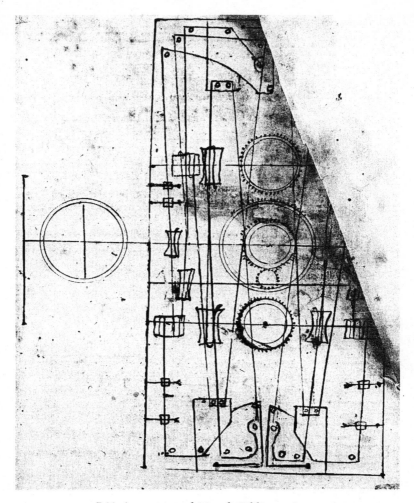

FIGURE 7.11 Automaton, al-Murādī. Biblioteca Laurenziana,
Florence, MS Orient. 152, f. 11v.

of the main wheel for Model 4, however, which is very similar to
Model 5, is almost intact. The setting of three sets of teeth is described:
one set is on the outer perimeter, and two are on the inside, 'facing the
axle'. Without any question, therefore, these machines contained
segmental gears. It is not so certain that they contained epicyclic
gearing, but taking the illustrations and the surviving parts of the text

together there seems little room for doubt. Surely no-one interested in the history of machines and clockwork can examine Figure 7.11 without a sense of excitement, since it shows a system for transmitting torque that is much more complex than any other power-driven gears known to have existed so early. In Hellenistic times there were instruments with complex gearing, but these were delicate manually operated devices, not water-powered machines in which the main gear-wheel was 72cm in diameter.

There are some descriptions in the treatises of musical automata, but these are often simple, single-note devices, such as the mechanical whistle used to simulate the sound of the trumpeter in al-Jazarī's first clock. He does, however, describe several machines specifically designed as musical automata, although he is more concerned with describing the production of a flow of air for operating the instruments than with the instruments themselves; indeed the latter are hardly described at all. The production of a continual flow of air, in al-Jazarī's machines and others, involves the use of two tanks, one of which is always in operation. One such system can be seen in Figure 7.12, which is an illustration of the machine described in Category 4, Chapter 8. At the top of the picture, on the right, is a supply channel, below which there is a pipe balanced on a fulcrum; it has a receiving channel on its upper side. At each end of this pipe are calibrated orifices. Below each of these orifices is a tipping bucket, each of which discharges into a large funnel which leads into a tank. These tanks are fitted with siphons and each has a mechanical flute mounted on a pipe opening into the top of the tank. Let us assume that water is discharging into the right-hand tipping-bucket. After a predetermined period the bucket tilts and discharges its contents into the funnel, whence it runs into the tank. As soon as the end of the siphon is covered the air is forced through the mechanical flute, which plays. Meanwhile, the extension on the back of the tipping-bucket has struck the pipe, tilting it and causing it to discharge into the left-hand bucket. When the water in the right-hand tank reaches the top of the siphon this evacuates the water from the tank and the flute ceases playing. Simultaneously, the left-hand bucket discharges through the funnel into the tank, and the left-hand flute begins to play.

As mentioned earlier, al-Jazarī gives no details of his automatic instrument. Some 350 years earlier, however, the Banū Mūsà described an automatic flute in considerable detail. This is in a separate treatise from the *Book of Ingenious Devices*. The flow of air is produced by using two air chambers, but the system differs from al-Jazarī's. The important part of the treatise lies in the description of the instrument itself. A cylinder of about 27cm diameter was mounted

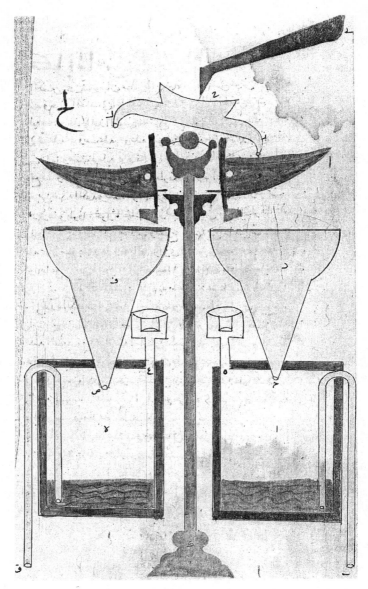

FIGURE 7.12 Musical automaton, al-Jazarī Category IV, Chapter 8.
Bodleian Library MS Greaves 27, f. 96v.

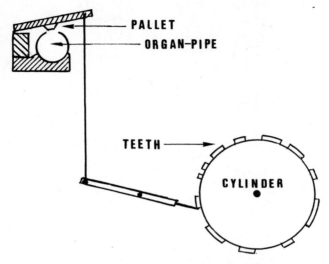

PALLET
ORGAN-PIPE

TEETH

CYLINDER

FIGURE 7.13 Musical automaton, Banū Mūsà.

horizontally on an axle which rotated in two bearings. At one end of the cylinder a large gear-wheel was mounted on the same axle. This meshed with a smaller gear-wheel on the axle of a water-wheel about 70cm in diameter. When the water-wheel turned the cylinder also turned.

The cylinder was installed alongside the pipe of the mechanical flute. This had nine holes, eight of which could be opened and closed by pallets while the ninth was always open. The pallets were connected through a linkage system to levers which engaged teeth on the perimeter of the cylinder. These teeth were arranged so that they played a particular melody (see Figures 7.13). The cylinder could be moved laterally so that two or three melodies could be played with the same instrument. The treatise also contains a section on the musical theory of the flute, referred, as is usual with Arabic musical theory, to the lute. This is clearly a very sophisticated instrument. Similar devices appeared in Europe in the Renaissance and later. A mechanical organ described by Athanasius Kircher in 1650, for example, uses a very similar system for rotating the cylinder, although its method for producing a current of air is cruder than that of the Banū Mūsà.

FOUNTAINS

We sometimes come across references to beautiful fountains in the works of Arabic geographers or travellers, when they are describing the

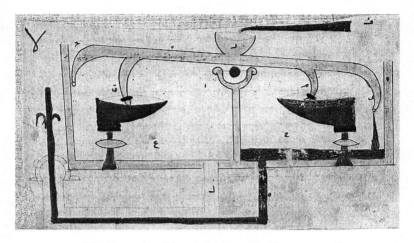

FIGURE 7.14 Fountain, al-Jazarī Category IV, Chapter 1. Bodleian
Library MS Greaves 27, f. 89v.

palaces or pleasure parks of cities such as Damascus, Baghdad or
Cordoba. They do not, however, give us any details. For this kind of
information we are dependent, as in so many other constructions,
upon the works of the Banū Mūsà and al-Jazarī. The Banū Mūsà
describe five fountains, one of which we have already met in the
previous chapter in connection with radial flow horizontal water-
wheels. This fountain is typical of all the Banū Mūsà's fountains in
that the shape of its discharge varies at intervals. Al-Jazarī included six
fountains in his work, and these are all also alternating devices. The
water issued for a while as a single jet (say), then as a spray, before
reverting to the original shape. Al-Jazarī criticised the Banū Mūzà's
fountains on the grounds that the intervals between changes of shape
would have been too short. He was quite correct in this criticism and,
as usual, his own designs are models of precision engineering. Figures
7.14 and 7.15 show the first of his fountains which contain all the
essential features of the other five. Referring to Figure 7.15, there were
two adjacent tanks x and h, upon whose dividing wall there was a
fulcrum which supported the balanced pipe jy. At the top of the pipe
was a funnel z, into which the water supply f flowed continuously.
Ends j and y of the pipe were open. Close to each end a short pipe led
out from the bore of the main pipe. On the end of each short pipe was
a drilled piece of onyx, calibrated to drip water out into a tipping-
bucket at a known rate. From the bottom of the tank h a pipe e ran
underground, reappearing at the fountainhead, where the water

146

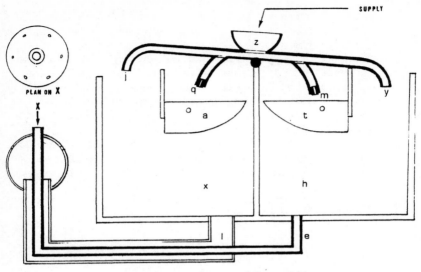

FIGURE 7.15 Line drawing of Figure 7.14.

emerged as a vertical jet. From the bottom of tank x a wide pipe l ran out, surrounding pipe e for most of the latter's length. Let us assume that end y of the pipe was discharging into tank h while orifice m bled some of the water into tipping-bucket t. The main flow ran through pipe e and emerged as a single jet. After a set interval the bucket tipped, tilting the pipe towards tank x. The water emerged from the fountain-head as a number of curved jets, until tipping-bucket a tipped, and the extension on its back pushed the pipe back towards tank. And so on, as long as the water supply was not interrupted.

The other fountains had certain variations, Different shapes of fountainhead were used; sometimes there were two, requiring two concentric pipes to be led out from each tank. Floats were used in some models instead of tipping-buckets; vertical rods soldered to the tops of the float pushed the balanced pipe when the water reached a certain level.

MISCELLANEOUS

The Banū Mūsà were concerned with public works and three of their devices reflect their interest in civil engineering projects. One was a 'hurricane lamp' whose flame was shielded by a vane which always turned so that it was at right angles to the wind direction. The second was a 'gas mask' that incorporated bellows and was used to protect men working in polluted wells. The third was a grab, which was

147

constructed in exactly the same way as a modern clamshell grab. It was used in mines and elsewhere to extract materials from under water (see Figure 11.1).

Al-Jazarī's last category consisted of five items that he classified as miscellaneous. These comprised two locks, an alarm clock, a protractor and a monumental door for the prince's palace at Āmid. One of the locks is particularly interesting, since it incorporates four combination locks on the lid of a chest, which are surprisingly modern in design. Each consisted of a number of concentric discs on a spindle. Each disc had to be moved to a pre-set letter before the lock would open; the lid of the chest could only be lifted when all four locks were open. The door is of significance in the history of technology because it embodies a method of casting that was unknown before this time. It was made of brass and copper and some of the brass sections were cast in closed mould-boxes in green sand.

8

Bridges and Dams

Five types of bridge are illustrated in diagrammatic form in Figure 8.1. In '*a*' a simple beam bridge is shown. Almost certainly this was the earliest type of bridge: in its most primitive form it was simply a log or a stone slab laid across a ditch or a small stream. From these beginnings came the first real bridges, with prepared abutments and spans consisting of several beams on top of which timber planking was laid. Handrails would often be provided. The problem with beam bridges, at a time when the only available materials were stone or timber, was that span lengths were limited to about 15 metres for timber, including abutments, and usually about 5 metres for stone. There were, however, some remarkable multi-span stone bridges built in China from the eleventh to the thirteenth century. These had spans up to 70 feet (21.3 metres) involving the handling of stones weighing up to 200 tonnes. This type of construction was, however, extremely wasteful in materials and labour. Also, a heavy load was placed upon the foundations, which often failed. Such structures were unknown in the Islamic world where multi-span beam bridges were generally built of timber.

The origins of the ancient cantilever bridge and its modern counterpart are quite different and demonstrate one of the dangers to which the historian of technology is exposed, namely that of assuming that because two structures look similar the older must be the ancestor of the younger. The modern cantilever bridge is a development of the continuous bridge: the introduction of hinges at certain points in a continuous bridge produces a statically determinate structure. In medieval times continuous spans were not possible, since structural steel and reinforced concrete were unknown. The ancient cantilever bridge was not based upon any analytical consideration. Rather it was a development from the beam bridge. Where an obstacle – a ravine or a stream – was to be crossed, and if its breadth was greater than could be bridged by a single timber span, then the abutments were built out from the banks to narrow the gap so that it could be bridged by wooden beams. The builders of bridges in the mountainous parts of Central Asia, for example, could do without the extended abutments if the gap between firm banks was narrow enough for a single-span bridge (Figure 8.1.b).

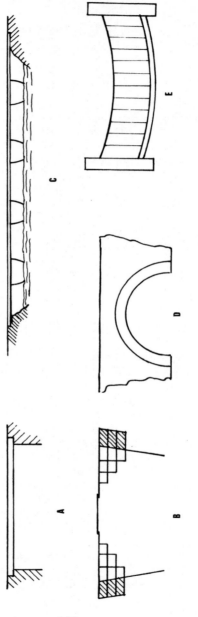

FIGURE 8.1 Types of bridges.

150

The pontoon bridge (Figure 8.1.c.) was in use by the ninth century BC at the latest. It is not an easy task to build any other kind of bridge over wide, deep rivers such as the Nile, Tigris and some rivers of Central Asia. Medieval technology did not permit the construction of single-span bridges long enough to cross the large rivers. If multi-span bridges – beam, arch or suspension – were erected, the foundations and substructures of the piers in deep water, particularly if the current was rapid, posed difficult engineering problems. The solution was therefore frequently the construction of pontoon bridges.

The arch had been known since Sumerian times. The Muslims were of course able to inspect the many fine arch bridges built by the Romans, Persians and Byzantines in the lands occupied in the Arab conquests of the seventh and eighth centuries. Many notable arch bridges were built by the Muslims both in stone and in brickwork (Figure 8.1.d).

Suspension bridges had been in use long before Islam in the mountainous regions of Central and East Asia. There is no description of them in Muslim writings and we must rely for our information on Chinese sources (Figure 8.1.e).

Beam and Cantilever Bridges

For reasons already given there is no point in trying to distinguish between the two sub-types. Moreover, because they are smaller and less spectacular than other types, especially masonry arch bridges, they rarely receive mentions in the Arabic sources. Ibn Ḥawqal, writing in AD 988, mentions a wooden bridge over the river Ṭāb, on the frontier between the provinces of Fars and Khuzistan. It was 10 cubits above the surface of the water and was used by both riparian dwellers and travellers. There must have been many thousands of beam bridges for crossing various types of obstacle, but they are unrecorded.

For information about beam/cantilever bridges we must turn to modern descriptions of this centuries-old type of construction. In the Hindu Kush region of north-eastern Afghanistan and ranges to the east they, along with suspension bridges, were the usual method of bridging streams and ravines before the introduction of modern steel and reinforced concrete structures. When in 1221 the Taoist Chhang-Chhun was on his way to visit Genghiz Khan in Samarqand he and his party followed a road through a defile in the Tien Shan mountains which had no fewer than 48 timber beam bridges of such a width that two carts could drive over them side by side. Fortunately we have detailed descriptions of the construction of timber bridges in Badakhshān, north-eastern Afghanistan, in 1963 (see Bibliography, Kussmaul and Fischer). The bridges are frequently damaged or totally

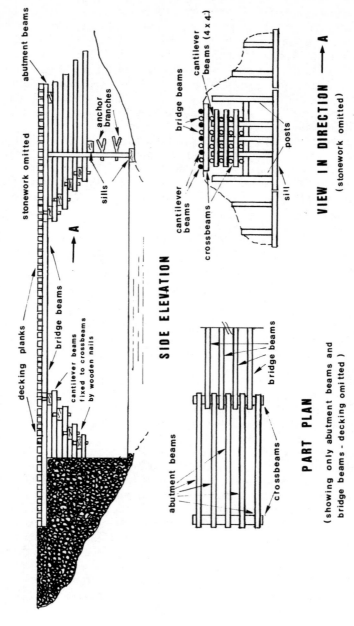

FIGURE 8.2 Wooden bridge, Afghanistan.

destroyed by floods, especially at times when heavy rainfall coincides with the melting of the winter snows. The bridges are not usually repaired; rather a new one is built at a nearby location. Material from the old bridge may be utilised for the new construction. The work, which is the responsibility of the local community, is undertaken early in the year or in the autumn. The latter is the preferred period, after the harvest has been threshed and when the water in the streams is shallow enough to be fordable.

The maximum span of these bridges is about 15 metres, including projecting abutments, although they rarely reach that length. The limit is of course imposed by the safe tensile stress of the timber beams. To keep the unsupported span to a minimum, sites are chosen where the gap is narrow, preferably where at least one bank is composed of solid rock. It is normal practice to narrow the gap by building cantilevered timber abutments. Indeed, the peoples of the region sometimes construct these types of abutments even when they are not strictly necessary, as if they regarded them as essential parts of a 'proper' bridge.

The design of a typical bridge is shown in Figure 8.2. The construction of each abutment begins with the laying of a wooden sill at ground level. Five vertical posts are fitted into mortices in this sill. They are spaced at interval of about 1.50 metres and they are about 5 metres high. The first part of the abutment is then built from stones and earth. The posts are anchored back into this fill with forked branches. When the abutment has reached a height of about 1.70 metres a second sill is laid behind the posts and the first row of abutment timbers is laid. There are four or five of these, from 8 to 12 metres long, extending through the abutment and projecting from its front wall for about 1.0 metre.

A transom is laid across these timbers, close to their free ends, and attached to each timber by wooden nails, both beam and transom having first been drilled to receive these nails. After further filling with earth and stones a second row of timbers is laid and connected by a transom in the same way. This row projects about 80 cm further than the first. Similarly a third and fourth row are added. The last row therefore projects about 3.0 metres from the face of the abutment (1.0 + 3 x 0.8). The total height of the cantilevered section depends, of course, upon the thickness of the beams and transoms. A fourth transom is fixed to the topmost row of timbers and the top beams of the abutment are fixed to this with wooden nails. There is a similar arrangement towards the rear of the abutment. The four main bridge beams are then laid across the span, each one between a pair of abutment beams. The distance between these beams is about 80 cm,

153

giving a total width of a little less than 3 metres (including the semi-diameters of the two outer beams), but a working width rather less than this. The abutments are completed with dry-stone walls at front and sides, the work on these walls proceeding as construction progresses.

The carpentry on these bridges is pretty rough. The timbers are stripped of bark and their tops and bottoms are flattened so that they lie flat against the earth or against other timbers. Apart from the danger of destruction by flooding, the bridges are not long-lasting because of the eventual rotting of the wood, especially the forked branches anchoring the vertical posts. The small size of these structures and their semi-permanent nature militate against their being recorded by geographers or travellers. Chhang-Chhun's description of the bridges he crossed on his way to Samarqand is an exception. These were, however, considerably wider and more impressive than those just described. This was probably because they were built and maintained at the expense of the State as part of the Mongol highway system, rather than being the responsibility of isolated local communities.

Pontoon Bridges

Pontoon bridges – bridges of boats – were an important and widely used method of crossing rivers in the classical and medieval period, not least in the Islamic world. We are dependent upon literary sources for our information, but there are a considerable number of reports in Arabic writings. The idea for pontoon bridges may have originated when boats were placed side by side at a jetty or landing stage, and planks were placed across the gunwales of adjacent boats to make it easier to walk from one boat to another. This type of bridge can be constructed quickly, and it is still the only type of bridge suitable for crossing rivers more than about 50 metres wide during military operations. It is quite simple to build a pontoon bridge in still water, but the skills of watermanship are needed when a current is flowing, to manoeuvre the boats into position and anchor them at the correct distance apart, ready to receive the beams and decking for the roadway. Anchors are not sufficient to hold a bridge in position for long periods in a swiftly flowing river, and it is therefore necessary to stretch a chain or heavy cable across the river upstream and secure it to an anchorage on each bank. For added security another cable may be laid on the downstream side. Each boat is made fast to the cables. The disadvantages of pontoon bridges are that they require constant maintenance, that they are liable to damage by floating debris or floods, and that they form an obstacle for river traffic.

In the Islamic world pontoon bridges were very common in Iraq, for crossing the two main rivers and the major irrigation canals. In the tenth century there were two bridges over the Tigris at Baghdad, but only one was in use; the other, having fallen into disrepair, was closed because few people used it. The traveller Ibn Jubayr, writing towards the close of the twelfth century, describes a bridge of large boats over the Euphrates at Ḥilla. It had chains on either side 'like twisted rods' which were secured to wooden anchorages on the banks. He also mentions a similar, but larger, bridge over a canal near Baghdad. There were also pontoon bridges on the rivers of Khuzistan, the province adjoining Iraq, and on the Helmand river in Seistan (now western Afghanistan). There was a pontoon bridge at Fusṭāṭ (now Old Cairo) in Egypt for many years. In the first half of the tenth century, al-Iṣṭakhrī says that one bridge crossed from the city to the island and a second bridge from the island to the far bank of the river. About two centuries later, al-Idrīsī describes the same arrangement, adding that there were thirty boats in the first bridge and sixty in the second. Many floating bridges are mentioned in the account by Chhang-Chhun of his travels in 1221. A famous one over the Amu Darya was built by Chang Jung, the chief engineer of Chagatai, Genghiz Khan's second son.

Arch Bridges

Many masonry arch bridges built by the Romans and the Sasānid Persians were still in use in Islamic times – indeed a number of them, the bridge over the Guadalquivir at Cordoba for example – are still carrying motor traffic. These bridges often impressed the Muslim geographers, who speak of them with admiration. Al-Idrīsī said that the bridge at Cordoba surpassed all others for beauty and solidity of construction. He went on to give details of the number and size of its arches, the width of its roadway and the height of its parapets. The bridge at Sanja over the upper Euphrates, which has also survived, was regarded by the Muslim writers as one of the wonders of the world. It was built by Vespasian and has a single arch of 112 feet span.

A famous bridge, said to have been built by the Sasānid king Shāpūr II, crossed the Diz river near Jundīshāpūr in Khuzistan. Its remains can still be seen. It was mentioned by several Muslim writers. In the fourteenth century it was described as having 42 arches, being 320 paces in length with a roadway 15 paces wide. Other Sasānid bridges included one 3,000 cubits in length over the Ṭāb river in Fars, and one at Ahwāz in Khuzistan built of kiln-dried bricks.

It is hardly surprising that the tradition of building masonry bridges was uninterrupted by the Islamic conquests. In the first centuries of Islam the constructors were usually from the indigenous peoples, since the Arabs were unfamiliar with bridge-building techniques. At the town of Arrajān in the Iranian province of Fars there was a famous arch bridge. It was described by al-Iṣṭakhrī in the tenth century as having but a single arch, eighty paces across in the span, and sufficiently high for a man, mounted on a camel and bearing aloft a banner, to pass easily under the keystone. It was said to have been built by a certain Daylamite (from the province of Daylam at the south-west corner of the Caspian), physician to al-Ḥajjāj, governor of Iraq under the Umayyad caliphs. There was a bridge over the Harāt river (now in Afghanistan) which, according to al-Muqaddasī in 990, was unequalled in all Khurāsān for beauty. It was built in Islamic times by a Magian (i.e. a Zoroastrian) and bore his name on an inscription.

There were, of course, many arch bridges built by the Muslims. On one of the rivers of Fars (the geographers disagree as to the actual name of the river) a bridge was built by a certain Abū Ṭālib. The bridge is described by al-Muqaddasī as having been built in his day, 'and there is none to equal it in all Syria and Mesopotamia'. A bridge with a special purpose was described by Ibn Jubayr who attributed its building to the prince Aḥmad b. Ṭūlūn (d. 884). It was a bridge of forty arches 'as large as the arches of a bridge can be'. It formed the first part of a causeway six miles long leading from the west bank of the Nile near Fusṭāṭ in the direction of Alexandria. Its purpose was to enable the army to move over the Nile floods to repel any attack coming from the west.

Other notable arch bridges in the Islamic world included those built in Artuqid times in eastern Anatolia: Diyar Bakr 1063, one over the Batman-Su river 1147, with gates and Customs houses, and one at Hasankeyf (twelfth century). Under the Mamluks notable bridges were built at Ludd in Palestine and at Yubna near Cairo. In Ottoman times a bridge built at Uzunköprü in Thrace had 174 arches and was 1,266 metres long. It formed part of the road network of the empire. The great Turkish architect Sinan directed the design and construction of a number of large arch bridges in the sixteenth century.

Apart from arch bridges over wide rivers, they were also required over irrigation canals. As far as the irrigators were concerned the main purpose of the bridges was to avoid the banks of the canals being damaged by fording people and animals; the convenience of the travellers was a secondary consideration. Since in many major irrigation schemes the canals were navigable, only arch bridges left the waterways clear for boats. There are therefore many references to arch bridges over canals in Spain, central Iraq, Khurāsān, Soghdiana and elsewhere.

The only description giving any detailed information about the construction of arch bridges in the classical Islamic world concerns a

FIGURE 8.3 Pul-i-Kāshgān bridge, Iran.

bridge near the town of Īdhaj in the Īranian province of Fars. The passage occurs in the geography of al-Qazwīnī (d. 1283). The bridge was called the Bridge of Khurra Zad, the mother of the Sasānid king Ardashīr (d. AD 241) in whose reign the bridge was originally built. By the tenth century it was in ruins and much of the lead used in its joints had been removed by the local inhabitants. The rebuilding was undertaken by 'Abd Allah al-Qummī, the wazir of the Amīr al-Ḥasan al-Buwayh (d. 977). 'Abd Allah collected craftsmen from Īdhaj and Isfahān. The work took two years to complete and cost 350,000 dinars.

The crossing was over a valley that was usually dry except at flood times when it became a swirling lake 1,000 cubits wide and 150 cubits deep. At the beginning of the construction workmen were winched down in baskets to build the lower sections of the piers. The masonry consisted of stone blocks, bonded together with iron clamps set in lead. The space between arch, spandrel walls, abutments and roadway was filled with slag from iron workings. Īdhaj is identified with the modern village of Mālamīr about 100 km east of Shustar (Sir Aurel Stein, *Old Routes of Western Iran*, Macmillan, 1940, 128).

There seems to have been a good deal of bridge building in the late tenth/early eleventh centuries in western Iran. Near the modern town of Khurramabad runs the river Kāshgān, and three Sasānid bridges over this river were restored in Islamic times. One of them, Pul-i-Dukhtar ('The Daughter's Bridge') had, in 1936, one arch intact, through which the motor road ran. This was near the town of Jaydar (*ibid.*, 182–6). Another ruined bridge, Pul-i-Kalhūr, was about twelve miles above the Pul-i-Dukhtar. The best preserved of these bridges, however, at the time of Stein's survey and indeed as late as 1972 (Syvia A. Matheson, *Persia, An Archaelogical Guide*, Faber, 1952, 83) was the Pul-i-Kāshgān, built over the Kāshgān river on the road to Kudasht about 56 km (35 miles) west of Khurramabad.

As can be seen from Figure 8.3, five of the arches had survived more or less intact. On the left bank the pier carrying the terminal arch was built straight against a wall-like cliff some 70 feet high. On the right bank, no less than nine massive piers carrying arches were needed to allow traffic to reach the full height of the bridge. Altogether there were 11 piers and hence 10 arches, and the total length of the bridge was about 900 feet. The arches were uniformly pointed and in each case had been formed by a triple course of burnt bricks. The heights of the arches varied from 49 to 62 feet.

Both the Pul-i-Kashgān and the Pul-i-Kalhūr are precisely dated by inscriptions, the former to 1008/9 and the latter to 984/5. They were built on the orders of Badr b. Ḥasanwayh (d. 1014) a well-known Kurdish chief who was recognised in 980 by the Buwayhids as lord of Kurdistan. They were part of the communications system which linked his stronghold near present-day Khurramabad to the plains of Khuzistan. In addition to these two bridges, the pointed arch occurs in the Pul-i-Dukhtar and at least one other bridge in the region. The significance of this type of arch in the history of building construction will be discussed in Chapter 12.

Suspension Bridges

The type of suspension bridge that was in use throughout Central Asia several centuries before Islam consisted of a deck made of as many as six bamboo cables a short distance apart with a deck of transverse planks laid upon them. Ropes stretched alongside on either hand to form a rail were added and the bridge was then fit for pack-animals as well as humans, if too many did not come on at one time. These bridges would have been of the catenary kind, where the walkway is on the natural curve of the cables, not the type in which the road is horizontal or even slightly cambered.

A Chinese source written about AD 90 refers to this kind of bridge in the Hindu Kush mountains: 'There the gorges and ravines allow of no connecting road, but ropes and cables are stretched from side to side and by means of these a passage is effected'. The very name Hindu Kush (Hsien-tu) means 'suspended crossings or passages'; a testimony, according to Joseph Needham, to the antiquity of the invention (*Science and Civilisation in China*, Vol. 4, pt. 3, pp. 187–8). There can therefore be no doubt that suspension bridges were in use in Central Asia in Islamic times. They are, in fact, essential for communications throughout the mountain belt of Asia from the Himalayas to the Hindu Kush. The cantilever/beam type is limited to spans of about fifteen metres, whereas single-span suspension bridges may be 100 metres or longer.

DAMS

As in the case of other technologies, the Muslims fell heir to long traditions of dam building in the lands they occupied in the first two Islamic centuries. Dams were almost always associated with irrigation systems: the diversion of rivers into irrigation canals was by far the commonest reason for their construction. The expansion of existing irrigation networks to meet the needs of great cities such as Baghdad, Samarqand and Cordoba will be discussed in the next chapter. Our purpose here will be to describe some of the dams that were built as elements of these expanded networks, and much of the information contained in this section is derived from the work of Norman Smith (see Bibliography). Although the Muslims learned the basic techniques of dam construction from the works of their predecessors, they did more than simply preserve a tradition and hand it on unchanged to their successors. Several innovations in the design and use of dams can be attributed directly to the Muslims, and were later to be incorporated in dams in Europe and the New World.

In fact, the Arabs did not need to go beyond the confines of Arabia for a knowledge of dam construction. The famous dam at Marib in the Yemen, whose destruction was recorded in the Koran, was built to intercept the flood from the rainstorms which from time to time fell in the high mountains of the Yemen. The dam was rebuilt several times after its first construction, perhaps as early as 750 BC. In its final form it was an impressive masonry structure of very high quality, the carefully cut and fitted blocks using lead dowels in their joints, but no mortar. It was fourteen metres high and 600 metres long, with elaborate waterworks including sluices, spillways, a settling tank and a distribution tank. Although the tradition is that the dam failed due to one catastrophic flood, it seems more likely that it went out of service – towards the end of the sixth century AD – because there were no longer the financial and technical means to maintain it.

Other masonry dams were built in Arabia in the pre-Islamic period and in the first Islamic century, including one at Ṭā'if which has survived and bears an inscription dating it to 677/8. All these dams were built to conserve soil and water. They were not diversionary dams like those in the irrigation systems based upon rivers.

In Sasānid times the Persians constructed irrigation networks, or rather enlarged ancient networks, based upon the rivers Tigris and Euphrates. The Muslims in turn enlarged these networks and this involved the construction of several new dams, one of the most impressive being over the 'Uzaym river east of the Tigris. The main body of the dam was a masonry wall 575 feet long which at the western end turns through a right angle and continues for 180 feet, to form one bank of the canal called Nahr Batt. ('Nahr' can mean either a river or a canal). The dam has a maximum height of fifty feet, but this rapidly reduces towards the sides. The cross-section of its central section has a neat trapezoidal profile, ten feet thick at the crest and fifty feet thick at the base. The water face was vertical and the air face was built to a uniform slope with the masonry stepped. The alignment of the structure was not straight, and this reflects an attempt to utilise the natural shape of the site as advantageously as possible. This was a common practice in dam construction in ancient and medieval times. The dam was built of masonry blocks throughout, and these were connected with lead dowels poured into grooves. We have already come across the use of lead to bond masonry in the dam at Marib and the Īdhaj bridge. The use of lead seems to have been a common practice in the Middle East both in pre-Islamic and Islamic times. It occurs in dowels as in the present case, or as a mortar to fix iron clamps. Either method might or might not be used in conjunction with lime or cement mortar.

In the year AD 260 the Roman Emperor Valerian, with an army of 70,000 men, fell prisoner to the Sasānid king Shāpūr I. For the next seven years the Romans, who presumably included engineers in their ranks, were engaged upon a massive project of hydraulic engineering on the Karūn (or Dujayl) river in Khuzistan. These works included the diversion of the river into an artificial cut – the Ab-i-Gargar – to leave the bed of the Karūn dry during the construction of a huge dam with a masonry bridge on its crest.

To this system the Muslims added a dam on the Ab-i-Gargar called Pul-i-Bulaiti. This dam was used to provide the power for irrigation and milling. The mills were installed in tunnels cut through the rock at each side of the channel. This is one of the earliest examples of hydro-power dams. Another example is the bridge-dam at Dizful which was used to provide the power to operate a great noria fifty cubits in diameter which supplied all the houses of the town. The wonderful mills below the dam at Ahwāz were mentioned by al-Muqaddasī. Many of these hydraulic works in Khuzistan – Sasānid and Muslim – can still be seen, but properly resourced restoration works are needed to ensure the survival of the remaining structures.

An important dam was built by the Amīr 'Aḍud al-Dawla, of the Buwayhid dynasty, who held the real power in Iraq and Iran from 945 until 1055. This dam, known as the Band-i-Amīr, was built in 960 over the river Kūr in Fars, between Shirāz and Iṣṭakhr (the ancient Persepolis). To quote al-Muqaddasī:

'Aḍud al-Dawla closed the river between Shirāz and Iṣṭakhr by a great wall, strengthened with lead. And the water behind it rose

160

and formed a lake. Upon it on the two sides were ten water-wheels, like those we mentioned in Khuzistan, and below each wheel was a mill, and it is today one of the wonders of Fars. Then he built a city. The water flowed through channels and irrigated 300 villages.

The dam still exists, though heavily silted up. It is some thirty feet high and 250 feet long. On top of it is a pointed arch bridge, of later construction than the dam itself. The dam is built of masonry blocks throughout and did not have a rubble core. In addition to the lead dowels, cement mortar was used in the joints, binding the whole structure together and making it watertight. It is not surprising that the Band-i-Amīr has had such a long and useful life.

The Romans were as assiduous and skilful in dam-building as they were at other types of civil engineering. Their dams included several in Syria, one at Leptis Magna in Libya, one at Kasserine in Tunisia and a number in the Iberian peninsula, two notable examples being at Merida, both of which have survived. From the end of Roman rule in the fifth century until the Muslim conquest in AD 711 the peninsula was ruled by the Visigoths. It is known that they practised irrigation, but there is no record of dam building or other engineering works. It is likely, however, that the Roman dams were kept in working order. In any case, the conquering Muslim armies included contingents from Syria, Iraq and the Yemen, among whom there were undoubtedly engineers skilled in hydraulic works. These engineers brought irrigation techniques to Spain and thereby laid the foundations of the agricultural prosperity which is one of the most impressive features of Islamic Spain. Nothing so elaborate and efficient had been seen before in Europe. The major irrigation schemes were in the great river valleys of the south, an environment similar to that of the Arabs' homelands in the Middle East.

Cordoba was the capital of Islamic Spain for nearly 500 years and it is here, on the river Guadalquivir, that we find what is probably the oldest surviving Islamic dam in Spain. According to the twelfth-century geographer al-Idrīsī it was built of Qibtiyya stone and incorporated marble pillars. It stands just down stream from the Roman bridge – the Puente Romano. It follows a zig-zag course across the river so that its total length is about 1,400 feet even though the river is only about 1,000 feet wide. This shape indicates that the builders were aiming at a long crest in order to increase the dam's overflow capacity. Today the remains of the dam are only a few feet above the river bed, but in its prime it was probably about seven or eight feet above high-water level and eight feet thick. There is rubble masonry everywhere but we may assume that this was originally faced with masonry blocks

FIGURE 8.4 Cordoba: detail of dam and millhouse.

– the Qibtiyya (or Egyptian) stone described by al-Idrīsī. As already mentioned in Chapter 6, al-Idrīsī mentions three millhouses below the

FIGURE 8.5 Cordoba: general view of dam, millhouses
and Roman bridge.

dam, each of which contained four mills. The millhouses still exist but
no trace of the original machinery remains. Also below the dam, and
powered by the head of water it provided, was a large noria that raised
water from the river and discharged it into an aqueduct which then
carried it into the city. The aqueduct and noria have been restored,
although the wheel is not operative. Here again, therefore, we have an
example of the Muslims' use of dams for powering mills and water-
raising machines. As an additional bonus, the Cordoba dam has for
1,000 years protected the Puente Romano piers from scour.

The river Turia flows into the Mediterranean at Valencia. In the
tenth century there were many small dams on the river and eight of
these, spread over six miles in the province of Valencia, are of particular interest. All of them are similar in size, shape and design. The one
at Mestella, the fifth in the series, can be considered as typical. It is 240
feet long and 7 feet high. The water face is vertical, the air face stepped,
the crest is 4½ feet wide and the base thickness 18 feet. The core of the
dam consists of rubble masonry and mortar, and the structure is faced
with large masonry blocks with mortared joints.

At one end the dam abuts on a masonry wall which extends
downstream some seventy feet and is everywhere the same height as
the dam and similarly built. Between this wall and the river bank a
proportion of the Turia's flow is directed to the mouth of the irrigation
canal. Two sluices are built into this wall, one half-way along, the
other near the canal mouth. They served two purposes: during normal
operation they were used as escapes to allow surplus water to drain

FIGURE 8.6 Mestella dam, Valencia.

back into the river; and occasionally they would both be opened to their full extent in order to desilt the approaches to the canal mouth. Such scouring sluices, closed with planks carried in grooves, are absolutely essential. Silt is bound to collect above dams of this type and must periodically be removed if the canal intakes and the canals themselves are not to become hopelessly choked and obstructed. All the Islamic dams on the Turia, and most others elsewhere, were equipped with desilting sluices. They were a Muslim development which later Christian Spanish dams were to utilise on a grand scale.

These eight dams all have similar foundation works, which at first glance appear to be too massive for the superstructures. The masonry of each dam extends some fifteen feet into the river bed. Below this the whole structure is supported by rows of wooden piles, the tops of which are built into the lowest courses of the masonry. The combined depth of masonry and piles is 20–25 feet. The reason for building such solid foundations becomes clear when the behaviour of the Turia is considered. The river's flow for most of the year is only about 400 cusecs, but there are occasional dangerous floods when the flow is more than a hundred times greater. The dams are then submerged to a depth of nearly twenty feet and must resist the battering of water, stones, rocks and trees. Because they are so low and flat and are provided with deep and very firm foundations, the Turia

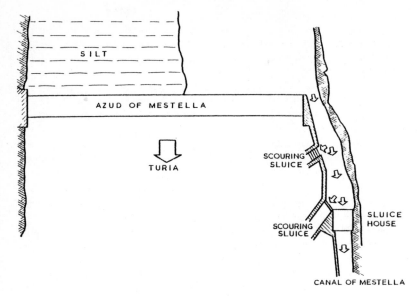

FIGURE 8.7 Mestella dam: desilting sluices.

dams have been able to survive these conditions for a thousand years.

The dams on the Turia may appear to be small, unspectacular and a not particularly notable factor in the history of dam building; but in fact, for the task they were required to perform and for the conditions under which they were required to operate, they turn out to be extremely practical. They continue to meet the irrigation needs of Valencia even today, and it is interesting to note that not only have no more dams been added to the system, but to add at all to it would be pointless anyway. Modern measurements have shown that the eight canals between them have a total capacity slightly less than that of the river. This raises, of course, the question whether or not the Muslims were able to gauge a river and then design their dams and canals to match. At present it is not possible to answer such a question with confidence. It should be remembered, however, that the art of dam building had been practised for several millenia in the Middle East before the Turia dams were planned. It would be surprising if the knowledge accumulated over such a long period did not include empirical methods for estimating the flow of rivers.

From the many other dams built in Islamic Spain, one further example will demonstrate the Muslims' mastery of constructional techniques. The river Segura, in its lower reaches between Murcia and

165

the sea, provides irrigation for Murcia and its environs. Unlike the Turia, which is only a little lower than its adjoining flood-plain, the lower Segura runs in a deep channel. A series of dams would not therefore have been a practical solution, since each would have had to have been of considerable size. One properly sited dam was the answer. It had to be built upriver at a point which would allow, in the first place, a structure of manageable size. Secondly the dam had to be far enough upstream to be at a higher level than the area to be irrigated, so that gravitational flow would guarantee a supply of water. These two factors governing the choice of dam site had to be weighed against a third consideration: length and route of the supply canals. All these considerations had to be carefully balanced, and it is clear that the siting and construction of the dam met the necessary criteria.

The dam was built just below a sharp bend in the river where the valley is particularly narrow. In recent years parts of it have been rebuilt and altered, so that the following description is based upon accounts of the nineteenth century when it was still very much in its original form.

The main body of the dam was 420 feet long and 25 feet high. For three-quarters of its length it was 160 feet thick at the base, reduced to 125 feet for the other quarter. The two portions of the dam were separated by a low wall running down the face of the structure. The longer of the two sections had a crest two feet lower than the shorter, and it seems clear therefore that the dam was intended to discharge its overflow in two stages. The short section of the crest would only come into action when the long portion was already covered by two feet of water.

Given that the height of the dam was only 25 feet, base thicknesses of 160 feet and 125 feet may seem excessive, and so far as resistance to fracture and overturning is concerned they were. The reason for such vast thicknesses was probably due to the foundation conditions. The bed of the river is very soft and weak, and thus far from ideal for the foundations of a dam. The Muslims therefore gave the structure enough weight to prevent it from sliding along the soft river-bed.

The large surface of the dam's air face was put to good use. Water flowing over the crest initially fell vertically through a height of 13–17 feet on to a level platform, running the length of the dam. This served to dissipate the energy of the water spilling over the crest. The overflow then ran to the foot of the dam over flat or gently sloping sections of the face. In this way the whole dam acted as a spillway and the energy gained by the water in falling 25 feet was dissipated *en route*. Thus the risk of undermining the downstream foundations was greatly reduced. As usual, rubble masonry and mortar were used for the

FIGURE 8.8 Orihuela dam near Murcia.

interior of the dam, and the whole was finished with large masonry blocks. At the right-hand end the dam connects with a long wall, in line with itself and designed to direct flood-waters over the crest so that they could not erode the dam's right-hand abutment. This flood diversion wall is of interest because, unlike the dam, it has not been recently rebuilt and is believed to be original Muslim work.

For our final examination of a dam we return to Iran in the Ilkhanid period. First of all, we must define the three basic types of dam: 'gravity dams', 'arched dams' and 'arch dams'. The first type, which includes the vast majority of dams built in Antiquity and the Middle Ages, resists the pressure of the water by its weight alone. The second type is really a modification of the first; its arched plan is dictated by foundation conditions, but the main resistance to the pressure is still due to gravity. There are a few examples of early arched dams, for example a Roman one at Glanum in southern France. The arch dam is more slender than the other two types and does not depend solely upon its weight. The arch itself carries the forces due to water pressure along horizontal lines to the sides of the structure. At the sides the predominantly horizontal forces are resisted by normal forces and shear forces. Underneath the arch dam the only vertical forces are those required to support its own weight. Clearly, therefore, the site of an arch dam must be chosen where the banks will provide secure anchorages.

167

At the end of the thirteenth century a dam was built at Kebar, about fifteen miles south of Qum in central Iran. It was built in a roughly V-shaped gorge which suddenly narrows, about half-way down, to a deep gully, much deeper than it is wide. The rock is limestone and there were no foundation problems. The dam, which has survived intact, is 85 feet high and 180 feet long at the crest. The crest thickness varies between 15 feet and 16½ feet. The air face is vertical, except near the base where there is a slight slope in the downstream direction. Much of the water face of the dam is today obscured by the vast amounts of silt and debris which have collected in the reservoir. Where it can be observed at the top the water face is vertical, and it seems reasonable to suppose that this face of the dam is vertical throughout its height. The Kebar dam is a very thin structure, too thin to act as a gravity dam. It is in fact an arch dam, the oldest surviving example of this type of structure so far located. The radius of curvature of its air face is 125 feet at all points, the dam constituting what is known, in modern terminology, as an arch dam of constant radius.

The dam has other points of interest in addition to its status as the earliest known arch dam. Up both sides of the dam and in the narrow bottom of the ravine the limestone is cut away to form grooves into which the dam is built. There has been no cracking or slipping and the dam has remained watertight throughout. It has a core of rubble masonry set in mortar. The faces are finished with roughly dressed rectangular blocks of varied size; they have mortared joints, but are not closely fitted. The mortar which was used is called locally *saruj*. It was and still is made from lime crushed with the ash of a desert plant. The addition of ash makes the lime hydraulic and results in a strong, hard and impervious mortar ideal for dams, and undoubtedly an important factor in the Kebar dam's long life.

To summarise the developments in dam construction and usage in the medieval Islamic world we have, first of all, the various constructional techniques which have ensured the survival of so many dams. The massive foundations of the Turia dams, the design of the Murcia dam to prevent slippage and undermining of the foundations, and the measures taken to keep the Kebar dam watertight, including the use of hydraulic mortar, all point to a knowledge of the techniques of construction in hydraulic conditions of various kinds. The number of the Turia dams, which almost exactly corresponds with the flow of the river, suggests that the Muslims were able to gauge rivers and design their dams and canals to suit. The Kebar dam is the first known example of a true arch dam. Many Muslim dams in Spain incorporate desilting sluices, an essential feature if the dams and the mouths of their canals are not to become hopelessly silted up. Finally, the Muslims made use of dams as a source of hydropower to drive mills and water-raising machines: cases we have cited include the Pul-i-Bulaiti and the Dizful dams in Khuzistan, the Band-i-Amīr in Fars and the dam at Cordoba.

It is impossible to say which of these developments were originated by the Muslims. Given that dam building had been an established practice in both Egypt and Sumeria for at least three millenia before the advent of Islam, it seems certain that sound techniques of hydraulic engineering were passed on to the Muslims from their predecessors. These techniques probably included good constructional practices and perhaps also the gauging of rivers and the use of special materials of construction such as lead and lime mortar. The introduction of desilting sluices, the arch dam and hydropower seem to have made their first appearances in the Islamic world, and it is therefore difficult to see how these can be other than Muslim inventions.

9

Irrigation and Water-supply

IRRIGATION SYSTEMS

We are concerned here with the engineering elements in the two related technologies of irrigation and water-supply. Indeed, so closely are they related that several of their constituents are identical. This applies to the main arteries bringing water to the distribution networks – canals and qanats – and to the methods of impounding and storing the water. As we shall see, the same arteries were sometimes used to serve both purposes. Irrigation and water-supply stimulated the development of other technologies, which are dealt with in other chapters of this book: water-raising machines in Chapter 6, dams in Chapter 8, and surveying in Chapter 10. Some aspects of these technologies will, however, be mentioned in this chapter.

A causal connection between government and large-scale hydraulic schemes was discussed and supported by F. Wittfogel (see Bibliography) in very profound and detailed studies. Wittfogel's findings have been challenged, but there seems little reason to doubt that his main thesis, that there is a correlation between large-scale public works on the one hand and strong, stable government on the other, has been established. In Chapters 6 to 11 of this book we are concerned with the history of Islamic engineering from a technical standpoint, without paying formal attention to the societal and political aspects of the subject. It is, however, impossible to avoid touching upon these aspects tangentially. The instances that we shall discuss of large-scale hydraulic works all support Wittfogel's correlation hypothesis. It seems to be the case, however, that it was the maintenance of existing systems, even more than the construction of new ones, that necessitated centralised irrigational bureaucracies.

Before examining the hydraulic systems of medieval Islam we need to identify the four different types of irrigation. *Basin* irrigation consists of levelling large plots of land adjacent to a river or canal, each plot being surrounded by dykes. When the river reaches a certain level the dykes are breached, allowing the water to inundate the plots. It remains there until the fertile sediment has settled, whereupon the surplus is drained back into the watercourse. The regime of the Nile, with the predictable arrival of the flood, made Egypt particularly suitable for basin irrigation, before the construction of the high dam at Aswan. *Perennial* irrigation was, and is, practised extensively in the

Iraqi plain and elsewhere. As the name implies, it consists of watering crops regularly throughout the growing season by leading the water into small channels which form a matrix over the field. Indeed, a network of waterworks is typical of perennial irrigation. Water from a main artery – a river or a major canal – is diverted into supply canals, then into smaller irrigation canals, and so on to the fields. In many cases the systems operate entirely by gravity flow, but water-raising machines are used to overcome obstacles such as high banks, natural or artificial. Perennial irrigation from wells, using devices of varying degrees of sophistication to raise the water, has also been practised from very early times.

Terrace irrigation was used at an early date in Syria and Palestine, and in India, China and pre-Columbian America. This last locale is important, since it indicates that the technique did not diffuse from a single point of origin. Terrace irrigation is a method used in hilly country and consists of the formation of terraces stepped down a hillside. The effort is high in relation to the levels of production, but if the land is the sole livelihood of a family or a community there is no alternative. Irrigation is by means of stored rainfall, wells, springs and occasionally qanats.

Wadi irrigation, which has already been mentioned in connection with the dam at Marib in the Yemen, was also extensively practised by the Nabateans in southern Palestine and Jordan. From the second century BC until about the beginning of the first century AD they produced a flourishing civilisation based upon wadi irrigation. Whereas irrigation in the Yemen depended upon a single large dam, the Nabateans built thousands of little barriers sited across wadi after wadi in order to divert or capture the one or two weeks of runoff occurring each year. Neither the Marib system nor the Nabateans' elaborate works were emulated in the Islamic world. Apart from Egypt, all the major systems in the Muslim countries, from Spain to Central Asia, were based upon perennial irrigation.

Whatever the level of irrigation activity in the Iberian peninsula in Roman and Visigothic times, there can be no doubt that this was greatly increased after the Muslim conquest. One confirmation of this is that the Muslims introduced a number of new crops into Iberia. Some of these, such as rice and sugar-cane, could only be grown under irrigation, while others were temperate species that could only be stabilised in a semi-arid environment by irrigation. Another testimony comes from the many words in modern Spanish concerning agriculture and irrigation that have been taken directly from Arabic. And of course we have seen in the previous chapter how the Muslims built dams and irrigation canals to establish

171

new systems in Valencia and Murcia, to name but two areas.

When the Muslims conquered Spain in AD 711 the Arab Empire was ruled by the Umayyad dynasty from Damascus. In 750 the Umayyads were overthrown in the East by the 'Abbāsids, who moved the capital to Baghdad, but the Umayyads held on to the Iberian peninsula, where their Amirs (later Caliphs) ruled from Cordoba. This is one of the factors which accounts for the 'Syrianisation' of the Spanish landscape, another being the similarity of the climate and hydraulic conditions in parts of Spain to the conditions obtaining in the Ghūta – the large oasis surrounding Damascus, watered by the Barada and other rivers. It is likely that the Syrian pattern was imposed upon the cultivators, mainly Berbers, by the Umayyad Amirs in the first quarter of the ninth century. In any case there were few large rivers in the Berbers' North African homelands, and they were therefore willing to apply the more appropriate eastern methods in Spain, where river irrigation was possible on a much larger scale. In places where the rivers supplied sufficient water, for example the regions of Valencia, Gandia and Murcia, the methods of irrigation and its administration were based firmly upon Syrian models. Further south, in the oasis-like communities of Elche, Novelda and Alicante, where the water sources were typically springs rather than rivers, irrigation water was also distributed by canals; but the administrative arrangements were different from those in the river valleys. As the Christians gradually reconquered the Iberian peninsula, the Muslim irrigation systems were taken over more or less intact.

The irrigation systems of the eastern Caliphate reached their highest state of development in the tenth and eleventh centuries, after the power of the 'Abbāsid caliphs had been eroded, but while the Islamic world, as a cultural entity, stretched from the Atlantic to Central Asia. One of the most important of these systems was in central Iraq. The story is complicated by major shifts in the courses of the Tigris and Euphrates, and by variations in the area of swamp and lagoons which lies to the north-west of Basra.

In general, the Sasānid kings had devoted considerable attention to the construction and maintenance of canals for irrigation and drainage, and to keeping the dykes in repair. This was a difficult task, since the plain below Baghdad is flat and the two rivers are subject to disastrous floods. One such occurred about the year AD 629, resulting in major changes in the courses of the two rivers, and in a great extension to the swamplands. Figure 9.1 shows the topography of Iraq in medieval times. The Great Swamp then covered an area of about 200 miles by 50. At its northern end the Euphrates discharged into the swamp through its main course, which flowed past the city of Kūfa; its

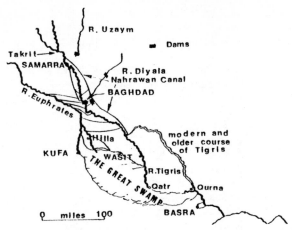

FIGURE 9.1 Irrigation network in central Iraq.

present course, flowing past Hilla, was then a great irrigation canal called the Nahr Sūra. The Tigris flowed well to the west of its present course, which was also its course before the floods of the seventh century. It flowed past the city of Wāsiṭ (both Kūfa and Wāsiṭ, once great cities, have now disappeared) and entered the Great Swamp at Qatr. Both rivers emerged from the swamp a few miles above Qurna, where they combined, as they do today, to form the waterway known as the Shaṭṭ al-'Arab, then called the Blind Tigris. Along the northern edge of the Great Swamp, from Qatr to a point upstream from Qurna, a line of lagoons linked by open channels made navigation possible from Baghdad to Basra. It is not known precisely when the Tigris shifted back to its older bed and when the Euphrates took its present course, but there seems to have been a gradual change, starting about 1200 and being completed in the sixteenth century.

The Muslims inherited the Sasānid irrigation system, the major expansion occurring after the founding of Baghdad in AD 762. The basic Sasānid network was dictated by topography, since there is a slight eastward tilt in central Iraq and hence the gridiron of large canals ran from the Euphrates into the Tigris. The main artery for the irrigation of the lands to the east of the Tigris was the great Nahrawān canal, which left the Tigris a short distance below Takrīt and rejoined the river about a hundred miles below Baghdad. The upper part of the canal was known as "the cut of the Chosroes", since this part of it had been excavated under the Sasānid kings. The rivers 'Uzaym and Diyāla discharged into the Nahrawān from the east, and these rivers were dammed by the 'Abbāsid engineers to provide water for a huge

173

irrigated area. Important canals taking off from the west of the Nahrawān included the Khālis and the Bīn; the waters of these made possible a closely-cultivated area north of Baghdad, and in part supplied the city itself.

In the south of Iraq, due to the influence of the tides on the Shaṭṭ al-'Arab and the lower reaches of the Tigris and Euphrates, there is a particularly favourable situation for irrigation. Thanks to a system of canals specially adapted to the situation, there is no need to use machines to raise water to the fields, since there is always sufficient raised by the tides for purposes of irrigation. The cleansing of the canals is done automatically by the movement of the tides, and drainage is effected during the ebb tide. There is therefore no danger of salination, despite the presence of dissolved salts in the water due to the proximity of the sea. The Basra area presents a marked contrast to central Iraq during the summer months, since the vast plantations of date palms provide shade for flourishing vegetable gardens, whereas further north the dust is pervasive and the canals are half empty, the water being brackish.

The historian al-Balādhurī (d. 892) has left us an account of the foundation of Basra and the measures subsequently taken to supply the city with water for irrigation and drinking. When 'Utba b. Ghazwān was the commander of a Muslim army in southern Iraq in 638 he selected the site of Basra, after consultation with the caliph 'Umar I, as an encampment for his troops. It was located about ten miles to the west of the Shaṭṭ al-'Arab, and in the early years it was simply an army camp consisting of huts made of reeds, which were dismantled when the troops were absent on campaigns. During this period drinking water had to be transported from the Shaṭṭ al-'Arab, and although attempts seem to have been made to excavate canals from the site to the river in the caliphate of 'Umar I, neither of the two main canals was completed until after 660, when the Umayyads assumed power. One of these great canals, the Nahr Ma'qil, came down from the north-east and carried shipping from Baghdad; the other, the Nahr al-Ubulla, carried ships going south-east to the Gulf. The canals were linked by another canal, upon which the city itself was located. A great many irrigation canals were then excavated. Al-Balādhurī usually gives us the names of the excavators, but these were not the surveyors or engineers, but rather Arab notables from the army or the civilian community. Certain riparian rights seem to have been granted to these men. Basra became, in the eighth century, a thriving centre for agriculture and the most important city in Iraq for commerce, finance and learning. Although it was eventually eclipsed by the rise of Baghdad it was still prosperous in the tenth century; the geographer al-Iṣṭakhrī described its enormous network of canals and its abundant agricultural produce.

One of the most fertile provinces of the eastern Islamic world was Khurāsān, then very much larger than the modern Iranian province of that name, since it included parts of present-day Afghanistan and what was until recently Soviet Central Asia. The region includes a number of great rivers: the Helmand rises in the mountains of Afghanistan and flows eastwards into the Zara lake; the Harāt river rises in the mountains of Ghūr and after flowing west turns north and eventually loses its waters in the desert; the Murghāb, which also rises in the mountains of Ghūr and flows west then north, becomes lost in the Ghuzz desert, at about the same latitude as the Harāt river, approximately seventy miles to the eastwards of the latter. These rivers, and others in Khurāsān, were exploited extensively for irrigation in medieval times, as of course was the Oxus (or Amu Darya) which forms the northern border of Khurāsān.

The Arabic geographers of the tenth century devote a good deal of space to describing the irrigation systems of Khurāsān. One of the most vivid descriptions concerns the hydraulic works on the river Murghāb. Al-Muqaddasī, writing at the close of the century, calls the Murghāb the river of the two Marvs and describes it as flowing past Upper (or Lesser) Marv towards Lower (or Great) Marv. One march south of the latter city its bed was artificially dyked with embankments faced by woodworks which kept the river-bed from changing. In the tenth century this embankment was under the control of a specially appointed Amir who acted as water-bailiff. He had 10,000 men under him, each with an appointed task, and is said to have had more authority than the prefect of Great Marv. This workforce included horse guards and a team of 300 divers. Each diver had with him a supply of wood for repairing the dykes, and when it was cold they covered their bodies with wax before entering the water. On the embankment there was a gauge which registered the flood-height; in a year of abundance this would rise to sixty barleycorns above the low level, and the people then rejoiced, while in a year of drought the water would only attain the level of six barleycorns.

At a distance of one league south of Great Marv the waters of the river were dammed back in a great round pool, whence four canals radiated to the various quarters of the city and the suburbs. The height of the pool was regulated by sluices, and there was a great festival when, at high flood-time, the various dams were cut and the waters were divided up according to rule. Of the four canals the Nahr al-Mājān appears to have carried the main stream of the Murghāb, and after passing through the suburbs of the city, where it was crossed by many

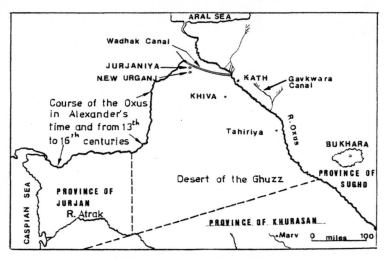

FIGURE 9.2 Irrigation network in Khuwārazm.

bridges of boats, it came out again into the desert plain and flowed on until the residue of its waters were lost in the swamp.

The province of Khwārazm, an oasis on the lower reaches of the river Oxus, offers several interesting features. It is evocatively described in the last eighteen lines of Matthew Arnold's poem *Sohrab and Rustum*, which is based upon an episode in the *Shāhnāma*, the epic poem by the great tenth-century Persian poet Firdawsī. Although the end of Arnold's poem is one of the great moments of English poetry, it gives a false picture, probably unwittingly, of Khwārazm, since it conveys the impression that much of the area was wasteland. In fact, the cultivation of the delta began at Ṭāhirīya (see Figure 9.2), some 300 miles from the river's mouth. Moreover, the population were by no means all agriculturists and bureaucrats. Khwārazm was a centre of learning and produced a number of notable scholars. The great mathematician Muḥammad b. Mūsā al-Khwārazmī (see Chapter 2) flourished at a time when the rulers of the province – the Khwārazm-Shāhs – were only just becoming Muslims. In the following century, the tenth, Abu 'Abd Allah al-Khwārazmī wrote his pioneering encyclopaedia of the sciences, *Mafātiḥ al-'Ulūm* (see Chapter 4). Al-Bīrūnī (d. after 1050), probably the greatest scientist of medieval Islam, was born in Kāth, eastern capital of the province.

The chief products of Khwārazm were cereals, fruit and textiles. The land was extremely fertile and grew large crops of cotton, as well as pasturing huge herds of sheep and cattle. Irrigation was of course essential for crop cultivation and a number of large canals led off from both banks of the river, each main canal being the basis of a network of canals, as is usual with perennial irrigation.

Figure 9.2 is an outline map of Khwārazm as it was in the tenth century. It would be impossible to show all the many towns, hundreds of villages and complete network of canals; in any case much of this topographical data cannot be identified. Only the major towns and cities and one or two of the main canals are therefore shown. Several of these were substantial waterways. From the eastern bank of the Oxus the large canal called the Gāvkhuwāra was taken. It was navigable for boats, being twelve feet deep and thirty feet across; it went northwards and irrigated all the lands up to the level of Kāth. About six miles to the north of Kāth the great Wadhāk canal branched off from the west bank of the river. It was navigable as far as Jurjānīya, the western capital of Khwārazm. The irrigation system of the province necessitated, of course, the construction of many diversion dams, large and small.

In the last decades of the fourth century BC, when Alexander the Great made his conquests in western Asia, the Oxus is described as flowing into the Caspian. When the change of course from the Caspian to the Aral took place is not known, but though at the present day the Oxus, like the Jaxartes (or Sir Darya), flows into the Sea of Aral, its old bed to the Caspian still exists and is marked on modern maps. In the earlier Middle Ages the course of the Oxus, as described by the Arab geographers of the tenth century, is in the main that of the present day, but the old bed leading to the Caspian is mentioned by al-Muqaddasī. Later, some two and a half centuries after the time of al-Muqaddasī, it seems certain that the Oxus once again resumed its old course. This we learn from the contemporary Persian authors. It is beyond doubt that from the early part of the thirteenth century to near the close of the sixteenth century the Oxus, except for a small fraction of its waters which still passed into the Aral Sea by the canals, reached the Caspian along the old bed of the time of Alexander the Great.

The Arab historian Ibn al-Athīr (d. 1233) in his chronicles explains the reasons for the change of course of the Oxus. In 1220 the Mongols, in order finally to capture the city of Urganj, after a five month's siege broke down the dykes and overwhelmed the city with the waters of the Oxus and its canals. The whole country was laid under water and the overflow began to drain off to the south-west, filling the old bed of the Oxus which it followed to the Caspian. The Aral Sea became an insignificant lake, as it had been in Alexander's time. It is ironic to realise that because of heavy extraction of water for irrigation in the second half of the twentieth century, very little of the waters of the

Oxus and Jaxartes reaches the Aral, which has again almost dried up.

One of the most important of the provinces of eastern Islam, also very largely dependent upon irrigation, was Sughd (the ancient Soghdiana) which includes the fertile lands lying between the Oxus and the Jaxartes. It was watered by two rivers, the Sughd (now the Zarafshān) upon which the cities of Samarqand and Bukhārā stand, and the river which flowed by the cities of Kish and Nasaf. The Sughd region had attained its greatest splendour in the ninth century under the Iranian Samānid Amīrs. In the following century, however, it was still incomparably fertile and rich, and is given glowing descriptions by the Arabic geographers of the tenth century, apparently without exaggeration. The Sughd river rises in the Alay mountains, an eastward extension of the Tien Shan range. At a large village called Waraghsar, a few leagues to the east of Samarqand, most of the canals watering the lands around Samarqand had their origin. Of the canals flowing to Samarqand, two were sufficiently large to carry boats. At Samarqand the river was crossed by a masonry bridge. Below the city many canals branched off to various districts, after which the river came to the neighbourhood of Bukhārā.

Bukhārā was a walled city about 150 miles downstream from Samarqand. Standing in a plain a short distance south of the main arm of the river Sughd, it measured a league across in every direction. Around the city were many towns, palaces and gardens, gathered into an area measuring twelve leagues in every direction and enclosed by a Great Wall that must have been over a hundred miles in circuit. Through this great enclosure passed the Sughd river, with its numerous canals. All the main canals, and the towns and villages which they irrigated, are enumerated by Ibn Ḥawqal; but it would be impossible now to reconstruct the major canal networks of the Sughd river.

THE MEASUREMENT OF IRRIGATION WATERS

The concept of rules governing the distribution of irrigation waters is at least as old as the Code of Hammurabi (c.2000 BC). The subject has been closely studied, both generally and for specific periods and locations, and there is no possibility of discussing the complex question of distribution systems within the scope of this work. All that can be said by way of summary is that distribution could be by proportion, by time or by measurement – sometimes by a combination of these methods.

In a proportional system the amount of water available in a river or feeder canal was divided into a number of notional units and each irrigator received an allocation of units in proportion to the size of his holding. The advantage of this system was that equitable distribution could be assured without measure of time or the use of delivery orifices. When water was abundant the farmer took whatever he required. When water was scarce a turn was imposed, and as the available water diminished the interval between successive turns became greater. But no measure was needed in this eventuality either, except for the original gauging of the stream and the measurement of land. The irrigator only had a certain amount of land and could not overwater his crops without harming them. Therefore the only control needed to ensure equitability of distribution was to see that no farmer watered again until everyone else had had a turn.

When distribution was by timing, it could be achieved by stipulating parts of a day, say from dawn until noon. For shorter periods some kind of timepiece was required. This often took the form of a bowl with an orifice in its underside, known as a *ṭarjahār*. It was placed empty on a pond or tank adjacent to an irrigator's land, and when it sank the period was over and the channel to that piece of land was blocked until the next time the farmer was due for watering. Use of the *tarjahār* for timing the allocation of irrigation water is reported from places as far apart as north-western Iran and North Africa. It was, of course, the component that was adapted by al-Jazarī as part of the water machinery in two of his clocks, as we have seen in Chapter 7.

Control by means of delivery orifices was the method used on the river Murghāb, for example. Ibn Ḥawqal tells us that every quarter in the Marv area had a little supply channel, dammed by a board in which there were holes of set diameters; no-one could alter these diameters. Everyone got equal shares, more in times of plenty, less when water was scarce. Presumably the precise allocations depended upon the height reached by the water on the level gauges, which we have already mentioned. This height may also have been used for assessing the land-tax, the *kharāj*, to be levelled on each farmer. Certainly, the most famous measuring device of all, the Nilometer, was used for deciding the amount of *kharāj* to be paid to the Sultan for the year.

There had been Nilometers in use in Egypt since early times. Several were built by the Muslims. The most famous of these, which still exists, was completed in 861–2 on the island of Rawda at Cairo by Muḥammad al-Ḥāsib, according to an inscription around the top of the pit. It consists of a tall graduated octagonal column which serves as a measuring gauge, standing in a stone-lined pit, roughly 6.20 metres square, with a staircase running down to the bottom. Below this is a cylindrical section with steps cut into its masonry walls. The four sides of the square pit are relieved by recesses, each covered by a pointed arch vault resting on a pair of engaged colonettes with clock-formed capitals and bases. This type of arch was, of course, an essential part of Gothic architecture, but the arches in the Nilometer are three centuries older than any Gothic example. The measuring column is a tall octagonal shaft measured into 16 cubits, averaging 54.05 cm, by transverse lines, and the ten uppermost are each subdivided into 24 'fingers' by 24 divisions, grouped four by four on either side of a vertical line. These details are taken from the report of a survey made by K. A. C. Creswell (*A short account of early Muslim architecture*, Harmondworth, 1958, 292–6). Creswell goes on to mention that the column had been broken in two places: '(1) in the twelfth cubit, the length of which has been reduced, between 1798 and 1853, to 22.5 cm, and (2) at the junction of the 16th and 17th [*sic*], the length of the cubits remaining unchanged'. The column rests on a pedestal 83 cm square and 1.17 metres in height and this rests on a millstone 1.50 metres in diameter and 32 cm thick. The length of the column before it was broken, including these supports, was 19 cubits. The millstone rests on a floor of wooden planking supported by four heavy timber beams. Connection to the Nile is made by three tunnels, all opening into the east side.

Descriptions by early Arab writers agree essentially with the foregoing details given by Creswell, except for the length of the column. According to Ibn Jubayr, writing late in the twelfth century, this was 22 cubits; a water-level of 17 cubits was most beneficial for agriculture but up to 19 was acceptable; the Sultan was entitled to levy *kharāj* if the level reached 16 cubits and the actual amount of tax levied depended upon the measured level above that point. Al-Idrīsī, writing perhaps three decades earlier that Ibn Jubayr, has much the same information, including the fact that the Sultan could levy *kharāj* once the level had reached 16 cubits. If the level exceeded 20 cubits it was detrimental because trees were uprooted and houses ruined, while a maximum level below 12 meant a year of drought and sterility. There is therefore an indication that the column was longer in the twelfth century than it is today.

Al-Muqaddasī gives little information about the construction of the Nilometer, simply saying that it was a pit in the centre of which was a long column divided into cubits and fingers. He tells us something, however, about the importance of the device to the people of the Nile Delta. When the water started to rise, the supervisor reported daily to the Sultan the mark reached by the water on the measuring column. No public announcements were made until the level reached 12 cubits. Thereafter the crier made his rounds every day, announcing 'Allah increased the blessed Nile today by such-and-such an amount'. The people rejoiced when the water reached 16 cubits, since they knew it would be a good year.

QANATS

The *qanat* is an almost horizontal underground conduit that conducts water from an aquifer to the place where it is needed. The qanat should not be confused with tunnels or covered aqueducts, which carry water from above-ground sources such as streams or lakes; the technique for constructing qanats is quite different and highly specialised. In Iran, where qanats are still an important source of water, their construction is in the hands of experts (muqannī), and the secrets of the profession are largely handed down from father to son. The construction of a new qanat requires a considerable outlay of capital, and there is always the risk that financial returns may be low if the eventual flow of water is inadequate. It is customary, therefore, for the landowner or other authority to engage a skilled surveyor, usually a former muqannī with great field experience and keen powers of observation, for the preparatory work. The termination of the qanat, either farmland to be irrigated or a community to be provided with potable water, or both, will be known in advance, as will the general location of likely aquifers. The surveyors then carefully examines the alluvial fans, looking for traces of seepage on the surface and often for a hardly noticeable change in vegetation, before deciding where the trial well is to be dug. A winch is set up at the selected point, and two muqannīs begin to excavate a vertical shaft about three feet in diameter, the spoil being hauled to the surface by two labourers and deposited around the mouth of the shaft. When the muqannīs reach the aquifer they proceed slowly until they reach the impermeable layer. The well is then left for a few days, during which time the water is hoisted up in leather buckets, and its quantities noted, while at the same time any fall in the level of water is observed. The surveyor then has to decide whether they have reached genuine groundwater, or just some water trickling in from a local clay or rock shelf. If necessary more trial wells are dug to find a genuine aquifer or to determine the extent of the one already found and its yield. The shaft with the highest yield is chosen as the 'mother well'; in some cases all trial wells are linked together with a conduit, thus forming a water-yielding gallery.

The next step is for the surveyor to determine the route, gradient and precise outlet of the qanat. The route will be selected according to considerations of terrain and, in some cases, questions of ownership. To start the survey, a long rope is let down into the mother well until it touches the surface of the water, and a mark is made on it at ground level. The surveyor then selects a spot on the route 30 to 50 metres from the mother well for the first ventilation shaft. A staff is held on this spot by a chainman (a surveyor's assistant; usually an intelligent labourer who has been given careful instructions in his duties – the word derives from the use of a chain for measuring). The surveyor then measures the fall with a level. Nowadays a modern surveying level may be used, but in earlier times one of the instruments to be described in Chapter 10 was employed. A second mark is made on the rope coinciding with the measurement on the staff; the distance from this mark to the lower end of the rope will be the depth of the first ventilation shaft. He continues to level in this way along the route, marking the rope at the location of each shaft, until he reaches the end of the rope. He has then reached a point on the ground which is level with the surface of the water in the mother well. For the mouth of the qanat he now chooses a place below this level, but higher than the fields, and divides the drop from the level point to the mouth by the number of proposed ventilation shafts and adds this amount to the previously surveyed depth of each shaft. In this way be determines the gradient of the conduit, which is usually from 1:1000 to 1:1500.

After completion of the survey, a number of guide shafts, about 300 metres apart, are driven under the supervision of the surveyor. Then the rope with the marked length of each vertical shaft is handed over to the muqannī. He now begins work with his assistants by driving the conduit into the alluvial fan, starting at the mouth. At first the conduit is an open channel, but it soon becomes a tunnel. Another team sinks ventilation shafts ahead of the tunnellers, and labourers haul up the spoil to the surface through these shafts. The tunnel is about one metre wide by one and a half metres high, and work can proceed fast through reasonably firm soil, but in soft, friable soil the roof is unsafe, and hoops of baked clay, oval in shape, have to be used as reinforcement. Two oil lamps are kept burning on the floor of the conduit; sighting along these, the muqannī keeps the tunnel in alignment, and they also serve as a warning of poor air, since they go out before there is danger of a man suffocating. As the work nears the mother well great care has to be taken in case a muqannī misjudges the distance and strikes the full well, in which case he might be swept away by the sudden flow. Once qanats are in operation they must be well maintained and kept thoroughly clean, although the frequency of cleaning depends upon the type of soil through which the qanat has been excavated (see Figure 9.3).

Qanats have a long history. They were probably invented in Armenia in the eighth century BC and in the ancient world they were known in Achaemenid Iran, in Egypt and in Arabia. The medieval Muslim geographers made frequent references to qanats. They supplied much of the water in many cities and farming districts in Iran, including the provinces of Quhistan, Kirmān and Seistan, and the cities of Rayy

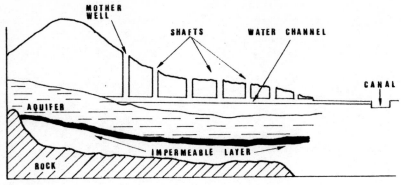

FIGURE 9.3 Qanat.

(near modern Tehran) and Nīshapūr in Khurāsān. In Nīshapūr the qanats were supervised by inspectors and guards. In North Africa the city of Tangier was supplied by several very long qanats. They were introduced to Spain by the Umayyads.

Estimates for the number of qanats in modern Iran vary between 30,000 and 50,000 with a total discharge of 600/700 cubic metres per second. The city of Tehran has thirty-six qanats, and many other towns in the country owe their existence to them. There are still some in use in North Africa and in south-east Arabia, where they are known as *aflāj* (sing. *falaj*). The qanat may therefore be considered as one of the most successful of man's inventions, since it has been in continuous use for over 2,500 years.

WATER-SUPPLY

Given the importance of irrigation in the agriculture of many parts of the Islamic world, it is perhaps inevitable that this aspect of hydraulic engineering has received more attention from historians than the supply of water for other purposes. Moreover, because the same carriers – rivers, canals and qanats – were often used, as mentioned earlier, for several purposes, there is a tendency for water-supply to be subsumed with irrigation. The supply of water for non-agricultural purposes was, however, an important feature in Islamic life. The availability of water is not taken for granted in many regions in the Islamic world, as it is in wetter climates. Arabs, especially desert dwellers, have discerning palates for the quality of water; a source of sweet water is a highly prized possession in any community. But water is not only important for domestic purposes. The great Islamic cities of the Middle Ages had numerous public baths; those in Baghdad were counted in the year 993

FIGURE 9.4 Islamic aqueduct bridge over Canal de Quart, Valencia.

and found to number 1,500. Every mosque had fountains or cisterns for ritual ablutions. Nor should we forget the aesthetic pleasure taken by Muslims in the creation of ornamental water-gardens. As we noted in Chapter 6, water power was used in a number of industrial applications, for instance in paper-making and in the fulling of cloth. In this case, however, special works were usually unnecessary, since the facilities were located on the banks of running streams.

Aqueducts were not built on the same scale by the Muslims as they were by the Romans. The topography of much of the Middle East militates against their construction. In alluvial plains, such as those of Iraq and Khuwārazm for example, there is no source of water other than the great rivers – Tigris, Euphrates and Oxus. In Spain, on the other hand, the Muslims sometimes used the Roman aqueducts which brought water considerable distances. Al-Idrīsī tells us, for instance, that a Roman aquaduct brought water to a large reservoir at the town of Almuñecar. The Muslims themselves built aqueducts in the peninsula, notably one bringing water from the Sierra Nevada to the wonderful gardens of the Alhambra and the Generalife at Granada. They also built a channel to bring water from the nearby sierra to the mosque in Cordoba. The Muslims constructed many short aqueduct bridges to carry the water raised by norias into the nearby towns and gardens. Such structures were built, for example, at Cordoba and Toledo, and at Ḥama in Syria. In general, however, above-ground masonry aqueducts were not a common method of water transport in the Islamic world.

The Muslim geographers, when describing a city, town or rural community, almost invariably tell us where the inhabitants' water supplies came from: springs, wells, canals, qanats or rivers. Naturally, wells were a common source in all kinds of locations. Many villages depended upon wells for both potable water and irrigation, but they were also very common inside towns, in private premises and in public buildings. Individual supplies from wells were often used for convenience even when the community was supplied with running water through artifical conduits. Even so, channelled supplies were usually necessary, especially for major urban centres.

We do not know how often conflicting interests of the various users were reconciled, but it was apparently not the case that the demands of irrigation were always paramount. On the contrary, the city was often upstream of the farmlands, and the demands of the former were met before the water flowed on to the latter. At Damascus in the tenth century the canal called Nahr Yazīd was taken from the river Barada and flowed through dwellings, streets and baths before reaching the Ghūta, the large oasis downstream from the city. Al-Muqaddasī spoke of the many beautiful fountains in the city, and two centuries later Ibn Jubayr said that Damascus had 100 baths and forty houses for ritual ablutions. Since domestic usage must have been substantial it seems that a large amount of water was utilised in the city before the channels reached the Ghūta. Of course, a good deal of this water must have found its way to the farmlands after it had been used for the first time in the city – it would still have been fit for irrigation. Similar supplies were to be found in other cities: for example, from open channels in Niṣibīn in northern Syria, Fez in Morocco, Elche in Spain, Zaranj in Seistan; from qanats in Rayy and Nīshāpūr. Samarqand seems to have been especially well supplied; in the tenth century there were said to have been 2,000 points for the dispensing of iced water.

It was a common practice for water that entered towns in canals or qanats to be collected in cisterns. Thus in the city of Zaranj in the tenth century the water was collected in two large cisterns. It discharged from these into small cisterns in people's dwellings. The use of cisterns, for both water-supply and irrigation, was highly developed in the Qayrawān region of Tunisia in the first four centuries of Islam. Fortunately, one of the most impressive of these installations exists intact. There are two large cisterns, dated to the year 863, about a kilometre from the north gate of Qayrawān. The smaller one receives the water of the Wadi Merj al-Līl when it is in flood, the rim of the basin being below the level of the bed of the wadi. This cistern, although it is practically circular, is really polygonal, being composed of seventeen straight sides averaging 6.25 metres. Each corner is strengthened, externally and internally, by a round buttress. This cistern is the basin of decantation, where the mud settles. One of its sides is in contact with the sides of a much larger basin, to which there is a channel of communication in the partition wall, several metres above the bottom. This larger cistern has forty-eight sides, with a rounded buttress at each corner internally and externally and, in addition, an intermediate buttress externally in the centre of each side. The total depth is about 8 metres. The interior diameter is just under 130 metres, of the lesser cistern 37.40 metres. The masonry is of rubble covered with a very hard coating of cement. These two cisterns have a truly monumental aspect. On the side opposite the smaller basin are two oblong covered cisterns into which the water passes from the great cistern by openings several metres from the bottom, being thus decanted for a second time (Creswell, *op. cit.*, 291).

The fact that hydraulic works often served several purposes should not make us believe that one of these purposes was necessarily more significant than another. Water supplies for the manifold needs of urban communities were often considered by the Muslims as important as the supply of irrigation water.

10

Surveying

For information about surveying in Islam we are dependent upon two valuable treatises, together with scattered references in works on geometry and the use of the astrolabe. The first of the two treatises is called *Inbāṭ al-miyāh al-khafiyya* (*The Search for Hidden Waters*, an edition of which was published at Hyderabad, Deccan, in 1945). It was written by a certain al-Karajī, a native of the town of al-Karaj in the Iranian province of Jibal (the Media of the Greeks). Little is known of his career; much of his life appears to have been spent in Baghdad, but eventually he returned to his native province, where he must have died after 1019, the probable date of his *Search for Hidden Waters*. This is an excellent manual on hydraulic engineering that includes, in addition to a chapter on levelling, a section dealing in a very practical way with the construction of qanats.

The second treatise was written by an unknown author in Iraq, probably in the second quarter of the eleventh century. It is entitled *Kitāb al-ḥāwī li l-aʿmāl al-sulṭāniyya wa rusūm al-diwāniyya* (*Book comprising public works and regulations for official accounting*). It includes a section dealing with commercial and fiscal problems and another concerned with irrigation. This latter has been published by Claude Cahen (see Bibliography). It is divided into three parts: a brief survey of water-raising machines, a longer section on levelling instruments and their use, and a series of problems concerned with the construction and maintenance of canals, dikes and embankments. The second section is obviously of interest to us, and the third section has some instructions on quantity surveying that are probably unique in Arabic writings.

Al-Bīrūnī and other scholars wrote works on the uses of the astrolabe that include instructions for its application to geodetic surveying. As mentioned in Chapter 2, one of the meanings of the words *misāḥa* is 'land surveying'. The Egyptian writer Ibn Mammātī (d. 1209) devotes the seventh treatise of his book *Qawānīn al-Dawānīn* (*Rules for government*, edited by A. S. Atiya, Cairo, 1943), to the measurement of land. Unfortunately however, as with other works of this nature, he tells us how to calculate areas once they have been measured but gives no details of the instruments and methods used in the surveys.

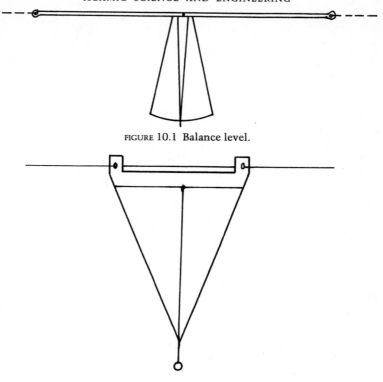

FIGURE 10.1 Balance level.

FIGURE 10.2 Triangle level.

LEVELLING

The levelling instruments described in the *Kitāb al-ḥāwī* had probably undergone little change since ancient times, and it seems likely that they were the standard equipment in a somewhat conservative profession. If we examine them first, we can then see how al-Karajī developed other instruments and techniques from these traditional origins.

The first instrument was known as the 'balance' (*mīzān*). This consisted of a rod about one and a half spans (36 cm) long, in the centre of which a pointer was suspended to a fulcrum, like the tongue of a balance. A fixed plate marked with a vertical centre-line was soldered to the centre of the rod, both of whose ends were formed into rings (Figure 10.1). The second was an isosceles triangle made of metal or wood, having suspension hooks in its short side. In the same side was a hole to which a plumb-line was attached; this hung below the apex of the triangle, where a plumb-bob was suspended (Figure 10.2). The third instrument was called the 'reed' (*qaṣaba*). As its name implies it was a long narrow tube, in the centre of which was a hole that penetrated into the bore.

For each of these instruments two levelling staffs were required. The *Kitāb al-ḥāwī* specifies that these were to be of equal length and were graduated into 'fists' – *qabḍa* – each of about 12 cm, subdivided into four 'fingers' each.

To level with the first instrument one took a cord about 15 cubits, i.e. 7.2 m long, and threaded it through the holes so that the balance was in the centre of the cord. One assistant – chainman – was ordered to take one end of the cord and one of the staffs to the start of the survey. A second chainman was sent along the line of the survey, taking the other end of the cord and the other levelling staff with him. The cord was stretched between the staffs, whose verticality was checked by means of plumb-lines. Usually the cord was held initially between the top of the graduations of the staffs, in which case the tongue would probably have been at an angle to the inscribed centre-line of the plate. The end of the cord was then gradually lowered to one of the staffs until the balance was brought to the horizontal. The difference in level between the two stations could then be obtained from the difference in the readings on the staffs. This figure was noted. At the end of the survey the algebraic sum of the rises and falls gave the total rise or fall along the line of the survey. Levelling with the second instrument was very similar; one brought the triangle to the horizontal by bringing the cord to coincide with the inverted apex.

To use the reed level, the end of the tube were held against the staffs which were of course held vertically. A third man, equipped with a jar of water and a rag of cotton or wool was stationed at the centre of the tube. Having soaked the rag with water he squeezed it into the central hole. If the water came out from both ends simultaneously with both ends of the tube held against the uppermost of the graduations then the ground was horizontal. If it issued from one end only, then the end from which it did not issue was lowered while the man at the centre continued to squeeze water into the hole, until the water issued at an equal rate from either end. As previously, the readings on the staffs were noted and the levelling continued to the end of the section to be surveyed.

Al-Karajī's description of levelling methods starts with the same three instruments. In the case of the first two, his methods are very similar to those appearing in the *Kitāb al-ḥāwī* except that he specifies a total distance of 30 cubits between the staffs, i.e. the sum of the lengths of the instruments and two separate lengths of cord was 30 cubits, or about 14.4 metres. The staffs were each 6 spans, or about 1.44 metres, long.

With regard to the tube, al-Karajī mentions the reed, but says that by his time it was obsolete. This indicates that the engineers of qanats

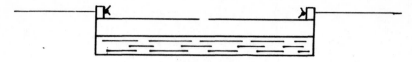

FIGURE 10.3 Water level.

(muqannī, see Chapter 9) were more advanced than the conservative engineers of the Iraqi governmental irrigation service. The reed was replace by a glass tube, only one and a half spans long. It had, like the reed, a hole in its centre and also holes in each end. The three holes were in alignment, and cords were attached to the two outer ones. As mentioned above, when the cords were held tautly against the staffs, the total distance between the staffs was thirty cubits. The procedure was then the same as for the reed. As an alternative to the tube a water-level was used. This consisted of a short glass cylinder with one hole at the centre and having handles at either end to which the cords were attached. Before levelling began the cylinder was filled to half its capacity with water; straight horizontal marks were inscribed longitu-dinally along the cylinder at at the half-way positions (Figure 10.3). During levelling, therefore, all that was necessary was to bring the marks in line with the surface of the water. The instrument was clearly very similar to a modern spirit level.

The traditional methods discussed so far were probably perfectly adequate for hydraulic surveys; but they must have been rather slow and tedious, not to mention their expensive use of labour. The use of the reed required three chainmen in addition to the surveyor, while the other two needed two chainmen. Also, having fixed distances for each pair of sights would have made things very difficult in broken terrain. To obviate these problems al-Karajī invented some new instru-ments and methods, some of which bring us very close to modern methods of levelling.

One of his innovations concerned the graduation of the levelling staffs. He specified that these be divided sexagesimally, and that if possible the subdivisions be subdivided sexagesimally also. The idea of sexagesimal divisions is very interesting; the staffs were thirty cubits, i.e. sixty spans apart, and the sexagesimal division of the staffs would have facilitated calculations.

The first of the new instruments was a variant of the traditional balance arm. A plate of wood or brass was constructed in the form of a long rectangle with two suspension lugs on one of its short sides. Near the top of the plate, midway between the two lugs, a hole was drilled into which a plumb-line could be inserted. The plate was divided longitudinally by a line inscribed on its centre-line, so that when the

190

plate was horizontal the plumb-line coincided with the inscribed line. For this device the cord was replaced by a chain of brass or iron. This was 60 spans long, consisting of 60 links of 1 span each; it terminated in a ring at each end. Until recently, for linear measurements on the ground, the 66' long Gunters chain was widely used in English-speaking countries. The reason for the choice of length was that 10 square chains = 1 acre. There is therefore a close corollary between this system and al-Karajī's sexagesimal division. Both were intended to facilitate calculations.

To calibrate the plate a horizontal area was selected, upon which two points were marked one chain-length apart. The staffs were graduated into sixty equal parts; each was held vertically at one of the marks by a chainman. The chain was held between the upper ends of the graduations of the staffs, and the plate was suspended to its centre. A plumb-line, extending below the plate, was tied to the hole already made in its centre. One of the chainmen then moved his end of the chain one division down the staff. Of necessity, each movement of the end of the chain down the staff meant that the staff had to be moved a short distance nearer to the other staff. The movement of one division caused a displacement in the plumb-line, and a mark was inscribed at its new position The end of the chain was moved down division by division and the corresponding marks were inscribed on the plate – all these marks were, of course, on one side of the centre-line. A similar procedure was now followed with the other staff, producing marks on the other side of the centre-line. The graduation of the plate along a straight line produced unequal divisions corresponding to equal divisions of the staffs. The author therefore recommended that the plate be graduated on a circular arc, so producing equal divisions.

During levelling the surveyor directed the chainmen to hold the chain at the top of the graduations. At each station he simply recorded the reading against the plumb-line on one side or the other of the centre-line of the plate. The algebraic sum of the readings gave the rise or fall over the complete line of the survey. The author comments that the graduation of both staffs and plate had to be done with great care and accuracy. With this proviso, this method would certainly have speeded up the survey, as opposed to bringing a chain or cord level by moving one of its ends each time up or down a staff.

The next instrument brings us closer to modern methods of levelling. It was a square or circular plate made of wood or brass and perfectly flat. In fact the illustrations show a circular plate and this was probably the usual shape. (See Figure 10.4.) A fine hole was made in its centre. Then one made a perfectly straight copper tube, one and

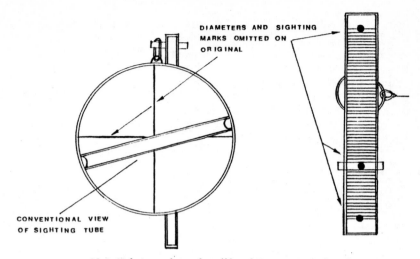

DIAMETERS AND SIGHTING
MARKS OMITTED ON
ORIGINAL

CONVENTIONAL VIEW
OF SIGHTING TUBE

FIGURE 10.4 Sighting tube and staff by al-Karajī. Note that the
divisions of the staff are conventional and do not correspond to the
divisions stipulated in the text.

a half spans long with a very narrow bore; it was slightly longer than
the diameter of the plate. In its centre was a spigot that fitted into the
hole at the centre of the plate, so that the tube turned freely. It was,
says the author, similar to the alidade of an astrolabe. Two diameters
at right angles were inscribed on the plate; at the end of one of them
was a staple into which a ring was fitted.

A wooden 'gallows' was then made for suspending the level. The
gallows was perfectly straight and about four spans long, just long
enough for the surveyor to be able to look through the sighting-tube,
squatting on his heels, when the level was suspended to the gallows.
The author makes it clear, in fact, that the apparatus was to be
constructed to suit the measurements of the surveyor.

Now a single level staff was made. This was a piece of wood about 9
spans (2.16 metres) long, absolutely straight and smooth and of
uniform rectangular cross-section. At either end a distance of one
gabḍa (12 cm) was left blank. The remainder of the staff was divided
into 60 divisions, each division being subdivided into as many
subdivisions as possible. The last line at the top and bottom of the
graduations had a red circle about 2.5 cm (one inch) painted in its
centre. Now one made a copper cursor to slide along the staff as a
sighting mark; its centre was also marked with a red circle. Presumably, although the text does not say so, marks on the sides of the cursor
would have indicated the position of the centre of its circle in the

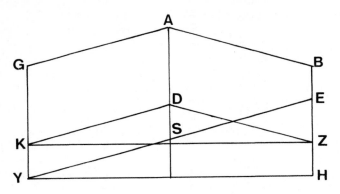

Figure 10.5 Geometry for Figure 10.4.

graduations of the staff.

Next one took a cord of silk or linen, well twisted and of a maximum length of 100 cubits or about 50 metres, since at this distance a person of normal vision could distinguish the marks on the staff. A ring was fixed to each end of the cord. One of them was permanently attached to a staple at the side of the graduated staff and the other was held by the surveyor.

Now it must be admitted that the instructions for the use of the level, staff and cord are somewhat confused. The basis of the system may be briefly described, however, with reference to Figure 10.5. Let us assume that at the start of the levelling the surveyor was above the level of the foot of the staff. Holding the ring he drew the cord tight and held it so that it was in his estimation more or less horizontal. He dropped a pebble and where it struck the ground he placed the foot of the gallows, at point E. The staff was held vertically, its length being represented by the line AS. The centre of the sighting-tube is represented by point B. The surveyor then sighted the circle at the top A of the graduations. The angle of the tube was recorded, and the surveyor then moved to the lower side of the staff, which was held in the same position. The cord was again held horizontally, a pebble was dropped and the gallows was placed where it struck the ground at point Y, K being the centre of the tube. The staff was sighted through the tube, at the same angle as had been used in the first sighting. The chainman moved the cursor along the staff until the surveyor signalled to him that its circle was in the centre of the tube, at D. Now it is quite easy to prove that the difference in level between the two stations, i.e. EH, is the same as the distance AD on the level staff.

The method described next is that used in modern levelling, except of course that there was no telescopic or electronic equipment. The sighting-tube, plate level and gallows were exactly as described in the previous section. The graduated staff had a single round mark painted on it at exactly the same distance from the ground as the centre of the plate suspended to the gallows. To carry out the levelling the sighting-tube was brought to the horizontal along one of the diameters of the plate, and the staff was viewed through it from as great a distance as possible. (It would have facilitated the operation to have provided the level with a wind-shield, so that it oscillated as little as possible.) If the circle on the staff coincided with the line of site then the distance from the ground was the same in both cases. If the point visible in the sighting-tube was a certain distance above the painted circle, then this was a measure of the vertical distance of the foot of the gallows above the foot of the staff. The reverse applied when the line of sight met the staff below the painted circle. In modern terms this is the 'line of collimation, or 'height of instrument' method of levelling. There is no essential difference between this and the 'rise and fall' method. Both involve the meticulous recording of all the figures taken along the line of the survey, then at the end taking the algebraic sum of the figures to determine the total rise or fall from start to finish. The author says that the method is preferable to the previous one because there is no need of chain or rod, and because the surveyor himself can choose the most convenient distance for sighting. If the line of sight was above or below the staff, then for a foresight the chainman moved closer to the surveyor, for a backsight vice versa. The section ends with a paragraph enjoining the utmost accuracy in constructing and graduating the instruments, in carrying out the levelling and in making the calculations. Nothing is said, however, about 'checking back', i.e. levelling back to the original start point to verify that there is no discrepancy. This is one of the simplest and most trustworthy methods of checking the accuracy of levelling.

Yet another method of levelling is suggested for the same instrument. We revert to the use of a chain 100 cubits in length. The staff is ten spans long. The plate is square, having a large circle in its centre left blank, apart from two diameters at right angles. There is a pointer on the end of the sighting-tube – probably a long triangle of thin metal fixed below the tube. The staff was divided sexagesimally. For the purposes of graduation a level piece of ground was chosen where the feet of the gallows and the staff could be placed at the same level, one chain-length apart. As before, a mark was made on the staff at the level of the centre of the sighting-tube. The tube was sighted on to the first mark at the top of the staff and a mark was made on the plate at the

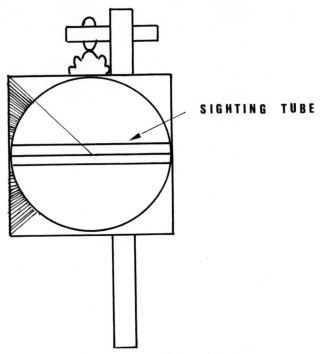

SIGHTING TUBE

FIGURE 10.6 Sighting tube.

position of the pointer. The procedure was repeated for all the divisions on the level staff. The author points out that because the gallows is shorter than half the length of the level staff, there will be fewer divisions below the centre of the plate than above it; this is correct, although it is incorrectly illustrated on the drawing taken from the text. After all the marks had been made the sighting-tube was removed, a ruler was laid from the centre of the circle to the first mark and a line was inscribed along this radius from the circumference of the circle to the edge of the plate. 'No 1' was marked on this line. Lines were inscribed for each of the marks on the plate corresponding to each of the divisions on the level staff. (See Figure 10.6.)

The method of levelling with this equipment was as follows: the gallows with the plate suspended to it was set up vertically and the staff was held vertically one chain-length distant. The tube was then sighted on to the red circle on the staff. If the division on the plate was then below the horizontal this showed the amount by which the foot of the gallows was above the foot of the staff. (Figure 10.7 shows the

195

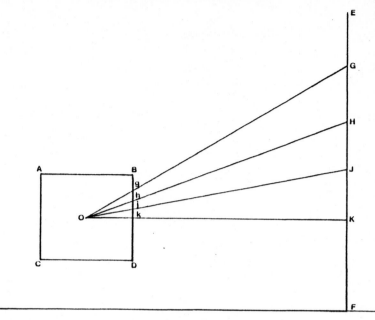

FIGURE 10.7 Geometry for Figure 10.6.

principle, using just four sightings; triangles OGK and Ogk, OHK and Ohk, etc. were similar.) The number of the division with which the pointer coincided was written down; this was a direct measure of the difference in level between the two points. If the pointer was above the horizontal the gallows was of course lower than the staff. Again, an algebraic sum of the readings gave the total rise or fall over the complete distance levelled.

To appreciate why this method should have been used when the previous method is so much more direct we must remember that without a telescope the surveyor probably could not read the number of the divisions of the staff. In the previous method the sighting-tube was horizontal and the chainman moved the cursor until the surveyor signalled that the circle on the cursor was in his line of sight. At this juncture either the chainman was relied upon to read the number of the graduation and call it out to the surveyor, or the surveyor had to walk to the staff each time, relying upon the chainman to keep the cursor still until he had taken the reading. In the other method the surveyor could read the graduation direct on his instrument.

The methods of levelling described by al-Karajī were applied, among other thing, to levelling along the route of a qanat, as described in the

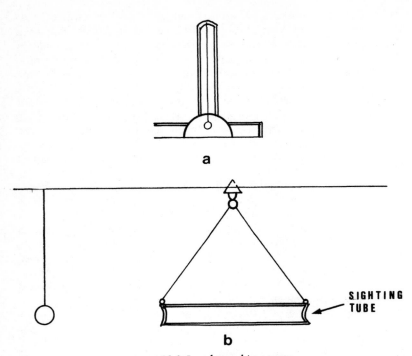

a

b

FIGURE 10.8 Levels used in qanats.

previous chapter. Additionally, some method of maintaining line and level within the tunnel, as work proceeds, is necessary. Two instruments are described by al-Karajī. The first is a simple level consisting of a square piece of timber about 3 cubits long and 4 fingers, i.e. about 8 cm. square. In the centre a piece of timber of the same cross-section, about 1 cubit long, is jointed at right angles to the first. When in use the long member is laid on the floor of the conduit while the short one is vertical. In its centre is a hole to which a plumb-line is attached, and a vertical centre-line is inscribed down the face of the upright member. As excavation progresses the level of the floor is frequently checked by ensuring that the plumb-line and the inscribed line coincide (Figure 10.8.a).

The second instrument is a sighting-tube made of brass, about 1½ spans long and with an inside diameter of about 1½ cm. At each end there is a ring to which a light iron chain is attached. The two chains are brought together in a ring which is stapled to a wooden wedge. Before being used the tube was checked for straightness and circularity. About 1½ cubits of the conduit were excavated and the wedge to which the tube was attached was hammered into the centre of the roof.

At the entry to the conduit a ball was suspended centrally by a cord, at the same level as the bore of the tube, which was of course horizontal. As excavation continued the conduit was kept in alignment and level by sighting on to the ball and then in the forward direction, the tube also being moved along the roof of the conduit from time to time (Figure 10.8.b). It should be mentioned that the correct line to the next ventilation shaft was first marked on the surface by running a cord across the centre of the shaft already excavated to the centre of the well to be excavated. This line was transferred from the surface to the conduit by dropping two cords from the upper cord down the existing shaft. If the correct line and level were then maintained in the horizontal gallery, this would meet the next shaft accurately.

Despite the directions given by al-Karajī it would not have been possible, from these instructions alone, for an inexperienced man to have excavated a qanat. Although the use of the various instruments for levelling on the surface could easily have been carried out, after a certain amount of instruction, an an intelligent trainee, the underground work was a different matter. The tunnelling techniques could only be learned from long apprenticeship under masters of the profession. In fact the excavation of qanats was, and remains, a skill handed down from father to son.

TRIANGULATION

Triangulation methods were in common use by the Muslims, for determining the heights and depths of objects and the widths of obstacles such as wide rivers that could not be measured directly. The usual instrument for carrying out these observations was the back of the astrolabe. It was mentioned in Chapter 3 that the squares on the back of the instrument were known as 'shadow squares', since they simulated the gnomon and its shadow, i.e. the tangent function of an angle. One square was usually divided into tenths, the other into twelfths, the subdivisions being known as 'fingers'. It was immaterial which square was used, since it was the angular relationships that mattered. When the alidade was sighted on a tall object – a tower for example – the sides of the triangle formed by the object and its horizontal distance from the observer were duplicated on the shadow square. If the horizontal distance 1 were known and the 'tenths' square, say, was being used, all that was necessary was to read off the number of 'fingers' on the scale, where it was cut by the alidade. If this number were n then the height h of the object is given by

$$h = \frac{1.n}{10} \quad (1)$$

plus the height of the observer's eye.

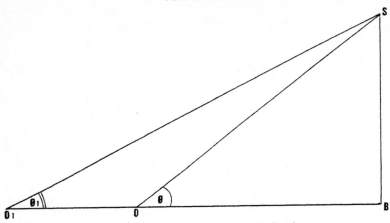

FIGURE 10.9 Geometry for measuring heights.

From Figure 10.9 we can express the relationships in modern terminology. If BS is the object to be measured and OB is known, then BS =
OB tan φ (2), which is identical with (1). If OB is not known, angle φ is
first measured, the theodolite is moved back from O to O_1, and the
angle φ, to the top of the object is measured. Then:

$$BS = \frac{OO_1.\ \sin \phi.\ \sin \phi_1}{\sin (\phi - \phi_1)}$$

Although Muslim astronomers and mathematicians were perfectly
capable of making calculations of this nature, it was more practical for
surveyors in the field to be provided with constructive methods for
using the shadow squares, obviating the need for calculations and the
use of tables of trigonometric functions. The best way of illustrating
these methods is to take some examples from a work of al-Bīrūnī.
Although the work is concerned mainly with astrology, the section
from which these examples are taken was clearly meant for the use of
surveyors. The text and illustrations are taken directly from a manuscript of the treatise (see Bibliography).

Width of a river or piece of ground
To find the breadth of a river or a piece of ground the other extremity of
of which it is impossible to reach so as to measure it in the usual way,
stand on the bank, hang the astrolabe on the right hand and move the
rule till you sight the other bank; then turn around without changing
your position and without altering the rule look through both sights
for a mark which you can recognise and measure the distance between

199

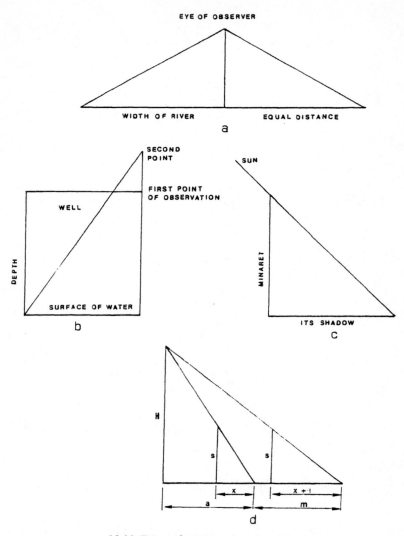

FIGURE 10.10 Triangulation methods by al-Bīrūnī.

your position and the mark. The breadth of the river is the same. The same method can be used for a piece of land (Figure 10.10.a).

Depth of well

To find the depth of a well, stand on the margin with the astrolabe in the left hand, the quadrant of altitude towards you, and move the rule till the opposite margin of the water or the bottom is seen through both sights. Then note the number of fingers in the quadrant of shadow to which the rule points, place its tip at one finger less, and go straight up higher until the opposite margin is again sighted without disturbing the position of the rule. Measure the distance between the two points of observation and multiply by the number of fingers of shadow noted. The result is the depth of the well, while that distance multiplied by twelve (or ten if the other square is used) gives the diameter of the well (Figure 10.10.b).

Height of minaret the base of which can be reached

To find the height of a minaret or wall the base of which it is possible to reach, take the altitude of the sun and continue observation till it attains 45°, then measure the shadow, this gives the height of the minaret. If the sun does not reach 45° at the desired time, place the point of the rule at 45° and move forwards or backwards till you find a point where the top of the minaret is sighted, then measure from that point to the base of the minaret and add your own height; the result is the height of the minaret (Figure 10. 10.c).

Height of minaret the base of which is inaccessible

To find the height of a minaret, column or mountain the base of which it is impossible to reach, stand where you are and move the rule until you see the top of the object through both sights just as you take the altitude of a star, then note the number of fingers in the quadrant of shadow to which it points and move forwards or backwards, according as the ground is most level; if forward, place the rule-point at one finger less, if backward at one finger more, and walk until the top is again visible through both sights. The distance between the two points of observation multiplied by twelve (or ten) is the height of the mountain, while the same distance multiplied by the number of fingers of shadow observed at the first point of observation gives the distance between that point and the base of the object. Similarly the height of any object in the air, such as a bird or a cloud which is so stationary as to allow of the altitude being taken from two different points, can be determined by the same method, as well as the distance between you and a perpendicular dropped to the ground from the object. In Figure 10.10.d, H is the height of the object, a is its distance from the observer's first position, s (=12) the side of the shadow square, m the distance moved backwards, x the first reading, x + 1 the second.

201

Then: H: a = s:x and H:a + m = S:(x + 1). Whence H = ms and a = mx. For the sake of clarity, s and x are exaggerated by comparison with the other dimensions.

It is evident that, although these examples show that the methods were based upon trigonometry, they were so designed as to make it unnecessary for the surveyors to have recourse to trigonometrical calculations. All they were required to do was to take sightings through the alidade of the astrolabe, make measurements of lengths and do some straightforward arithmetical calculations.

The measurement of land, mainly for taxation purposes, was clearly an important function for land surveyors in the Islamic world. Unfortunately, there is no known treatise which gives details of the methods of measuring and recording land surveys. The chain used by al-Karajī, consisting of sixty links, each one span long, terminating in a ring at each end, is very similar to the Gunter's chain familiar to (older) British engineers and surveyors. It seems highly likely that such measures were widely used by land surveyors, and that chain surveys were carried out in exactly the same way as in modern times. This kind of survey is a perfectly satisfactory method, particularly in flat lands such as Egypt, where no allowance need be made for gradients. Ibn Mammātī's chapter on *misāḥa* in Egypt contains some interesting remarks on how farmers were overcharged for land taxes because of the use of deliberately faulty formulae in calculating areas. His own calculations for areas of various shapes are accurate enough, but they could just as well have appeared in a work on plane geometry as in a treatise on surveying.

QUANTITY SURVEYING

The second 'Abbāsid Caliph, al-Manṣūr (ruled 754–75), having put down three serious challenges to his authority, was free to consolidate his rule in comparative peace. His most lasting achievement was the building of the new capital of Baghdad, the famous 'Round City', upon which work began in 762. Al-Manṣūr was noted for his hard work and almost proverbial meanness – he was known by the nickname Abu'l-Dawāniq, 'Father of the farthings' (presumably not to his face). When the city was being built he seems to have exercised an overall control of the work through teams of three, each responsible for one quarter of the city. One of these teams consisted of al-Musayib b. Zuhayr as leader, Rabī', a client of al-Manṣūr, and the architect 'Imrān b. Waḍḍāḥ. In addition to one quarter of the city, this group was also responsible for the construction of the Caliph's palace.

One day, apparently, al-Manṣūr was inspecting the work done up till that time on his palace. He thought that the quality was very good but that the cost was too high. He sent for al-Musayib and told him to instruct his chief builder to select a good master builder. He then told al-Musayib to agree a daily rate with the builder, which he then reduced by 20 per cent. (The rate was for a gang, not a single workman.) Manṣūr then instructed the builder to build an arcade of burnt bricks and plaster. This took just over one day, during which period Manṣūr checked the quantities of material used in the construction. He therefore had all that he required to work out the unit cost for this type of building: time, quantities, money and labour. These rates could then be applied to all future work and indeed to work already carried out, since al-Musayib had to disgorge some 6,000 dirhams that he had been overpaid. The new rates were then agreed not only with al-Musayib but also with the agents of the subcontractors. They were also agreed with the representatives of the builders and architects. Incidentally, this kind of strict budgeting rather spoils the stories of lavish expenditure in the *Thousand and one Nights* and its imitators. But interesting as this anecdote is, the administration of construction work in the public works departments in the Islamic world cannot usually have depended upon the personal interventions of rulers.

The *Kitāb al-ḥāwī* makes it clear that administration of the irrigation department in eleventh-century Iraq was closely controlled and regulated. In particular, in the final section of the treatise, considerable attention was paid to quantity surveying, setting out the methods to be used for the measurement, calculation and payments for all the excavation of canals. The section begins with definitions of the units to be used in measurements and calculations. The bulk unit of measurement was called the *azala*. This consisted of 100 cubic 'cubits of the balance', each of which was the height of a man up to the tip of his nose. This was about 1.44 metres, giving three cubic metres for one cubic cubit of this type and 300 cubic metres for an *azala*. We are then given the productivity of one excavator. These men, who are called 'spades' in the treatise, would nowadays be classified as 'navvies'. This is a precise definition that applies to a certain type of semi-skilled worker, not only having the muscular strength to keep up a steady rate of work, but also able to follow the lines and levels set out by the surveyors.

Several different rates are given for the productivity of a navvy but the most usual figure seems to have been three cubic cubits of the Balance daily, or about nine cubic metres, for each navvy. Obviously, this productivity would have depended upon the ground conditions, but this variable is not mentioned, so we must assume a fairly uniform type of soil. The figure of nine cubic metres seems high but not excessively so. In a later passage the author mentions sand as if it were the normal type of soil, so we may use the modern figure of 1.25 metres a manhour for excavation in sand. This would mean the navvies doing 7.2 hours of steady work in a day. The actual labour rates are unimportant provided quantities, labour and costs all tally, but it is useful to know that the author of *Kitāb al-ḥāwī* was using feasible quantities. (I am indebted to Col. Gerald Napier, of the Royal Engineers Museum, Chatham, for making available to me data about productivities.)

Each navvy was allocated a number of 'carriers', from one to seven, depending upon the distance for the spoil to be carried. About ten metres on the level was the limit for one carrier, less if there was a gradient. The spoil was carried in baskets, each basket containing about $5^1/_2$ kg of earth. The same method of transport, for concrete as well as for earth, was used in Syria in 1950s, but in this case the containers were flat rubber buckets; they were carried on the head. The ratio of carriers to navvies was for the purposes of calculation, and does not imply that each navvy was personally allocated one or more carriers by name. All the workers would have been organised into gangs, the navvies excavating the spoil into baskets, while the carriers circulated, carrying full baskets to the destination then returning with the empty baskets which they set down near the navvies before picking up full baskets to repeat the process. And so on.

The calculation for the quantity of soil to be excavated was of course very simple; one multiplied the breadth by the length and the depth. If the cross-section was trapezoidal one took the sum of the upper and lower breadths and divided by two. Somewhat different calculations, with different units, were required for embankments, when these were strengthened by bundles of reeds, which was usually the case. Measurements were made in 'black' cubits, which were half as long as the 'balance' cubits. As before, one worked out the volume, in this case taking the height of the embankment as the length of a bundle of reeds – one and a half black cubits.

If the volume is V, then for an embankment made entirely of reeds, the number of bundles, each of circumference c, is given by:

$$\text{Number of bundles} = V \div \frac{c^2}{4\pi}$$

One therefore multiplied the calculated volume V by 4π ($12^4/_7$ taking π as $^{22}/_7$) and divided by the square of the circumference. Since the circumference was 2 cubits, this merely meant multiplying the volume by π to give the number of bundles N. The ratio by volume of reeds to earth in an embankment was usually 1:1, so one then divided N by 2. The example given is: an embankment 50 cubits long, 20 wide and $1^1/_2$ high, giving a volume of 1500. This was multiplied by $12^4/_7$ giving 18,857 $^1/_7$, divided by the square of the circumference (4), giving 4714 $^2/_7$. Half of this is 2357 $^1/_7$, which is the number of reed bundles. The volume of earth is slightly over 750 cubic cubits.

One could, of course, simply multiply the volume directly by π, instead of by 4π then dividing by 4. This would, however, have been completely against the declared intentions of the author of *Kitāb al-ḥāwī*. In a revealing passage he tells us that the surveyor must be able to apply general formulae, not just know how to deal with particular instances. On another job, for example, the circumference of the revetment bundles might have been other than two, and one would have had to apply the general formula. There are many examples of calculations given in the section on quantities. The arithmetic is straightforward, but after this kind of instruction the trainee surveyor would have been able to cope with any measurements and calculations he would be likely to encounter in irrigation projects.

To calculate the cost of a project one first of all totalled the numbers of navvies and carriers needed to carry out the work of excavation and earth movement. These numbers were then multiplied by the daily rates to give the labour cost. The wages of foremen and their assistants were also included. To this figure, if the engineer was satisfied with the work, he could add a further 5 per cent. The bundles of reeds were paid for by number – it is not clear whether this was a separate subcontract or part of the excavation contract. The engineer (i.e. the Department's Resident Engineer) was entitled to $^1/_{40}$th of the total cost of the project.

This in outline was the system for measuring, calculating, costing and controlling projects in the irrigation department in eleventh-century Iraq. The text is corrupt in places and there are lacunae and some inconsistencies. Nevertheless it is quite clear that there was a system in being which used Bills of Quantities in much the same way as in modern civil engineering practice, and that the Bills of Quantities were the means by which valuations were made and accounts settled.

11

Mining

Information on Islamic mines occurs in geographical works, in books on mineralology, in alchemical treatises and in various other sources. Obviously, mining was an important activity in Islam, as it is in any civilisation. It will be possible to mention here only some of the more important minerals and mining centres.

Gold mines were found in western Arabia, Egypt, Africa and in some eastern Islamic lands. One of the most important of the gold mining areas was at Wādī al-'Allākī, which is a right-bank tributary of the upper Nile. It lay in the Buja country between Ethiopia and Nubia. The mines were in a desert area between the Nile and the Red Sea. The nearest towns were Aswān on the Nile and 'Aydhāb on the Red Sea. A second major gold mining area was called by al-Bīrūnī the Maghrib Sudan. This is the area south of the Sahara in Senegal and on the Upper Niger in Mali. According to al-Idrīsī, Wangāra was the most important gold mining centre on the Upper Niger. Salt, cloth and other commodities were exchanged for gold. Silver was either mined individually or in association with lead ores; the major silver mines were in the eastern Islamic provinces. Prominent among these were the mines of the Hindu Kush in the towns of Panjīr and Jāriyāna, both in the neighbourhood of Balkh. According to one report there were about 10,000 miners working at Panjīr. Other important silver mines were in Spain, North Africa, Iran and Central Asia.

Lead was obtained mostly from galena (lead sulphide), which was of very common occurrence. This lead ore is often associated with small amounts of silver. Only two other lead ores have any commercial value. One is cerussite (lead carbonate) and the other, which is of minor importance, is anglesite (lead sulphate). Lead ores, especially galena, were exploited in Spain, Sicily, North Africa, Egypt, Iran, Upper Mesopotamia and Asia Minor.

Copper ore deposits were exploited in various areas, including the important mines of Spain in the west and several in the east, such as those in Seistan, Kirmān, Marv, Farghāna, Bukhārā, Ṭūs and Harāt. The copper mines in Cyprus were always an important source.

The word calamine or tutia (Arabic *tūtiya*) was used to denote the natural zinc ores (especially zinc carbonate), or the white zinc oxide which was obtained during treatment of the ores. The major mines for

206

tutia were in the province of Kirmān in Iran. Tutia was also available in various mining areas in Spain.

Tin came from the Malaysian peninsula, which was known as Kala, hence the Arabic word *gal'ī* for the metal.

Iron ores were distributed throughout the Islamic world. There were five major iron mining areas in Spain. These included the mines near Toledo, and near Murcia. In North Africa, about ten mining areas were exploited in Morocco, Algeria and Tunisia. These included mines in Jabal al-Ḥadīd in the Atlas mountains, the Rīf, Gawr al-Ḥadīd in Algeria and Majjanat al-Ma'dan in Tunisia. Iron ores were produced and exported from Sicily. Egypt exploited those ores that were available, for example in Nubia and on the Red Sea coast. Syria was famous for its iron and steel metallurgy; iron ores were obtained in the south and in the mountain ranges between Damascus and Bayrūt. The Islamic countries in the east were better endowed with iron ores than Egypt, Syria and Iraq. The province of Fars had at least four important iron mining centres. There were also iron mines in Khurāsān, Ādharbayjān, Transoxiana and Armenia.

Mercury came chiefly from Spain. Al-Idrīsī mentions the mine to the north of Cordoba, where more than one thousand men worked in the various stages of mining the ores and extracting the mercury. Another source was Farghāna in Transoxiana.

Salt was produced in numerous localities. It was, of course, an essential commodity, and production was undertaken in some areas on a very large scale for export purposes, for example in North Africa, where the salt mines were on the desert edges in the south. Salt was carried by caravans south of the Sahara to be exchanged for gold. Thousands of men and camels were engaged in these operations. Other important salt mines or production centres were in Khurāsān, Arabia and Armenia.

The alum of Yemen was famous for its quality but according to al-Idrīsī the major source was in Chad. It was exported to Egypt and all the countries of North Africa. Among the many other minerals that were known and utilised was asbestos from Badakhshān, from which wicks and fire-resistant cloths were made. Coal was also known and utilised in some areas such as Farhāna, where it was mined and sold. It was used as a fuel for ovens and its ashes were used as a cleansing agent. The exploitation of petroleum deposits was mentioned in Chapter 5.

Precious stones of various kinds were mined. There are several Arabic lapidary works, of which the most famous is al-Bīrūnī's *Kitāb al-Jamāhir* (edited by F. Krenkow, Hyderabad, Deccan, 1936). Rubies were mined in Badakhshān and were also imported into the Middle

East from Sri Lanka. Diamonds came from the Indian sub-continent, agate and onyx from Yemen, emeralds and lapis lazuli from Egypt and turquoise from Nīshāpūr. Corundum came from Nubia and from Sri Lanka. Crystal was mined in Arabia and in Badakhshān. Diving for pearls was a flourishing industry and corals were obtained from the coasts of North Africa and Sicily.

In the period of the Umayyad and 'Abbāsid Caliphs, the output of the mines in their dominions was apparently sufficient to meet the demands for some of the most important metals. In later periods when the empire was fragmented into various kingdoms, one often warring with another, many of the Islamic countries needed one or several of the metals and had to import them from non-Islamic regions. This was due to the fact that the metalliferous ores were distributed over the Islamic countries very unevenly, as we have already seen. Some of them had rich deposits of several metals, others almost none. Certain regions on the fringes of the Islamic world were relatively rich in metals, notably Central Asia and Fars in the East and Spain in the West. In Spain there were mines of gold, silver, lead and iron in every district. It seems that mining, which had somehow declined in the Visigothic period, was revived and flourished under the Spanish Umayyads.

In the times of the Caliphs the output of gold in the Islamic countries was insufficient for the regular coinage of gold *dīnārs*, especially after Spain had become detached from the 'Abbāsid Empire. This is clearly borne out by the slow spread of gold coinage in the eastern provinces of the caliphal empire. In fact, the Islamic countries were always dependent upon the supply of gold from the areas which now form Senegal and Mali. On the other hand, there were in the caliphal empire rich silver or argentiferous lead mines which made it possible regularly to strike silver *dirhams*. Most of these were in the extensive province of Khurāsān the most renowned being, as we have seen, those of Panjīr. Spain, too, was rich in argentiferous ores.

The Arabic authors of the early medieval period leave no doubt that the copper production of the empire was not sufficient for the manifold uses of the metal. For copper was needed for the striking of locally-circulating small coins (*fulūs*), the roofing of mosques, the covering of gates of towns and public buildings, but above all for the thriving industry of fabricated copper utensils, e.g. kettles, receptacles and various other vessels. Copper was also needed to combine with tin and zinc to form the alloys bronze and brass respectively. So from early times, copper had to be imported from Europe. In the period preceding the Crusades, apparently great quantities of copper were imported from the Urals.

Metalliferous ores which contained lead and tin were not altogether lacking in the caliphal empire, but the demand for lead in particular was very great. It was used for the lining of aqueducts, for the installation of public and private baths and for the roofing of public buildings. It is doubtful whether the production was sufficient, and whether additional quantities had not therefore to be imported from non-Islamic regions. This was certainly the case so far as tin was concerned. The metal was produced in Spain and exported to the Islamic East, but even as early as the tenth century tin had to be imported from Devon and Cornwall in Britain, and from Malaysia.

Iron deposits were insignificant in the near East, but sufficient quantities could be procured from other provinces of the caliphal empire, and from neighbouring countries which were tributary to the Caliphs and their successors or otherwise dependent upon them. Of the other metals the ores of zinc came from the Iranian province of Kirmān and from Spain; and mercury, likewise, came from the fringes of the Islamic world, from Spain and Transoxiana.

When the empire of the Caliphs crumbled, the unevenness of the distribution of metal deposits resulted, of course, in some countries suffering a temporary or permanent lack of important raw materials. Although the countries which had belonged to the empire remained to a great extent an economic unity, exchanging their products and keeping their economic structures, the stopping of the supply of metals which served as raw materials for manufactured goods, and bullion for the mints, was used as a weapon in political struggles. Medieval statesmen were of course aware that cutting off the gold supply to the enemy meant weakening his financial resources, and that curbing his supply of iron dealt a blow to the production of arms.

Already in the second half of the tenth century, the supply of the mints of Iraq with bullion for the coinage of gold dinars was deficient, as the mines in the provinces which had remained under the sway of the ʿAbbāsid Caliphs, or were accessible to them, were poor. The dinars of the later Buwayhids of Iraq and south-western Iran were of bad alloy. Even the mines of Wādī al-ʿAllāki yielded in that period insignificant quantities of gold, so that in the Ayyubid and Mamluk periods Egypt was wholly dependent on the supply from West Africa.

Even the supply of the Islamic countries was in the later Middle Ages very irregular. In the eleventh and twelfth centuries there was everywhere a silver famine, so that the striking of silver dirhams had to be discontinued. There are several possible reasons for this phenomenon. Among the hypotheses based upon economic factors are the suggestion that the influx to Afghanistan and Iran of great quantities of gold from the Indian subcontinent, due to the campaigns of Maḥmūd of Ghazna, led to a corresponding export of silver to the newly-conquered provinces. According to another theory, the purchase of commodities by Muslim merchants in Russia resulted in the export of much silver coinage to Russia, where it was hoarded. It is possible, however, that the silver famine was due, at least in part, to the technological shortcomings of medieval mining. Indeed, al-Idrīsī mentions the fact that work on the 'Silver Mountain' between Harāt and Sarakhs had to stop because of technical faults and the lack of wood for smelting the ores.

Whatever the reasons for the shortages of silver, by the beginning of the thirteenth century silver coinage revived in Iraq, Syria and Egypt. This appears to have been made possible by Central Asian silver being brought in by the Mongol conquerors. In the first half of the thirteenth century great amounts of silver were available and it was consequently cheap. The bullion was supplied by mines in the Middle East and Central Asia. In the later Middle Ages, however, the mints and silversmiths of Egypt and Syria were supplied with silver from both Central Asia and Europe. Modern chemical analysis of Egyptian coins has shown that the bullion used by the Mamlūks for striking silver dirhams came from both those regions.

In the medieval period the Turkish and Iranian countries had abundant supplies of copper. In these countries and in some neighbouring ones, there were mines with copious supplies of good quality copper. Some of them were in Ādharbayjān, others in Armenia. Syria and Egypt, which lacked copper deposits, had to import it from Europe. The abundant issue of copper coins and the manufacturing of large numbers of copper vessels would have been impossible if the Venetians and Genoese had not carried to the East heavy shipments of German, Slovakian and Bosnian copper. The countries of North Africa, on the other hand, could supply themselves with copper from local sources. The Near Eastern countries also lacked lead and tin and had no option but to purchase these metals from southern European traders, who imported them from Serbia, Bosnia, Germany and England. The Persian countries were supplied by mines in Transoxiana.

Even so far as iron was concerned, the resources of the Near Eastern countries were seriously deficient and they were dependent upon a supply from Europe, where this export trade was stigmatised by the Church as treason against Christianity, and transgressors were threatened by ecclesiastical and secular authorities with severe punishment. Nevertheless, the Italian merchants supplied the Muslims with this (and other) forbidden merchandise, and the republic of Pisa, by a treaty concluded in 1171 with Saladin, formally undertook to sell iron to Egypt.

MINING TECHNOLOGY

As with modern mining there were two major types of operation – the underground and the open-cut. In underground mining, one method was to sink shafts vertically into the soil and then drive horizontal passages when the veins were reached. In Syria the shaft of the mine was called the *bīr*, i.e. the well, and the horizontal passage the *darb*, i.e. the road. In the Lebanese mountains, a typical shaft was only six or seven metres deep whereas the tunnels were very long. Al-Idrīsī saw the mercury mines to the north of Cordoba and was told that the depth from ground level to the bottom of the mine was 250 fathoms. Other mines of intermediate depth were reported. Thus in the silver mines in North Africa the average depth was twenty cubits. The technique of drilling vertical shafts and horizontal tunnels was a familiar one in the Islamic world since it was used in the construction of qanats.

More often, however, miners preferred to dig horizontal adits into the slopes of a mountain and follow the veins, rather than to sink shafts. This method could only be used if the terrain was suitable, but it was also easier and less expensive for a miner who was working for himself. It is noticeable that the reports of mines with vertical shafts usually apply to mines owned by the state. A vivid description of the 'private enterprise' silver mining activities in Panjīr is given by the historian Abu'l-Fidā' (d. 1331). He describes how a man would follow a seam in the hope of reaching silver. The same seam might be selected by another miner, starting from a different location. In this case the miner who first found the silver was entitled to all the produce, the other to nothing. Only if they arrived at the silver simultaneously was the produce shared. Fortunes could be won or lost in a very short time. The tunnels were lit by lamps; if these went out the seam was abandoned, since further progress in foul air would have been fatal.

Windlasses were used for hauling ores and materials out of the shafts. A simple but efficient form of windlass was used in the iron mines in Syria and is still used in the construction of qanats in Iran, for drawing water, and in the building industry. To operate this machine an operator sits on a bench on one side of the shaft or well, pulling the horizontal bars of the windlass towards him with his hands and pushing the opposite ones away with his feet at the same time. The material is loaded into a small bucket about 30-35 cm in diameter, which has two handles. The rope is attached to the bucket by hooks fastened at its end. More sophisticated capstans were also used for haulage, when loads were heavier.

The devices invented by the Banū Mūsà for use in public works, which were mentioned in Chapter 7, could have been of use in mining. In particular the clamshell grab would have been useful for dredging up

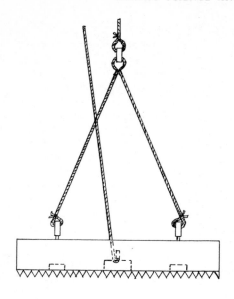

SIDE ELEVATION

END ELEVATION

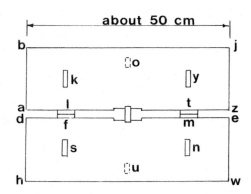

PLAN (ropes omitted)

FIGURE 11.1 Clamshell grab by the Banū Mūsà, Model 100. The hinged copper half-cylinders were lowered into the water by rope qx. When they reached the bottom, rope bm was pulled, bringing the two half-cylinders together. The grab was then raised by rope bm and its contents were examined on dry land.

212

ores that were under water, while their 'gas mask' would have enabled a miner to enter shafts or adits where the air was polluted, although he would still have had to leave the polluted area at frequent intervals. Al-Bīrūnī mentions a kind of rudimentary breathing apparatus for use by pearl divers. The diver wore an airtight leather helmet from which a tube led to the surface of the water, where its end floated between inflated bladders.

The main tool of the miner was the pickaxe. It had a sharp end to peck the stones and a flat end to hammer or drive wedges. There were also various hammers, chisels, wedges, crow-bars, hoes and shovels. Oil lamps were used for illumination. As with qanats, they were useful for aligning the direction of the digging and, as already mentioned, they were reliable indicators of the adequacy of fresh air supplies.

Ventilation was an important problem. In Panjīr, as we have seen, with thousands of small miners working for themselves in a frantic search for silver, capital investment was kept to a minimum and no provision for ventilation was usually made. The miners simply stopped the digging if the lamps stopped burning. In more organised mining work, especially in the state mines, a means of ventilation was always provided. This would have been essential, particularly in very deep mines such as those near Cordoba in Spain. Special ventilation shafts were provided or, when several shafts were needed for drainage, these could serve the dual purpose or drainage and ventilation.

Drainage was, of course, the other major problem in mining operations. Here again small miners could not afford to deal effectively with the problem. On the other hand in state-owned mines such as the silver mines at Zakandar in North Africa, drainage was carried out properly, as the geographer al-Qazwīnī (d. 1283) reports.

The contractual system seems to have been that the Sultan, who owned the mines, installed the drainage and ventilation systems and then let out the actual excavation of the ores and extraction of the silver to contractors. The Sultan installed water-raising wheels in three stages, since it was twenty cubits from the level of the water in the mines to the surface. The first stage raised the water to a certain level, where it was discharged into a tank, upon which a second wheel was erected. This wheel again raised the water to a tank, where the third wheel was installed. This raised the water to the surface where it was discharged into channels to irrigate farms and gardens.

It is not stated what type of wheel was used, but it is likely to have been a tympanum. A noria will only operate in running water and it is improbable that there would have been sufficient room to install a sāqiya. The lift of one-third of 20 cubits, or about 3.3 metres would be feasible for a typanum, although the drum would have been 9–10

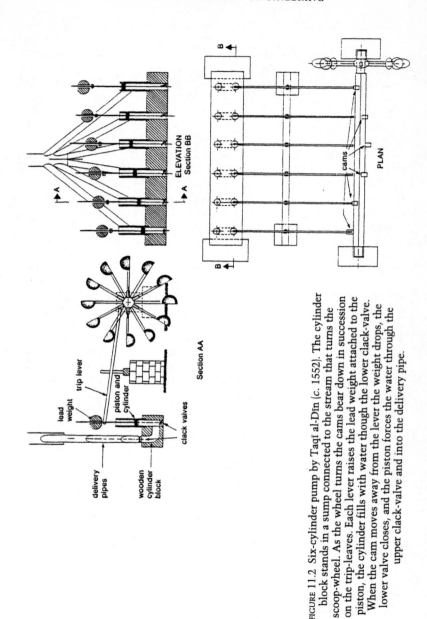

FIGURE 11.2 Six-cylinder pump by Taqī al-Dīn (c. 1552). The cylinder block stands in a sump connected to the stream that turns the scoop-wheel. As the wheel turns the cams bear down in succession on the trip-leaves. Each lever raises the lead weight attached to the piston, the cylinder fills with water though the lower clack-valve. When the cam moves away from the lever the weight drops, the lower valve closes, and the piston forces the water through the upper clack-valve and into the delivery pipe.

214

metres in diameter. Another possibility is the Archimedean screw, which we know to have been in use in Roman mines, but this seems precluded by al-Qazwīnī's use of the word *dawlāb*, which always means a wheel of some sort. Later, more sophisticated machines, such as that described by Taqī al-Dīn in the sixteenth century may have been used (Figure 11.2).

NON-FERROUS METALLURGY

Speaking about native gold which is collected from gold mines, al-Bīrūnī says that it is usually not free from impurities and therefore this gold has to be refined by smelting or by other methods. He gives details of the amalgamation process that was used in the mines on a commercial scale: 'After pounding the gold ore or milling it, it is washed out of its stones, and the gold and mercury are combined and then squeezed in a piece of leather until mercury exudes from the pores of the leather. The rest of the mercury is driven off by fire' (*Jamāhir*, 234). He further describes (236) how gold is mined from the deep waters of the Sind river:

> At its sources there are places in which they dig small pits under the water, which flows over them. They fill the pits with mercury and leave it for a while. Then they come back after the mercury has become gold. This is because at its start the water is rapid and it carries with it particles of sand and gold like mosquitoes' wings in thinness and fineness. Water carries these particles over the surface of the mercury which picks up the gold, leaving the sand to pass away.

Gold was tested by cupellation and by other methods. These included the touchstone, measuring the specific gravities, and by noting the speed of solidification of gold after it had been removed from the furnace.

Unlike gold, native silver was not found in alluvial deposits or in the sands and gravels of rivers, but it was to be sought in mountainous regions in embedded veins. In general, however, native silver was not abundant and the main source, as mentioned above, was from galena (lead sulphide) and to a lesser extent from other lead ores. The first step in the production of silver would be to obtain the lead from the galena. This was done by first roasting then smelting. The resulting lead could then be treated to extract silver. In Arabic literature, we find the result of some experiments indicating the amount of silver which could be recovered from an ingot of lead. Sometimes, silver was associated with gold in what is called electrum. Here also methods were adopted to separate the two precious metals.

Tin was brought to the Islamic world from Malaysia, Spain and

England. It was used in alloys. Its main use in the unalloyed state was the 'tinning' of water-containing vessels to inhibit corrosion.

Zinc was not known as a distinct metal by the early Islamic metallurgists and chemists. It was first known, and used extensively, mainly in combination with copper to form brass, through tutia, which is usually pure zinc oxide obtained from natural zinc carbonate. Various authors describe the method of producing the pure product from the natural one. The ore is placed in furnaces which contain long ceramic rods. Upon heating the ores, the smoke of tutia ascends and adheres in films to the rods. Al-Muqaddasī saw the 'curious tall furnaces in mountain villages' in the Iranian province of Kirmān. They later attracted the attention of Marco Polo when he visited the same area. By the sixteenth century, zinc as a distinct metal was known. Abu'l-Faḍl, secretary to the great Mughal Emperor Akbar, gives several compositions employing pure zinc. Antimony and arsenic. Antimony was obtained from antimony sulphide and was one of the constituents of copper alloys. Arsenic was unimportant as a metal, but we read of its preparation from its sulphides.

Copper was usually obtained from its sulphide ores. It seldom occurred as oxides or carbonates. These latter ores required only the simple treatment of heating with charcoal, while the sulphides required roasting, smelting with fluxes and partial oxidation. A useful discovery, however, took place in Muslim Spain. The sulphide ores, on exposure to air in the presence of water, are oxidised to soluble sulphates. The Muslims then found that if water containing copper sulphate is allowed to flow over iron, pure copper is deposited and the iron dissolved. As iron was cheap and abundant in Spain, this discovery yielded an efficient method of recovering copper from sulphide ore, and direct mining of copper ore became less necessary.

Bronze is an alloy of copper and tin. It was much used for plain kitchen wares and implements and was the alloy upon which the coppersmiths based much of their work. A small but important use of bronze was in the manufacture of hydraulic components such as valves and taps. Brass is an alloy of copper and zinc which is stronger, harder and less malleable than pure copper. Different kinds of brasses are obtained by varying the zinc content. A 20 per cent brass simulates the colour of gold. When zinc was not known as a metal, copper was heated in a mixture of powdered zinc ore and charcoal. A proportion of the zinc formed in the vicinity of the copper was diffused into it by cementation.

IRON AND STEEL METALLURGY

Three main types of iron and steel were utilised in Islamic metallurgical centres; wrought iron (narmāhin), cast iron (dūṣ), and steel (fulādh).

Wrought iron is soft – the word *narmāhin* means in Persian 'soft iron'. It is malleable but cannot be heat treated. It has many applications provided strength is not required, and it was used as a raw material for manufacturing steel.

Cast iron was a well-known material to Islamic chemists and metalworkers. Historians of technology seem to have been unaware, until recently, of its importance in the medieval Islamic world, both as an intermediate and as a final product. According to al-Bīrūnī it was the 'water of iron', and it was the liquid which flowed during the melting and extraction of the metal. Al-Jildakī, whom we have already met as an important alchemical writer of the fourteenth century, gives a description of the production of cast iron. The process takes place in purpose-built foundries, using as raw material a 'yellow earth'. This ore was placed in furnaces designed for smelting it, after it had been 'kneaded' with a little oil and alkali. Fire was then applied to it, the heat being intensified by a battery of powerful bellows, until it became molten. The metal was then allowed to flow down through strainers at the bottom of the furnaces where it was formed into ingots.

The properties of cast iron can be summarised from al-Bīrūnī's *Jamāhir* as follows; it is quick to flow like water when smelting iron ores; it is hard and whitish-silvery in colour and its powder has sometimes a pinkish reflection; it does not resist blows, but shatters into pieces – 'breakage and brittleness are typical of it'; and it is mixed with wrought iron in crucibles for making steel. Cast iron was exported to many countries as a raw material. In the fifteenth century there were at least two commercial brands, one from Iraq the other from the Iranian province of Fars. In Europe the production of cast iron began in the fourteenth century but it was not of sufficiently consistent quality for the casting of gun barrels until a century later.

In the same treatise in which he discusses the manufacture of cast iron, al-Jildakī describes how rods of cast iron are used to produce steel by carbonisation. The rods are placed in furnaces in the foundry and heat is applied to them, with a continuous blast of air until it (i.e. the iron) becomes like turbulent water.

> They nourish it with glass, oil and alkali until light appears from it in the fire and it is purified of much of its blackness by intensive founding, night and day. They keep watching while it whirls for indications until they are sure of its suitability, whereupon they pour it out through channels so that it comes out like running water. Then they allow it to solidify in the shape of bars or in holes made of clay fashioned like crucibles. They take out of them refined steel in the shape of ostrich eggs,

217

and they make swords from it, and helmets, lanceheads and all tools.

As reported by al-Bīrūnī, a similar method was used by a Damascene blacksmith named Mazyad b. ʿAlī. The crucibles, before being placed in the furnace, were filled with nails, horseshoes and other wrought iron objects as well as marcasite stone and brittle magnesia. The crucibles were then filled with charcoal, placed in the furnace and subjected to hot air blasts for a period, after which bundles of organic matter were thrown into each crucible. After another hour of hot-air blasting the crucibles were left to cool, and the 'eggs' were then taken from the crucibles.

In the same passage al-Bīrūnī also describes a method of producing molten steel in crucibles from a mixture of cast iron and wrought iron. This was the method of producing cast steel in Ḥarāt. Two qualities could be obtained. One resulted if the components were 'melted equally so that they became united in the mixing operation and no component can be differentiated or seen independently'. Al-Bīrūnī says that such steel was suitable for files and other tools. A second quality of steel was produced if the degree of melting of wrought iron and cast iron was different for each substance, 'and thus the intermixture between both components is not complete, and their parts are shifted and thus each of their two colours can be seen by the naked eye and is called *firind*' (*Jamāhir*, 256).

The *firind* is the distinctive pattern on the blades of 'Damascus' swords, which were in this context the most notable achievement in various metalworking centres in the Orient. The eminent historian of metallurgy, Cyril Stanley Smith, noted that 'In comparison with the relative neglect of structure by the European metallurgist, the enjoyment and utilisation of it in the Orient is impressive. In the Orient, etching to display patterns depending on composition differences was in use contemporaneously with the European pattern-welded blade, and was thereafter continually developed to a high artistic level' (p. 14; see Bibliography). It would be a difficult task to attempt to unravel the history of sword manufacture in the Middle East and Central Asia, and the results would probably prove inconclusive. Patterned swords were in use in Arabia before Islam. The poet Imru' al-Qays (d. *c.*550 AD) described the *firind* of the sword as resembling the tracks of ants. Another poet, a contemporary of Imru', describes the blade of the sword as if it were water whose wavy streaks are like a pond over whose surface the wind is gliding. Indeed, in Arabic poetry the beauty of the sword with the *firind* was always a source of inspiration. The provenance of the blades in these references is uncertain. At the battle of Yamāma in 633 the Muslims' opponents were armed with Indian swords, and there are many references to them in the works of Islamic poets. On the other hand, Yemenī swords were famous, as were those from Damascus. The poet al-Mutanabbī (d. 965) compared Arab swords favourably with those from India.

It is a reasonable conjecture that a single tradition of steel making, particularly in the manufacture of swords, had become established in the Middle East and Central Asia (including northern India) some time before the advent of Islam. Thereafter there was a flourishing business in the trading of steel within this extensive cultural area. Al-Bīrūnī mentions that steel eggs were cast in Harāt and then sent to India, and al-Idrīsī says that iron was exported from North Africa to India. Smith was therefore almost certainly correct when he wrote, 'The geographical distribution of these [Damascus] swords seems to have been practically co-extensive with the Islamic faith, and they continued to be made well into the nineteenth century' (ibid., 14).

For about a century and a half attempts were made in Europe to reproduce steel comparable in quality to Damascus steel. A large number of metallurgists carried out extensive research into steel making including eminent scientists such as Faraday. These attempts failed, and interest in the duplication of the blades declined as European steelmakers developed their own techniques; the introduction of the Bessemer and Siemens processes gave homogeneous steel more suitable to large-scale production.

The attempts to reproduce Damascus steel did, however, ultimately result in a closer understanding of this metal. It was shown that the blades are made of very high carbon steel (about 1.5–2.0 per cent) and owe their beauty and their cutting qualities alike to the inherent structure of the cakes of steel from which they are forged. The light portion contains numerous particles of iron carbide (cementite) while the dark areas are steel of normal carbon content. The structure is visible, of course, only after etching, which was done with a solution of some mineral sulphate.

12

Transmission of Islamic Knowledge to Europe

SCIENCE

The eleventh century witnessed in Europe a quickening of intellectual life. As trade and manufacturing grew, a 'middle class', residing in the towns, also began to appear. They expressed a rising interest in secular, materialistic matters. A growth in economic activity with the emergence of a wealthier middle class also enriched the resources of the Roman Catholic Church. Greater financial resources accrued to it under the centralisation of royal power, the construction of better transportation and communications systems and a more productive economy. These means were used, among other things, for making improvements in education.

The Church was almost the sole patron of scholarship and learning in medieval Europe. Cathedral schools had a narrow objective, the preparation of clerics and priests. The level of scientific learning in these schools was low: it consisted of basic arithmetical computations, the propositions of Euclid (without the proofs), an astronomy based mainly on the folklore of Germanic tribes, rudimentary geometry and chemistry consisting of basic metallurgy and the dyeing of cloth. Nevertheless, it was from the cathedral schools that the universities were to be established, and it was mainly from the cathedral schools and early universities that Islamic knowledge was to enter the Latin West.

The great period for the dissemination of Islamic science in the West was the twelfth and early thirteenth centuries. The translation movement of the twelfth century from Arabic into Latin, whether the translations were from Greek or Islamic works, gave the necessary impetus to the growth of European science. However, before the twelfth century, some isolated instances did occur of the diffusion into Europe of Islamic knowledge. The most notable of these are linked to the names of Gerbert of Aurillac – later Pope Sylvester II – and of Constantine Africanus. Gerbert, who died in 1003 after a short papacy, studied for several years in Christian Spain and became acquainted with Arabic literature, which he may have read through Latin translations of Arabic manuscripts. In addition to an interest in mathematics, he also seems to have been responsible for the first diffusions into Europe of the knowledge of the astrolabe. The earliest Latin treatises on the instrument, which were certainly of Arabic inspiration, were produced by a certain Llobet or Lupitus and his colleagues at the close of the tenth and beginning of the eleventh centuries, in the abbey of Ripoll in Catalonia. The abbey was visited by Gerbert in 967 and he probably took copies of the treatises with him into France. These early writings on the astrolabe are very elementary, deal only with the simplest problems, and contain many mistakes. They are also full of unassimilated Arabic words, sometimes so distorted as to make the meaning obscure. Properly presented European works on the astrolabe did not appear until the twelfth century (see below). Constantine Africanus, who died in 1087, is rather a shadowy figure. A somewhat suspect biography of him suggests that he travelled widely through North Africa and the Middle East, as was the practice of Islamic scholars, but for some reason he became *persona non grata* in his native Tunis and sought asylum in the Italian port of Salerno. He transcribed treatises by Ḥunayn and his son Isḥāq, but passed these off as his own and gave no credit for his sources. His translations were criticised for their over-liberal interpretation of the manuscripts. They were corrected by Stephen of Antioch around the year 1127. Stephen belonged to a new breed of translators who prided themselves on their accurate rendering of Arabic texts into Latin and cited proper sources when necessary.

The Crusades, although they fostered economic and commercial activity throughout the Mediterranean area, seem to have done little to stimulate intellectual exchanges. Rather it was in the countries newly conquered from Islam – Sicily, southern Italy and above all Spain – that the great work of diffusing Islamic knowledge into Europe took place in an organised, systematic manner.

The Norman conquest of Sicily from the Muslims was virtually completed in 1072 with the fall of Palermo. Thereafter the Normans and their Hohenstaufen successors were to rule Sicily and southern Italy until 1250. Ferdinand II of Hohenstaufen founded the University of Naples in 1224. To his palace school in Sicily he drew scholars – Muslim, Jewish and Christian – to engage in the translation of Arabic works into Latin. (It was in Sicily also at this time that the first school of Italian poets appeared). In 1227 Michael the Scot, one of the most noted scholars of the day, was attracted to his court.

The most important transfers of Islamic knowledge to the West, however, took place in the Iberian peninsula. The southward advance of the Christian armies was, fortunately, accompanied by a desire to assimilate the superior culture of the Muslims. The patronage of kings and bishops was important, for scholarship and translations were greatly benefited by the collaboration of Muslim, Jewish and Christian scholars. In fact, many of the translations had passed first from Arabic into Hebrew before being rendered into Latin, much as the translations in Baghdad, centuries before, had sometimes gone from Greek into Arabic through the medium of Syriac.

The most notable source of translations came into being in Toledo, immediately after its conquest in 1130, when the newly appointed archbishop, Raymond, founded a translation centre at his court. To this institution, during the course of the twelfth century, came eminent scholars such as Robert of Chester, Adelard of Bath, Gerard of Cremona and Michael the Scot. The most prolific of these men, and perhaps the most famous in the West, was Gerard of Cremona (1114–87). He became learned in Arabic but still was assisted by Spanish Christians and Jews in his rendering of Arabic books into Latin. Some eighty-seven translations are attributed to him, including works of philosophy, medicine, mathematics, astronomy and alchemy, from both Greek and Arabic originals. Many other translators, in Toledo and elsewhere, laboured to translate Arabic works into Latin. Indeed, so pervasive did Arabic works become in the later Middle Ages in Europe that many of the names became Latinised: Avicenna for Ibn Sīnā', Averroes for Ibn Rushd, Alhazen for Ibn al-Haytham, Albatenius for al-Battānī and many others. In his *Inferno*, written in the first decade of the fourteenth century, Dante places Ibn Sīnā' and Ibn Rushd among the virtuous pagans: 'Averrois, che il gran commento feo ... ' (Canto 4, l. 144).

Of the many works rendered into Latin at this time, we must inevitably exclude from our consideration all those of Greek origin, and those which deal with subjects such as philosophy, metaphysics and medicine which are outside the scope of this work. Even so, such a large number of works remain that simply listing them would occupy many pages. We shall therefore mention only a few that had a seminal influence on the development of European science.

The works of Muḥammad b. Mūsā al-Khuwārazmī exercised a profound influence on the development of mathematical thought in the medieval West. Many of his main works were translated into Latin in Spain during the twelfth century. His algebra was translated partially by Robert of Chester as *Liber algebras et almucabala*; shortly afterwards Gerard of Cremona made a second version of it, *De jebra et almucabola*. In this way a new science was introduced into Europe, and with it a terminology that was completely developed, needing only for words to be replaced by symbols for it to be recognisable as the modern science of algebra. The two technical terms that appear in the titles of the early translations were used until the time of Canacci (fourteenth century), who began to use only the first term;

two centuries later the term *mucabola* (Arabic *muqābala*) had fallen completely into disuse.

Almost at the same time as the *Algebra* was being translated, John of Seville published a Latin version of the *Arithmetic*, made from the lost Arabic original of al-Khuwārazmī. John's work was entitled *Liber algoarismi de practica arithmetrice*. This work describes the existence of operations carried out by nine or ten numbers – a place-number system that was already known in Spain in the tenth century. The *Liber algoarismi* and similar works explain the operations of adding, subtracting, multiplying and dividing; they show how decimal and sexagesimal fractions should be used, and also the Egyptian fractions, i.e. those with 1 as numerator from which others can be obtained by addition (e.g. $\frac{1}{3} + \frac{1}{15} = \frac{2}{5}$; $\frac{1}{4} + \frac{1}{28} = \frac{2}{7}$). This system was introduced into Europe through various Spanish versions including that of Fibonacci (c.1170–c.1240). The operation was sexagesimal fractions, necessary for astronomical computations, were rapidly taken into the courses of instruction in universities.

Another very influential work of al-Khurārazmī was his *Zīj al-Sindhind*, astronomical tables translated into Latin by Adelard of Bath. The translation of tables of trigonometric functions by Gerard of Cremona, which derived from al-Khuwārazmī and other Arabic writers, were known in Europe as the Toledan tables of Gerard. Many other translations of trigonometric functions, and the associated tables, derived from Arabic treatises, became available in this period. Until that time, trigonometry was unknown in Europe.

In astronomy, Ptolemy still exercised a predominating influence, which spread into Europe with Gerard's translation of the *Almagest*. During the twelfth century other volumes of Islamic astronomy made their appearance, due mainly to translations made by John of Seville and Plato of Tivoli. In the following century, in 1277, Alfonso X of Castile sponsored the publication of a large work, the *Libros del Saber de Astronomia* (referred to in Chapter 7 above), whose express purpose was to make Islamic knowledge available in Castilian. It consists of direct translations and paraphrases of Arabic works on astronomy, and also includes a section on timekeeping.

On the transmission of knowledge of the astrolabe into Europe, we have already seen that tentative steps were taken at the end of the tenth century. Among the many astronomical works, the *Planisphere*, or theory of stereographic projection, by Ptolemy, was translated by Hermann of Dalmatia. The treatise on the astrolabe by Māshā' Allah (Messahalla, who flourished in the late eighth century) was rendered into Latin by John of Seville. These, and several other translations from Arabic into Latin on the construction and uses of the astrolabe, stimulated the production of a number of original treatises by European writers. These included Raymond of Marseilles, before 1141, on the construction and uses of the astrolabe; Adelard of Bath, about 1142–6, on its construction; Robert of Chester, in 1147, on its uses; Abraham Ben Ezra, about 1158–61, on its uses. These treatises are much better than their predecessors of the tenth and eleventh centuries. Arabic words no longer appear as equivalents of Latin expressions, and the Latin terms themselves are those that were to be used from that time onwards in the definitive technical vocabulary of the astrolabe. The twelfth-century treatises, in their discussions on the uses of the instrument, reveal an awareness of its resources and present problems in a logical sequence and in ascending order of difficulty. The geometric constructions on the back of the astrolabe were known in Europe by the tenth century, but are first clearly described by Raymond of Marseilles and came into general use in the thirteenth century.

Equatoria were described in at least three Islamic treatises, all originating in Spain. These were by Ibn al-Samḥ (c.1025), al-Zarqall (Azarquiel, c.1050) and Abu al-Salṭ (c.1110). The first European treatise was written by Campanus of Novara in Italy in 1264, and this was followed by various treatises written in England and France in the fourteenth and fifteenth centuries. Although an independent European invention cannot be ruled out, diffusion from Islam seems to be the most likely explanation for the origin of European equatoria.

Some of the most important Islamic works on physics did not reach Europe until modern times. These include all the treatises by al-Bīrūnī on physical subjects and al-Khāzinī's *Balance of Wisdom*. (Indeed, the latter work has yet to be properly edited in Arabic and there is no translation into any European language.) Much of the knowledge of mechanics and hydraulics probably reached the West through translations from the Arabic of Hellenistic scientists such as Archimedes and Pappus.

Unquestionably, the most important work on physics to reach the West in medieval times was the *Kitāb al-manāẓir* (*Optics*) of Ibn al-Haytham (Alhazen). The influence of this work, with its intromission theory of vision and its completely new methodology, can hardly by exaggerated, both in Islam and in the West. Through a medieval Latin translation, later published at Basel (1572), the *Optics* made a profound impression, among others, on Roger Bacon, John Pecham and Witelo.

There appears to have been no knowledge of alchemy in the West until it was introduced from Islam, a process beginning in the twelfth century. It was in Spain in 1144 that Robert of Ketton completed the first translation of an alchemical work from Arabic into Latin. Among alchemical works Gerard of Cremona translated a book of al-Rāzī and is also believed to have translated one of the works of Jābir. There were many other translations of alchemical works made at the same period.

Although one or two genuine works of the Jabirian corpus were translated into Latin, other works in Latin that carry the name of Geber are without known Arabic originals. It is of course possible that the study of as yet unedited works of the Jabirian writings may reveal a direct connection with the Latin Geber, but this seems to be unlikely. That the 'Geber' treatises are based upon Arabic alchemical theory is not questioned, and it seems likely from various turns of phrase that their authors knew Arabic. The general style is, however, quite different from that of any known writings in the Jabirian corpus, nor do they contain any typical Jabirian ideas such as the theory of the 'balance' or the use of alphanumerology. These works were probably by one or more European scholars, but whatever their origin they became the principal authorities in early western alchemy and held that position for several centuries.

Early medieval Europe was by no means lacking in skilled artisans such as dyers, painters, glass-makers, metalworkers, jewellers and others. For example, the many fine exhibits of Anglo-Saxon work in the British Museum notably in jewellery and illustrated manuscripts, leave no doubt of the standards of excellence of the craftsmen working in England from the seventh century to the eleventh. As we shall see in the field of engineering, technology in Europe did not undergo the same period of decadence as science. Chemical technology, and the artifacts made from its producers, was a continuous tradition from Antiquity through classical times into the Middle Ages and beyond, and eventually led to the development of ideas and apparatus from which scientific chemistry evolved.

The chemical technology of Europe in the Dark Ages and early medieval times was based upon indigenous and imported ideas and practices, the outside influences being mainly Byzantine. After the rise of Islam, Islamic influences began to appear in European chemistry. The Arabic alchemical works were, of course, an important element in these transmissions since, as we have seen, the processes and equipment that they embodied were relevant not only to alchemy in the narrow sense, but to the whole field of developing chemical technology. There were also Arabic works with little alchemical content that exerted much influence on European practices. Prominent among these was the drug list of the Spanish Muslim Abu'l-Qāsim al-Zahrāwī (Albucasis to the Latins, d. 1013), which was translated into Latin in the thirteenth century as *Liber servitores*. It describes the preparation of litharge, white lead, lead sulphide, copper sulphide, cadmia, the vitriols, crocus of iron and other substances.

There was only a handful of European chemical treatises in the early Middle Ages, and these cannot all be precisely dated because additions were made at later times to the original texts. The earliest of Latin medieval craftsmen's handbooks is *Compositiones et tingenda* (*Recipes for Colouring*). Its various parts were collected in Alexandria about AD 600 and were translated into Latin some 200 years later. Despite its pre-Islamic origin it shows some Arabic influence; certain of its terms for dyestuffs are Arabic or Persian. The *Liber sacerdotum* contains 200 recipes, many going back to Alexandrian practice in the early Christian centuries and yet more ancient Egyptian methods. Its recipes were collected by an unknown Arabic writer and the substance of the collection was finally translated into Latin in the first part of the thirteenth century. The text is full of strange expressions, many of them badly transliterated Arabic worlds and some of them corrupt Greek words that have passed through Arabic. It even contains a Latin-Arabic glossary of metallurgical terms.

The scarcity of European literary material on the crafts until the thirteenth century changes from then on to an almost embarrassing abundance of treatises. The great European libraries contain many thousands of manuscript collections, dating from about 1200 to 1500; Britain alone has several hundred. Thenceforward European chemistry was much less subject to outside influences. In time it developed into a truly scientific discipline. Islamic ideas were, however, one of the roots that enabled the new science to flourish. As with other sciences and technologies, evidence for Islamic influence is the abundance of Arabic words in the chemical vocabularies of European languages. Examples in English are alkali, alchemy, alcohol, athannor, elixir, naphtha and many others.

ENGINEERING

In the sciences, as we have seen, transmission of Islamic knowledge to Europe was very largely by literary means. It is beyond question that transmission occurred on a large scale: anyone wishing to examine the diffusion of a particular science can trace its passage from its Arabic sources, through the Latin translations, and eventually into other European languages. Admittedly this is not an easy task, demanding a knowledge of the subject in question together with a competence in Arabic, Latin and several modern European languages. But it can be done, although so far there have been all too few attempts to undertake comprehensive studies of this nature.

With engineering the situation is completely different. Technology did not derive from or depend upon, written transmissions, but was largely a response to social and economic demands. (Even today, technologies cannot be learned entirely from books.) Instead of large quantities of literary materials, edited and unedited, there are very few works in Arabic dealing with engineering, and the treatises that have survived were never translated into Latin nor, until recent times, into any modern European language. Research into diffusions from Islam to the West is therefore difficult. It must be done by tracing the spread of constructions from the points in time and place of their first known appearance until they are in common use over extensive areas. These kinds of investigation are seldom straightforward. They depend upon references, often brief and obscure, in the writings of geographers, travellers and historians; iconographic evidence from inscriptions and illustrations in manuscripts; and some archaeological findings. This information can be supplemented from technical treatises, but these, as we have seen, are very scarce.

One has to be cautious in the use of these data. We cannot always assume that diffusions came from Islam into Europe simply because the constructions appeared earlier in Islam. Ideas may have come from Byzantium, for example, or have been due to the persistence of traditions from the classical world which came to light again when knowledge was more widely disseminated after the end of the Dark Ages. Transmissions may also have occurred when craftsmen examined the constructions of their predecessors or even took them over in working order. Finally, we must always consider the possibility of inventions occurring independently in different cultural areas.

Not surprisingly, in view of the foregoing, investigations into the transfer of engineering technologies seldom arrive at firm conclusions. Nevertheless, informed speculation should continue. Fresh light can be thrown upon diffusions by new discoveries in literature, iconography or archaeology (although industrial archaeology in the Middle East is in its infancy). Some questions may ultimately be resolved, others moved closer to resolution. For the time being, we can summarise the present state of knowledge in some of the more important engineering subjects.

Of the traditional water-raising machines the *shādūf* had come into widespread use in the Old World before the advent of Islam, and has been in continuous use in many areas until the present day: in east Asia, the Indian subcontinent, the Middle East and Europe. As late as the 1960s examples were reported from Touraine, Hungary and Bosnia.

Tracing the spread of the *sāqiya* and the noria is complicated by the confusion of writers, both medieval and modern, about nomenclature. In the present work the designations adopted are those prevalent in

Syria, where the *sāqiya* is invariably the animal-driven machine, the noria the current-driven. With many writers, however, the two expressions are virtually interchangeable. Also, at a fairly recent date, the term 'Persian wheel' made its appearance, again applied indiscriminately to either machine. This adds to the confusion and has led some writers into the error of assuming that because of this expression one or other of the machines was of Persian origin. This last point does not concern us unduly since, whatever their origins, both machines were in common use in the Middle East in pre-Islamic times. Despite the difficulties with evidence, it is beyond doubt that the *sāqiya* was introduced to the Iberian peninsula and then spread into other European countries. In the fifteenth century there are attestations from Italy, in the sixteenth and seventeenth from several other parts of Europe. From the eighteenth century onwards the report of travellers frequently mention *sāqiyas* in Europe, the Middle East, India and the New World.

The story of the noria is similar, but it was perhaps rather less common than the *sāqiya*: it needs running water to operate it, and the initial capital outlay for the larger machines is considerable. Nevertheless, it was diffused throughout the Islamic world in medieval times. As mentioned in Chapter 6, the splendid machines at Ḥamā on the river Orontes in Syria can still be seen, and the one at Murcia is still in operation. It was known in eleventh-century France and is depicted in fifteenth-century German manuscripts. It persisted in parts of Europe until very recently, for instance in the remoter parts of Bavaria and in Bulgaria. Like the *sāqiya* it crossed the Atlantic, but it was not in common use in the New World. Isolated wheels are found in Central and South America, such as the fine iron 'Spanish water-wheel' at Falmouth, Jamaica; a crude wheel south of Santiago, Chile; and the wheels on the lower Sao Francisco river in Brazil. Even in the nineteenth-century USA steam-driven norias delivering 2,000 gallons on each revolution were at work in the eighties for emptying copper sulphate into Lake Superior.

There is no evidence for al-Jazarī's water-raising machines or the ideas embodied in them having been transmitted to Europe. In particular, the crank in his fourth machine, and the fifth machine as a whole, with its conversion of rotary to reciprocating motion, its true suction pipes and its use of the double-acting principle – all these could have been of great importance in the history of machine design. Oddly enough, when the European piston pump makes its appearance in the fifteenth-century writings of Taccola (c.1450) and Martini (c.1475) the suction stage is already incorporated. Indeed it predominates, in that the forced or delivery stage of the pumps' action is little more than the stroke of the piston. It is very unlikely that either of the two engineers in question had any knowledge of al-Jazarī's work. Further research may one day identify the sources of the new machines.

Whereas it is certain that the traditional water-raising machines were diffused from Islam into Europe, no such certainty exists in the case of water power. The three basic types of water-wheel, and their application to grist milling, were known in Europe in classical times and persisted through the Middle Ages and beyond, until they were supplanted by steam power in the nineteenth century. Much the same pattern applies to Islam. As stated in Chapter 6, the industrial applications of water power appear to have been introduced roughly simultaneously in Islam and in Europe. It cannot be proved at present that there were diffusions in either dirrection. In the case of windmills the same uncertainty applies. The vertical axle mills of Iran and the horizontal axle mills of Europe were separate developments. The possibility that the idea of using wind as a source of power entered Europe from Islam will probably always remain conjectural.

There is no evidence that the Islamic treatises on Fine Technology were ever translated into any European language before modern times. Many of the devices of the Banū Mūsà and al-Jazarī were to be important elements in the development of European machine technology. It would be possible to list all the Islamic ideas that later appeared in the West. For example, feed-back control, 'reinvented' in the eighteenth century for steam engines; tipping-buckets, used in eighteenth-century rain gauges; casting in closed mould-boxes with green sand, first described in 1540 in Biringuccio's *Pyrotecnica*; and so on. A list of this nature, however, would be of little value, since any conclusions drawn from it without other evidence would entail *post hoc* reasoning. It is more instructive to select one important machine invented in Europe in the late Middle Ages, identify those of its elements that were previously known in Islam, and consider whether those elements could have been transmitted to Europe. The machine to be considered is the mechanical clock. The result will still be conjectural, but it will at least provide a credible hypothesis which could form the basis of further investigation.

The essentials of the mechanical clock in its early form were the weight-drive, the 'going train' of gears and the verge-and-foliot escapement. The mechanical escapement was one of the fundamental inventions in the history of technology. A vertical bar – the verge – was attached to the centre of a swinging horizontal arm – the foliot. Two pallets on the verge entered, in turn, the teeth of a crown wheel, which was on the axle of the weight-drive. This was an effective means of slowing down the speed of descent of the weight. There were movable weights on either end of the foliot; moving these towards or away from the centre altered the timing of the clock. Some form of marking the passage of the hours was also necessary: the tower clocks of medieval Europe, in addition to dials, usually incorporated elaborate biological and celestial automata. The mechanism for striking the hours was activated by the 'striking train' which included segmental gears-wheels.

The heavy floats in Riḍwān's and al-Jazarī's clocks can be regarded as weights, with escapements provided by the feed-back control systems. The mercury clock in the *Libros del Saber*, however, has a proper weight-drive. Although its escapement was still hydraulic it was effective in this type of clock, which had been known in Islam since the eleventh century. The clock had an astrolabic dial, a component that also occurs in a fourteenth-century water-clock in Fez, Morocco, parts of which still exist. In addition to various types of automata, Islamic water-clocks normally had audible time-signals: devices such as, for example, balls dropping on to cymbals. Gears were used in Islamic instruments such as astrolabes and geared calendars, but the first known examples of complex gear-trains transmitting heavy torque occur in the automata of al-Murādī's treatise, written in Muslim Spain in the eleventh century. These gears incorporated segmental gears, essential elements in the striking-trains of mechanical clocks. It can be seen, therefore, that all the elements of the mechanical clock, except the verge-and-foliot escapement, were present in various types of Islamic water-clocks.

If we now turn our attention to Europe, we find that the earliest description we have of a European water-clock appears in Latin in Ms Ripoll 225 from the Benedictine monastery of Santa Maria de Ripoll at the foot of the Pyrenees. Estimates for its date vary from the middle of the tenth century to some time in the eleventh. The description of the main water machinery is missing but the section describing the striking strain is complete. Although this is not very clearly described, it appears that cams on a wheel driven by the water machinery released weights at intervals, and the release of the weights caused the rotation of iron arms that struck bells. An illustration in a manuscript dated about 1285 shows a water-clock in a monastery in northern France. It is not possible to determine the precise operation from the illustration, but it seems that there was a reservoir below which an inflow clepsydra was suspended. A chain or cord from this receiver passes round the axle of a wheel. The wheel is divided into fifteen segments, and between each pair of segments is a hole and a projection on the perimeter. A row of bells above the wheel indicates that this was a chiming clock.

The word *horologium* can mean either water-clock or mechanical clock, an ambiguity that has caused difficulties in establishing a date for the invention of the latter. It could not have been earlier than 1271, since in a treatise written in that year Robert Anglicus tells us that the makers of horologia were trying to make a weight-driven clock. 'But they cannot quite complete their task which if they could it would be a really accurate horologium'. This is a clear indication that the invention of the escapement was approaching at that time, and also implies that the invention was made by a clockmaker who was already familiar with the construction of water-clocks.

We know that advanced devices were constructed in Muslim Spain, as attested by the mercury clock in the *Libros del Saber* and by the devices described by al-Murādī. It is significant that al-Murādī, in the introduction to his treatise, says that he was writing it in order to revive a subject that was in danger of being forgotten, implying that this kind of technology had long been known in Muslim Spain. We therefore have the situation in which sophisticated water-clocks were made in the Iberian peninsula, coupled with the fact that the first known European description of a water-clock was written in the monastery of Ripoll, the very place from which the knowledge of the astrolabe had passed into northern Europe. Moreover, knowledge of the astrolabe was probably disseminated into Europe by Gerbert d'Aurillac, later Pope Sylvester II, after he had visited Ripoll about the year 967. Since the church was keenly interested in fining a means for timekeeping, it is likely that information about the new Islamic water-clocks was carried to Europe by a churchman – either Gerbert himself or a later visitor to Ripoll.

If we assume, on available evidence, that the European clock-makers came into possession of all the essential elements of Islamic hydraulic timekeeping between the tenth and twelfth centuries, then we may assume that an anonymous genius in northern Europe, late in the thirteenth century, invented the mechanical escapement and applied it to the array of mechanisms that were by then the common property of clockmakers. This hypothesis therefore proposes that the mechanical clock came into being when a single vital component was added in Europe to the elements that had been accumulated over the centuries by Muslim craftsmen and their Hellenistic predecessors.

For two types of bridge – beam and pontoon – there is no point in discussing diffusions into Europe from outside. Beam bridges are known in all cultural areas and are an obvious solution for crossing obstacles. Pontoon bridges were known in classical times but they do not seem to have been common in medieval Europe, although some were built. The first Rialto bridge in Venice, for example, was a pontoon bridge built in the thirteenth century.

Villard de Honnecourt (c.1235) drew several types of cantilever bridge, as did Leonardo. The structure which Trajan threw across the Danube in AD 104 may have been a multi-span cantilever bridge, but it seems to have been an isolated example in the classical West. Simple cantilever bridges had been built throughout the Middle Ages in the Savoy Alps. The point of origin of this type of bridge, if indeed it originated at a single locality, cannot be established, although the mountains of Central Asia seem to be the most likely candidate.

Suspension bridges made their first appearance in Europe in an illustration in a work by Faustus Verantius dated 1595. This was a design using a system of linked iron rods suspending a flat deck, but no bridge of this type was built in Europe in this century or the next. Accounts of Chinese iron-chain suspension bridges reached Europe in the seventeenth century, but the earliest iron-chain suspension bridge, of the catenary type, was built in England in 1741. The first suspension bridge capable of carrying vehicles was not built until 1809 over the Merrimac river in Massachusetts. From then on, of course, many suspension bridges were built in Europe and the USA. The original stimulus for constructing this type of bridge came from China, even though all the stages in the process of transmission have yet to be elucidated.

The existence of pointed arches in certain Islamic masonry bridges is of importance in the history of architecture. As mentioned in Chapter 8, there are substantial remains in western Iran of such bridges; in one of these at least, the Pul-i-Kāshgān, several arches were standing in 1936 (see Figure 8.3). This bridge is dated by an inscription to 1008/9, the Pul-i-Kalhūr to 984/5. The Pul-i-Dukhtar was also reconstructed at about this time, although the exact date is unknown. The bridges were rebuilt on the remains of Sasānid bridges. Assuming that the Islamic bridges were built upon the piers of the original structures, since a total reconstruction is very unlikely, then it is probable for structural reasons that the Sasānid bridges also had pointed arches. We shall not, however, base our chain of reasoning on such a conjecture, but depend upon the firm dates of the Islamic inscriptions.

The pointed, or ogival arch, by reducing the lateral thrust on foundations, enabled the architects of gothic cathedrals to lighten the walls and buttresses, which had to be massive to support semicircular arches. Furthermore, the ground plans of great churches were becoming more elaborate, and semicircular vaulting could not easily be tailored to cover such irregular areas. The glories of gothic architecture are therefore due in no small measure to the introduction of the ogival arch.

The ogival arch was known in Syria from AD 561. Creswell (102–4) lists a number of such arches built between 561 and 879, the first seven in Syria, others in Egypt and Iraq. In arches of this type the two halves are struck from a different centre; the less the separation of the two halves, the less the acuteness of the arch. The most acute of those listed by Creswell was in the Nilometer at Cairo, completed in 862, with a separation of one third of the span. The arches of the Pul-i-Kāshgān are slightly more acute than this.

The great historian of technology, Lynn White Jr. (see Bibliography), in tracing the passage of the ogival arch into Europe, located its origin in Buddhist India in the second century AD, whence it passed via Sasānid Iran into Syria and Egypt. It moved to Amalfi about 1000 – Amalfi had close commercial ties with Egypt at this time. White then makes a convincing case for the adoption of the ogival arch by church builders, first in a porch at the Abbey of Monte Cassino in 1071, then the incorporation of 196 pointed arches in the great new church at Cluny completed in 1120. In 1130 Abbot Suger of the French royal abbey of Saint-Denis visited Cluny, and between 1135 and 1144 he and his engineers produced at Saint-Denis what is generally regarded as the first true gothic church.

Some points of White's thesis can be queried, in particular the origin of the ogival arch in India. Also, its use by the Sasānids cannot yet be proved, although this may be established by research at present in progress. On the other hand, even White considered that it did not become a load-bearing member until its incorporation into the church at Cluny, whereas the arches in the Iranian bridges are clearly load-bearing. The view that gothic architecture was born of the efforts of medieval engineers to cope with the structural necessities of romanesque vaulting is widely adhered to in Europe. White's hypothesis, however, reinforced with the evidence of the Iranian birdges, seems to be difficult to refute.

A number of Islamic techniques of dam building were copied in Christian Spain. These include the incorporation of desilting sluices, the gauging of rivers and the extensive use of dams for hydropower. At present there is no evidence for the transmission of arch dams from Iran to the West.

Qanat technology was diffused by the Muslims through North Africa and the Iberian peninsula between the seventh and twelfth centuries. Two Spanish qanat systems constructed by the Muslims in Spain have been studied. The Madrid system, which still functions, brings water to the city from the Guadarrama. The system of Crevillante in the province of Valencia is less well known. It was some 1,500 yards long and had nineteen ventilation shafts. The Spaniards, having learnt the technique from the Muslims, were themselves constructors of qanats in the New World. The systems of Tehuacan and Parras in Mexico are almost certainly of Spanish origin. Similar works in Chile and Peru, however, appear to be pre-Columbian. Further research is required to resolve definitely the origins of these putative Inca systems.

Islamic irrigation systems passed into Spanish Christian possession as the Reconquest proceeded, some of them virtually unchanged until the present day. The Spaniards took Muslim methods of irrigation to the New World. In northern Europe, with its heavier rainfall, irrigation was never an important agricultural technique.

Practical simplified versions of Roman surveying techniques seem to have survived in Europe throughout the medieval period. On the other hand, triangulation had been introduced from the East in the astrolabic treatises of the Spanish Muslim astronomers Maslama of Madrid (d. c.1007) and Ibn al-Ṣaffār (d. 1035). Generally, when treatises on the astrolabe were translated into Latin, geodetic uses of the instrument were omitted and Christian treatises on the whole remained within the Roman tradition. An exception is the tenth-century *Geometria incerti auctori*, a compilation of Hispano-Arabic inspiration which is probably related to the Arabicised scientific corpus of the monastery of Ripoll. The *Geometria* deals with a variety of triangulation procedures that can be carried out with the astrolabe, similar to those described in Chapter 10. Simple triangulation was practised alongside the Roman surveying procedures in both Islamic and Christian Spain. The simpler Roman methods appear to have been used by individual farmers, while triangulation was associated with institutions that commanded the services of professional surveyors (such as the monastery of Ripoll, which was acquiring huge donations of land during the tenth century). Little is known of the history of surveying in other parts of Europe in the Middle Ages. It is assumed that the practices of the *agrimensores* continued in use in the erstwhile provinces of the Roman Empire. Triangulation procedures may have percolated into northern Europe at the instigation of the Church.

It is not always easy to extract information on mining from medieval European literature which deals ostensibly with the subject. This literature is usually of Arabic origin and often shades into alchemy. Later works, such as the eleventh-century treatise of Theophilus and the *Lapidario* of Alfonso X of Castile (completed 1279) were also partly inspired by Arabic originals. The latter gives details of many stones, including the production of argentiferous stibnite, said to be worked at various sites in Spain and Portugal. Its main economic use was the production of a 'beautiful gold-colour' on the surface of glass, which may have been used as early as the eighth century on mosque-lamps.

For early medieval Europe our information on the production of metals is very scanty. When mining came into prominence the greatest activity was in central Europe. Saxon miners led the way in the Middle Ages, not only in their own country but throughout almost the whole of Europe. Mining was begun by them at Schemnitz in Czechoslovakia as early as 745, at Goslar in the Harz in 970, at Freiburg in Saxony in 1170 and at Joachimsthal in Bohemia in 1516. The great textbook of mining was the *De re metallica* (1556) of Georg Bauer, known as Agricola. He was a Saxon who took a medical degree in Italy and settled at the famous mining centre of Joachimsthal. The book deals with every aspect of mining; one of its most important sections deals with the dewatering of mines by various types of pump. The German-led upsurge in mining, and improvements in mining technology, seems to have been an indigenous phenomenon. It is probable, however, that Roman and Islamic knowledge of mining techniques was part of the inheritance of the early Saxon miners.

The diffusion of Islamic scientific knowledge to Europe was mainly by literary means, which makes the tracing of the course of the various diffusions a relatively straightforward task. The impetus given by Islam to the development of the different sciences in Europe, and the value of the Islamic contribution to the Scientific Revolution from the sixteenth century onwards are questions that are beyond the scope of this book.

Because of the scarcity of written records on engineering matters, both in Islam and in Europe, all questions of diffusion must be, to a greater or lesser extent, conjectural. It is to be hoped that as more material – literary, inconographical or archaeological – come to light, some questions of diffusion may ultimately be resolved. It is important, however, not to evaluate Islamic engineering only with regard to its contribution to the development of its European counterpart. Engineers in the Islamic world were responding to the needs of society and in a number of fields, for example irrigation, masonry construction and milling, their responses were conspicuously successful.

Select Bibliography

There is no satisfactory work of a general nature dealing with the history of Islamic science or engineering. The method has therefore been adopted of listing first all works of wide application which contain information on various aspects of these subjects. An example is the *Encyclopaedia of Islam*. The reader can refer to the index of the first six volumes of this work in order to find entries of relevance to science or technology.

For the individual chapters the works cited are in most cases modern, the great majority being in English. Wherever possible books rather than articles have been listed, but there are cases in which no books adequately cover a given topic; recourse has then been had to the most authoritative article(s). In some subject areas, the only articles of any merit are to be found in one of the general works, which will therefore be cited in full. To take the *Encyclopaedia of Islam* once again as an example, Optics would appear as: Sabra, A. I., 'Manāẓir', *EI*, VI, 376–7, i.e. Author, title of article, abbreviation for *Encyclopaedia of Islam*, volume number, page numbers. The articles in *EI* always appear under transliterated Arabic titles: clearly 'Manāẓir' means 'Optics'. Cross references to the English equivalents are, however, given in the *Enyclopaedia* and in the Index to Volumes I–VI and Supplement 1–6.

It is intended that the bibliographies for each chapter, short though they are, will provide sufficient information to enable readers to follow up the subject matter of the chapter, without frequent cross-references to other parts of the Bibliography. Inevitably this means that certain works are listed more than once. In such cases the works are fully referenced for the first entry, but given only a short title for subsequent entries. Page references are usually given.

This book has obviously drawn upon a large number of source works in Arabic, but most of these have been omitted from the Bibliography although a few are referred to in the various chapters. There are also a few cases where the most satisfactory commentaries on a subject are to be found in editors' annotations to their translations of Arabic works. In these instances the translations – partial or complete – are listed in the Bibliography. Otherwise, for readers wishing to consult Arabic sources direct, it will be found that many of the works listed in the Bibliography contain comprehensive bibliographies of their own, including all the Arabic works which their authors consulted.

GENERAL

Dictionary of Scientific Biography, Scribners, New York, 1970–80.
The Encyclopaedia of Islam, 6 vols to date, Brill, Leiden, 1960–91, continuing.
Hassan, Ahmad Y. and Hill, D. R., *Islamic Technology*, Cambridge University Press, 1986.
Le Strange, Guy, *The Lands of the Eastern Caliphate*, Frank Cass, London, 1905; based upon the works of Muslim geographers, a valuable work for its references to various constructions.
Schacht, Joseph and Bosworth, C. E. (eds) *The Legacy of Islam*, 2nd Edn, Oxford University Press, 1979.
Singer, Charles, Holmyard, E. J., Hall A. R., and Williams, Trevor I. (eds) *A History of Technology*, Vol. 2, *The Mediterranean Civilizations and the Middle Ages*, Oxford University Press, 1956.
Taton, René (ed.), *Ancient and Medieval Science*, Thames and Hudson, London, 1963.
Vernet, Juan, *De 'Abd al-Raḥmān a Isobel I*, Barcelona, 1989.
White, Lynn Jr, *Medieval Technology and Social Change*, Oxford University Press, 1962.
———, *Medieval Religion and Technology*, University of California Press, Los Angeles, 1978.
Wiedemann, E., *Aufsätze zur Arabischen Wissenschaftsgeschichte*, Olms, Hildesheim 2 vols, 1970. (These are the collected papers contributed by Wiedemann to the Erlangen Society from 1902 to 1928. In Vol. 1 all Wiedemann's articles in other learned journals are listed. He is difficult to read as it is not always easy to distinguish text from notes. Also, he often omits full references. Nevertheless he covers a wide range of topics in science and technology and can never be ignored, although his results sometimes require modification in the light of more recent research.)

CHAPTER 1: INTRODUCTION

Hadas, M., *Hellenistic Culture*, Columbia University Press, New York, 1959.
Hussey, J. M. (ed.) *The Cambridge Medieval History*: IV, *The Byzantine Empire, Part II Government, Church and Civilisation*, Cambridge, 1967, 264–305.
Landels, J. G., *Engineering in the Ancient World*, Chatto and Windus, London, 1978.
Lloyd, G. E. R., *Greek Science after Aristotle*, W. H. Norton New York and London 1973.
Tarn, Sir William and Griffith, G. T., *Hellenistic Civilisation*, 3rd Edn, Edward Arnold, London, 1952.
Young, M. J. L., Latham, J. D. and Serjeant, R. B. (eds) *Religion, Learning and Science in the Abbasid Period* [*RLSAP*], Cambridge University Press, 1990: Goodman, L. E., 'The translation of Greek Materials into Arabic', 477–97.

CHAPTER 2: MATHEMATICS

Suter, H., 'Die Mathematiker und Astronomen der Araber und ihre Werke', *Abhandl. zur Gesch. der mathematischen Wissenschaften*, X, 1900.
Al-Uqlidisi, *The Arithmetic of al-Uqlidisi*, translated and annotated by S. A. Saidan, D. Reidel, Dordrecht, 1978. (One of the most important Arabic

arithmetical texts; the book is much enhanced by Dr Saidan's annotations.)

Youschkevitch, Adolf P., *Les Mathématiques Arabes*, translated by M. Cazenave and K. Jaouiche, C.N.R.S., J. Vrin, Paris, 1976. (This an excellent work, covering all branches of mathematics developed and practised by the Muslims.)

CHAPTER 3: ASTRONOMY

Kennedy E. S., with Colleagues and former Students, *Studies in the Islamic Exact Sciences*, American University of Beirut, Beirut, 1983.

King David A., *Islamic Mathematical Astronomy*, Variorum Reprints, London 1986.

———, *Islamic Astronomical Instruments*, Variorum Reprints, London, 1987.

King, David A. and Saliba, George (eds) *From Deferent to Equant: A volume of Studies in the History of Sciences in the Ancient and Medieval Near East in Honor of E. S. Kennedy*, New York Academy of Sciences, New York, 1987.

Michel, Henri, *Traité de l'Astolabe*, Librairie Alain Brieux, Paris, 1976.

Samsó, J., 'Marsad', *EI*, VI, 599–602.

Suter, H., 'Die Mathematiker' (see above, chp. 2).

CHAPTER 4: PHYSICS

There is no general work on Islamic physics as a whole and no comprehensive work on any of its main divisions. The most satisfactory method of learning about Islamic physics is to consult the articles written by Wiedemann in the *Aufsätze*. These can be found by reading the Table of Contents in each volume and by consulting the subject index in Vol. 2. This is a time-consuming and laborious task for which, of course, a facility in academic German is necessary. The following articles will also be found useful:

Anawati, G., 'Science' in the *Cambridge History of Islam*, Vol. 2b., ed. P. M. Holt and Ann K. S. Lambton, Cambridge, 1977, 741–79.

Arnaldez, R. and Massignon, L., 'Arabic Science' in Taton, *Ancient and Medieval Science*, Pt III, 385–421.

Al-Khāzinī, 'Analysis and Extracts from the Book of the Balance of Wisdom' by N. Khanikoff, *Journal of the American Oriental Society*, VI, 1859, 1–128.

Sabra, A. I., 'Manāẓir' in *EI*, VI, 376–7.

Vernet, Juan, 'Mathematics, Astronomy and Optics' in Schacht, *Legacy*, 461–88.

CHAPTER 5: CHEMISTRY

Hassan and Hill, *Islamic Technology*, 'Chemical Technology', 133–76.

Hill, Donald R., 'The Literature of Arabic Alchemy', *RLSAP*, 328–41.

Needham, J., 'The elixir concept and chemical medicine in East and West', *Journal of the Chinese University of Hong Kong*, 2, 1974.

Ullman, M., 'al-Kīmiyā' in *EI*, V, 110–15.

See also the relevant articles in Wiedemann's *Aufsätze*.

CHAPTER 6: MACHINES

Glick, Thomas F., *Islamic and Christian Spain in the Early Middle Ages*, Princeton University Press, Princeton, 1979, 230–8.

Haverson, Michael, *Persian Windmills*, CIP – Gegevens Koninklijke Bibliotheek, The Hague, 1991.

Hill, Donald R., 'Trebuchets", *Viator*, 4, University of California Press, Los Angeles, 1973, 99–114.

———, *A History of Engineering in Classical and Medieval Times*, Croom Helm, London 1984, 127–79.

———, 'Arabic Mechanical Engineering: Survey of the Historical Sources', *Arabic Sciences and Philosophy*, Vol. 1, pt 2, Cambridge University Press, 1991, 167–86.

Needham, Joseph, *Science and Civilisation in China*, Vol. 4, pt 2, *Mechanical Engineering*, Cambridge University Press, 1965. (Although Dr Needham's works are obviously concerned mainly with China, they contain a good deal of information about other cultural areas: consult Bibliography and Index.)

Schiøler, T., *Roman and Islamic Water-Lifting Wheels*, Odense University Press, Odense, 1973.

Smith, Norman A. F., *Man and Water*, Peter Davies, London, 1975, 3–18, 137–50.

CHAPTER 7: FINE TECHNOLOGY

Bedini, Silvio A., 'The Compartmented Cylindrical Clepsydra', *Technology and Culture*, 3, 1963, 115–41.

Farmer, H. G., *The Organ of the Ancients*, London, 1931.

Hill, Donald R., *Arabic Water-clocks*, Institute for the History of Arabic Science, Aleppo, 1981.

———, *A History of Engineering*, 199–245.

———, 'Arabic Fine Technology and its Influence in the development of European Horology', *Al-Abhath*, Vol. XXXV, American University of Beirut, Beirut, 1987, 8–28.

———, 'Arabic Mechanical Engineering', Cambridge, 1991.

Landes, David S., *Revolution in Time*, Harvard University Press, Harvard, 1983.

Turner, A. J., the *Time Museum*, vol. 1, pt 3, Rockford, 1984.

CHAPTER 8: BRIDGES AND DAMS

Creswell, K. A. C., *A Short History of Early Muslim Architecture*, Penguin Books, London, 1958.

Hill, Donald R., *A History of Engineering*, 47–75.

Kussmaul F. and Fischer, M., *Tadschiken (Afghanistan, Badakhshan) Bau einer Brücke*, Encyclopaedia Cinematographica, G. Wolf (ed.), Göttingen, 1971.

Mayer, L. A., *Islamic Architects and their Works*, Albert Kundig, Geneva, 1956.

Needham, Joseph, *Science and Civilisation in China*, Vol. 4, pt 3, *Civil Engineering and Nautics*, Cambridge, 1971, 145–210.

Smith, Norman A. F., *A History of Dams*, Peter Davies, London, 1971, 75–101.

Stein, Sir Aurel, *Old Routes of Western Iran*, Macmillan, London 1940, 182–7, 267–73.

CHAPTER 9: HYDRAULIC ENGINEERING

Glick, Thomas F., *Irrigation and Society in Medieval Valencia*, Harvard University Press, Harvard, 1970.
Goblot, Henri, *Les Qanats, Une Technique D'Acquisition de l'Eau*, Mouton Éditeur, Paris, 1979.
Hill, Donald R., *A History of Engineering*, 17–45.
Nordon, M. *L'Eau Conquise: Les origines et le monde antique*, Masson, Paris, 1991.
Smith, Norman A. F., *Man and Water*, 3–18.
Wittfogel, K., *Oriental Despotism*, New Haven 1957.

CHAPTER 10: SURVEYING

Cahen, Claude, 'Le Service de l'irrigation en Iraq au début du XIᵉ siècle', *Bulletin d'études orientales*, Vol. 13, 1949–51, 117–43.
Al-Karaji, *La civilisation des eaux cachées*, text established, translated and annotated by Aly Mazaheri, University of Nice, 1973.
Schirmer, H. "Ilm al-Misāha', *EI*, VII, 135–7.
Wiedemann, E., *Aufsätze*, Vol. 1, 577–96.
Wright, R. Ramsay *The book of Instruction in the Elements of the Art of Astrology*, reproduced from British Museum MS Or 8349 (ET facing Arabic text), London 1934.

CHAPTER 11: MINING

Al-Hassan, A. Y. and Hill, D. R., 'Ma'din', *EI*, V pt 2, 'Mining Technology', 967–73.
Ashtor, E., 'Ma'din', *EI*, V, pt 1, 'Economic Aspects', 964–7.
Singer et. al., *History of Technology*, Vol. 2, 1–41.
Smith, Cyril Stanley, *A History of Metallography*, Chicago, 1965.

CHAPTER 12: CONCLUSION

Daniel, Norman, *The Arabs and Medieval Europe*, 2nd Edn, Longman, Librairie du Liban 1979.
Stanton, Charles Michael, *Higher Learning in Islam*, Rowman and Littlefield, Savage, Maryland, 1990, 145–76.
Watt, W. M., *The Influence of Islam on Medieval Europe*, Edinburgh University Press, Edinburgh, 1972.
White, Lynn Jr, 'Cultural Climates and Technological Advance in the Middle Ages', *Viator*, 2, 1971, 171–201.

Index

The definite article '*al-*' is not taken into account in the alphabetical listing, but '*Ibn*' (son of) is.